THE CHURCH: COMMUNION, SACRAMENT, COMMUNICATION

Robert Kress

PAULIST PRESS
New York/Mahwah

Acknowledgments

I wish to thank Mr. Arnold Habig and the Habig Foundation of Jasper, Indiana for their gracious financial support in the preparation of this manuscript for publication.

I also wish to thank Editor James Provost for gracious permission to revise matter which first appeared in "Membership and Leadership in the Church," *The Jurist* 42 (1982) 29–69.

Library of Congress
Catalog Card Number: 84-61488

ISBN: 0-8091-2663-X

Published by Paulist Press
997 Macarthur Boulevard
Mahwah, New Jersey 07430

Printed and bound in the
United States of America

CONTENTS

ABBREVIATIONS

DS Henricus Denzinger and Adolfus Schönmetzer, ed. *Enchiridion Symbolorum* (Freiburg: Herder, 1967).

ET Karl Rahner, ed. *Encyclopedia of Theology* (New York: Seabury, 1979).

Barauna Guilherme Barauna, ed. *Elise de Vatican* 1-3 (Paris: Cerf, 1966).

SM Karl Rahner, ed. *Sacramentum Mundi* 1-6 (New York: Herder and Herder, 1968).

ST Karl Rahner, *Schriften zur Theologie* 1-15 (Einsiedeln: Benziger, 1954-1983).

TI Karl Rahner, *Theological Investigations* 1-18 (New York: Crossroad, 1961-1983).

HtG Henrich Fries, ed. *Handbuch theologischer Grundbegriffe* 1-2 (Munich: Kosel, 1962).

LTK Joseph Hofer and Karl Rahner, ed. *Lexikon fur Theologie und Kirche* 1-10 (Freiburg: Herder, 1957-1965) with a three volume supplement on Vatican II edited by Herbert Vorgrimler (1966-1968).

CTSA *Catholic Theological Society of America Proceedings* (Bronx: Manhattan College, annually).

Miller John Miller, ed. *Vatican II: An Interfaith Appraisal* (Notre Dame: University of Notre Dame, 1966).

NCE *New Catholic Encyclopedia* 1-17 (New York: McGraw–Hill, 1967-1979).

MS Johannes Feiner and Magnus Löhrer, ed. *Mysterium Salutis* 1-6 (Einsiedeln: Benziger, 1965-1981).

PG J.P. Migne, ed. *Patrologia Graeca,* 1-161 (Paris: 1857-66).

PL J.P. Migne, ed. *Patrologia Latina,* 1-217 (Paris: 1878-90).

INTRODUCTION

As the title indicates, this book is about the Church as communion, sacrament, and communication. All these terms are complicated, both in their basic meaning and because of their factual development in the course of the history of the Church and theology. Ecclesiology, the systematic theological study of the Church, can be regarded as both grandeur and misery. It enjoys a certain grandeur, because, in one sense, all the other theological specialties flow into it and find their unity and fulfillment there. On the other hand, ecclesiology is a misery for precisely the same reasons. The material to be covered in ecclesiology is so rich, so varied, that one is hard pressed to know what to include, what to exclude. It is not even easy to settle on a starting point, for many legitimate ones readily suggest themselves.

Because of various historical circumstances, ecclesiology had tended to start with the foundation of the Church by Jesus. The favorite scriptural text of this approach was Matthew 16:16–19, "So, I now say to you: You are Peter and on this rock I will build my Church." This approach was—and is—legitimate. It may very well have been the most appropriate one, given the controversies among Roman Catholics, Orthodox, Anglicans and Protestants,[1] Indeed, Martin Luther once said explicitly, "But what is the dissension about between the papists and us? The answer is: about the true Christian Church."[2] However, as history has shown, this approach has so focused on certain controversial questions among these churches that other equally important insights have been neglected. As a reaction, and remedy, more recent ecclesiology has emphasized the origin of the Church in the saving will of God. Here the starting point is 1 Timothy 2:4–6: "God our Savior: he wants everyone to be saved and reach full knowledge of the truth. For there is only one God, and one mediator between God and mankind, himself a man, Christ Jesus." Like Christ, the Church is seen to be the sacrament of this saving will of God, indeed of God's very own self.

It is on the basis of this second approach that I have arranged this book. We shall begin our ecclesiology not with Christ, Peter and the historical, human origin of the Church. Rather, we shall begin with God, Father-Son-Holy Spirit, and the transcendent, divine origin of the Church.

The inmost nature of the Church will be seen to reside in the very nature of God. The Church is the culmination of a long movement whereby the life

1

and being of God is shared with the non-godly. (In our usage this term has no moral connotations and overtones whatsoever. It simply designates that which is not purely and simply identical with God.) This Godly sharing is rooted in the triune nature of God. God the Father-Son-Holy Spirit is/are[3] the transcendent condition of the very possibility of the existence of the Church, and its historical founder, Jesus Christ. This outward sharing

> (1) begins in creation: cosmic and human nature as the image and likeness of God;
>
> (2) continues in salvation-history: the history of biblical and other religions;
>
> (3) intensifies in the incarnation: the embodiment and enhistorying of the Godly Son and Word in a human nature;[4]
>
> (4) matures in the Church: the embodiment and enhistorying of the Godly (Holy) Spirit in humanity;[5]
>
> (5) consummates in glorious and blessed vision: the new heaven and earth of the celestial city.   *escatology*

In a true sense, the Church is the history of the triune God's communion with the non-Godly. This history has often been described by the triad of nature, grace and glory.

The key concepts of this ecclesiology are communion, sacrament, communication. The inward communion of God Father-Son-Holy Spirit enables the outward communion of God with the non-Godly. As God's internal communion is symbolic, that is, sacramental (the second person in Word and Son), so is the divine communion with the non-divine. Insofar as the non-divine is human, the communion is called *theandric,* from the Greek words for God and man. The world is not only "where" God communicates with humanity. It is also, precisely as human, the sign and symbol of this theandric communion. So, we can, and must, already speak of the creation, of the world and humanity as the sacrament of God. This original sacramental theandric sharing is elevated and intensified in Christ and the Church.

God's inward communion is not a lifeless, static state of being, but an intensely "act-ual" communication.[6] So also is this act-ual God's communion with human beings. This theandric communication is threefold: God with human beings, whence results the Church; the Church within itself as the people of God; the Church, as the sacrament of salvation, with all humanity.

It is already clear that the word "Church" has various meanings. These are not contradictory or mutually exclusive. Rather, "Church" is a choice term to describe the communication of God with the non-Godly. Since this communication is historical, it is not always exactly the same at every moment. Likewise, the terms describing this historical communication will also not always have exactly the same meaning. We shall see more of this later. For now, we simply emphasize that the Church has both a divine and a human dimension.

In our presentation we shall emphasize the divine origin of the Church, for two reasons. First of all, one of the preferred "definitions" of the Church is the people of God. The Church is a gathering together of people whose specific identity is provided by its relationship to God. Of course, this people's identity depends on the nature or identity of the God whose people it is. Second, ecclesiology is a part or specialty of a more general enterprise known as theology, the study, that is, of God. Too often, past ecclesiology has not paid sufficient specific attention to the relation between God and the Church, between ecclesiology and the rest of theology. Like the Church itself, theology is a series of reforms and in need of continued reform. No single theology will ever be perfect. Even the Church itself hopes to be purely and simply "without spot or wrinkle" (Eph 5:27) only in its eschatological consummation. The purpose of this book is to retrieve some insights which have been neglected and to elaborate some which have been recovered for the sake of an ecclesiology which will correspond better to the needs, abilities and aspirations of our own age.

Among other possible approaches to the Church, this one will focus on the Church as the sacrament of God's communion and communication with the non-Godly. As the Second Vatican Council reminded us, "By its relationship with Christ, the Church is a kind of sacrament or sign of intimate union with God, and of the unity of all mankind. It is also an instrument for the achievement of such union and unity" (*The Church* 1; also 48). Precisely because the Church is the sacrament of salvation, a comprehensive theological term for theandric communion and communication, a successful general introduction to ecclesiology can also serve as an introduction to theology in general.

Vatican II also called for a revision of ecclesiastical studies in the preparation of candidates for ordination to the priesthood. It stressed that this preparation was to promote the organic unity of the spiritual, pastoral, philosophical and theological studies. It then stipulated that "from the very start of their training, ecclesiastical studies should begin with an introductory course of suitable duration. In this initiation [to] the mystery of salvation. . . ." Thus, "Seminarians should be thoroughly penetrated by the mystery of the Church . . ." (*Priestly Formation* 14; 9). There is no inherent reason restricting these admonitions to only seminarians, as distinct from other students of theology. Further, a purely "academic" theology with no relationships to the pastoral or missionary dimensions would be bad theology. As Karl Rahner noted in regard to the proposals for a kerygmatic in contrast to a scientific theology, "All theology must be salvation-history theology. There can be no such thing as a merely 'theoretical,' unengaged theology,"[7] The ecclesiology I shall present wants to be "theoretical" in the best sense of that term.

If it is, then it will also be spiritual, pastoral and missionary. It will want to be lived in everyday life and shared with others.

I have also endeavored to cultivate the ecumenical dimensions of ecclesiology. To do this, I have not proposed direct solutions to the classical controversial questions which have divided the Roman Catholic, Anglican, Orthodox and Protestant churches. I do not thereby think that these contoversies are passé and unimportant, irrelevant and insoluble. My approach is, rather, to find a wider horizon, within ecclesiology and theology, within which the classical controversial questions can be seen in better perspective.[8] Thus, one hopes, they may be relativized: without being erroneously explained away, as if they didn't exist; without total capitulation of any ecclesial community being required, as if it has been only erroneous. This relativizing is not intended as an escape from the reality of controversy, but as an ecumenical exercise in the principle of "Unity in Diversity, Diversity in Unity."[9] Jesus said, "There are many rooms in my Father's house" (Jn 14:2).[10] Ecumenical ecclesiology (theology) tries to find as many of these rooms as possible among the various churches as they now exist, even in their divided state. For it recalls another word of its founder, "Anyone who is not against you is for you" (Lk 9:50).

Finally, a cautionary word about the importance of ecclesiology. It is, of course, quite possible to be overly concerned with the Church and narrowly "churchy" matters. In today's heightened rhetoric of social concern and passion for social justice, any occupation with ecclesiological matters could seem to be preoccupation. Even such a balanced theologian as Karl Rahner has felt compelled to warn against "an introversion of the Church upon herself."[11] That such a danger exists is duly noted. It is also duly hoped that ecclesiology, properly performed, will not be "narcissistic."[12] Rather, it will aid the Church, as the sacrament of salvation, to be both symbol and agent of this salvation more effectively—for the glory of God and the salvation of God's world.

NOTES

1. Yves Congar, *Lay People in the Church* (Westminster, Md.: Newman, 1965) 38–58.

2. *Martin Luther: Selections From His Writings,* ed. John Dillenberger (Garden City: Doubleday Anchor, 1962) 242.

3. I am aware that the use of "is/are" here can cause consternation. I do it only to hint at a brief discussion about the one divine nature and the three persons in God in Chapter 1. This discussion is crucial for our presentation of the pastoral and ecclesiological importance of the doctrine of God as Trinity. Neither doctrinal heresy nor grammatical insouciance, but attention to the significance of the triune nature of God is intended.

4. According to Karl Rahner, the absolute bringer of salvation is not only "a historical moment in the saving action of God in the world . . . of the history of the self-communication of God to the world," he is also "a piece of the very history of the cosmos" (ein Stueck dieser Geschichte des Kosmos selbst ist"). . . . The fundamental statement of Christology is precisely the *Body*-becoming (Incarnation, *Fleisch*werdung) of God, his Becoming-*material* or matter." ST, V, 203–204; also 125.

5. Heribert Muhlen, *Una Mystica Persona* (Paderborn: Schoningh, 1964) 51–73, 216–285.

6. I have used this spelling of act-ual to make a point. The point is this—that being must be thought of as act, that is, as fullness of being. Act does not mean activity, especially not frantic activity. Too often, though, we tend to think of being in really minimalistic terms—to be simply means not not to be, a bare escape from nothingness, from not being at all. We must concede that the term can be used in this minimalist way. However, such minimalism in misleading. Being is really act or actuality in contrast to potentiality. When we think of being, we should not start with a rock. We should start with a person, and to start with a person means to start with a community, with a communion. When we think of person, we shouldn't think of someone asleep or barely hanging on. We should think of someone vital, fully alive, as we say. When we think of community, we should not think of a bunch of lethargic laggards, lounging about, just this side of dying from boredom. Again, act does not mean frantic and frenetic being. But it does mean fullness, energy, actuality, really and truly being. To convey this understanding I have chosen to spell the word, "act-ual." Thus, God who "bes" the most is also the most "act-ual." Non-Godly being is also "act-ual" insofar as it is like God. The more God-like, the more "act-ual," the more real, the more being-full. The activity of human beings in daily life is a reflection of this original actuality in being. This understanding of what it means to be is necessary if we are going to "understand" the triune God and this God's communion and communication, inwardly and outwardly. See William Hill, *The Three-Personed God* (Washington: The Catholic University Press, 1982) 246–250, 259–261. Emrich Coreth, *Metaphysics* (New York: Herder and Herder, 1968) 77–102.

7. LTK 6, 126.

8. See my "Leise Treten: An Irenic Ecumenical Hermeneutic," *Theological Studies* 44 (1983) 407–437.

9. Yves Congar, *De la communion des Eglises a une ecclesiologie de l'eglise universelle* (Paris: Cerf, 1962) 227–260.

10. The precise import of this statement is not immediately evident. The best interpretation seems to be that Jesus is instructing his disciples that, like him, they will have dwelling places in the glory of the Father, and that these places will last. They will be everlasting, that is, final resting places, not in death or nothingness, but in heavenly life with Christ and through him with the heavenly Father. In our sacramental understanding of the divine communion with the non-Godly and of salvation history, we believe that these many final dwelling places already exist in the world now. They exist in a preliminary way, but they truly exist. The graced life of this world is already an anticipation and pledge of the glorious life of the eschatological fulfillment of the next. In spite of the failings and faults of the present sinful, holy Church, it is not impossible, then, to regard even the divided ecclesial communities of the Church as the beginnings of these everlasting dwelling places with the Father-God of Jesus. This view is based

on the exegesis of John 14:1–6 by Raymond Brown, *The Gospel According to John XII–XXI* (Garden City: Doubleday, 1970) 616–628, and Rudolf Schnackenburg, *Das Johannesevangelium III* (Freiburg: Herder, 1975) 63–71.

11. *The Church After the Council* (New York: Herder and Herder, 1966) 93.

12. John Baptist Metz, in *The Crucial Question,* ed. Frank Fehmers (New York: Newman, 1969) 145, speaks of ''ecclesiological narcissism.''

GOD AND RELIGION

Before we begin our consideration proper of the triune God as the origin and pattern of the Church as communion, a twofold preliminary consideration requires our attention. It is our contention that human beings have a religion of some sort, and that all human beings believe in a God of some kind.[1] A brief treatment of these general considerations will set the scene for our consideration of the precisely Christian God and Christian Church.

RELIGION

The definition of religion has always been a troublesome undertaking. Even those who believe that all people are religious have difficulty in developing an adequate definition. Attempts to derive a definition from the etymology of the word have not been successful. We should note immediately that religion is a Latin and Western word. Other languages and cultures do not necessarily have a precise equivalent. Indeed, the etymology of the word itself is not clear. Does religion come from *religari* (to bind back again) or *relegere* (to pay special attention to) or *re-eligere* (to choose the same object repeatedly)? Famous thinkers like Cicero, Lactantius and St. Augustine have tried this approach.[2] St. Thomas Aquinas synthesized the three above suggestions into the following definition: "Properly speaking, religion designates the right order (relationship) to God, to whom we must be chiefly united (*religari*) as to our unceasing origin; to whom our choosing must also be diligently directed (*relegere*) as our ultimate end and goal; whom, should we have 'lost' him by sin, we must rechoose, regain (*re eligere*) by faith and witnessing the faith."[3]

Although St. Thomas composed this definition within a particular religious tradition, it can be easily modified to fit other religions. Nowadays one speaks of the phenomenological or anthropological definition of religion.[4] This approach focuses on the description of observable human behavior. It does not evaluate this behavior. It does not judge its truth or error, its goodness or badness. It simply states that people behave in such a way. It claims that there is a definite way of human behavior, distinct from all other observable ways of behaving, which can be called religious. The first hallmark of religion is totality.

Whether religion in general or a definite religion in particular is good or bad, true or false, religion embraces the whole of life. It describes whence one came, where one is going and how one should behave in between. Religion is concerned with the *whole* of life.

The second hallmark of religion is ultimacy. It describes human life on the basis of something ultimate, something non-negotiable. We humans organize our lives in many ways. But we all have one way which is the basis of all the other ways. There is a point at which we say "No further. This is it. Here I take my stand." Generally we do not have to make this "last stand" explicit in our thoughts. It simply functions in all our individual decisions and actions. It is this non-negotiable "last stand" that is source of that way of behaving which is called religion.

In view of this I suggest as an adequate definition: Religion is the organization of one's whole life, individual and social, on the basis of insights and values perceived to be ultimate.

"Organization" does not mean an elaborate computerization. It means how we spend our time and energy, what we do and don't do. "Individual" and "social" simply emphasize that it is our lives whole and entire which are organized by religion. "Insight" is another word for truth. Truth means basically that our thinking and the way things really are coincide. Truth gives meaning to life—it enables us to get things together, to put things in their proper perspective, to make sense out of things. "Value" is another word for good. Good describes what we want near to us, what we would like to have and be more of, given the proper conditions and circumstances. Good is that which makes life live-able. Good enables life to live, being to be. "Perceived" emphasizes that religion is at least partly a human action and work. It is something that human beings do. It grows out of human life and experience in the cosmic and human world. Hence, it is at least *a priori* possible that there can be a plurality of religions based, not on human ignorance and sin, but on different experiences of the world and reflection on these experiences. This does not exclude what we call divine revelation. Even special divine revelation has to happen in the world and be received by human beings.

Their experimental dimension will also necessarily play a role in any revelation God might choose to give. And there appears for the first time the word we usually expect to dominate any discussion or definition of religion—God.

GOD

Is God absent from my proposed definition? Yes and no. Yes, if the word itself is required. No, if the reality described by this word is acceptable. The traditional term for ultimate truth and good is God. However, anthropologically and phenomenologically, it is clear that people who do not believe in the traditional God of theism nevertheless still have ultimate insights and values in their lives.[5] It is also clear that these ultimate insights and values govern their lives and behavior as much as the traditional personal God governs the lives of traditional theists.

Some have suggested that these new, non-traditional religions be called pseudo-religions. Pseudo, however, has such negative connotations (false, fraudulent, deceptive, etc.) that this term is better left unused. Paul Tillich has suggested "quasi-religion" to describe these modern secular movements whose members are in a "state of being grasped by an ultimate concern, a concern which qualifies all other concerns as preliminary and which itself contains the answer to the question of the meaning of life."[6]

This approach does not judge the morality and truth of any particular religion or of religion in general. It simply states that there is an observable pattern of human behavior which is distinct from all other patterns. This distinct pattern, whose hallmarks are totality and ultimacy, is traditionally called religion. In support of this approach, we should note that a "traditional" religion, acknowledged by everyone to be a religion, does not profess belief in a personal god. This is, of course, Theravada Buddhism.[7]

The anthropological and phenomenological approach is not without its problems and disadvantages. It does, admittedly, refrain from the critical questions of truth and goodness. On the other hand, it does describe how people—all people—behave, however varied particular elements of this general pattern of behavior might be. Perhaps the most telling point in favor of the approach I am advocating is the universal concern for salvation—among people as people, but equally observable among people as organized religions, whether traditional theistic or non-traditional non-theistic.[8] It is better to avoid calling them atheistic. The suggestion of trans-theistic is interesting, but insufficiently explored to know whether it is reliable and helpful.

SALVATION

All human beings desire salvation. The whence, whither and how of this salvation are as varied as the people and their religions themselves. But salvation they do want, from situations perceived to be negative, sorrowful and painful.[9] Even the classical critique of traditional religion, represented by Friedrich Nietzsche, Sigmund Freud, Ludwig Feuerbach, and Karl Marx, is itself religious—and salvational, for it wishes to save human beings from both *de facto* misery and from the false and illusionary salvation offered by the traditional religions. They parody this illusionary and delusionary salvation as "Pie in the sky by and by when I die." That this secularist salvation may not appeal to traditional theists does not mean that it is not proposed as a salvation. That it replaces the Savior-God with a Savior-Man does not invalidate its claim to be a religion offering true salvation.[10] Secular ultimates may be immanent in the cosmos and its history, but they claim to be ultimate just as do the transcendent ultimates of more traditional religions.

Even in materialistic societies there is a "fundamental need for meaningful fulfillment beyond the mere satisfaction of material needs . . . they look to ends which transcend individual existence."[11] In one sense, human being and history can be described as the search for "what is permanent in the nature of things."[12] Consequently, some Christian theologians like Karl Rahner have been able to discern even in atheism an implicit desire for and an anonymous dynamism toward the truth that good Catholics believe they have received from God in Christ and his Spirit.[13] In this view the Church is not an isolated, elite conventicle of a chosen few in an otherwise godless, damned world. Rather, the Church is, as we noted in the Introduction, the sacrament of the salvation of the whole world, precisely because God wishes to save the whole world which God created to begin with.

The search for fulfillment and meaning, for the permanent and lasting, has been going on since the beginning of human history. In this search the idea of a "Beyond" has regularly arisen. People in general and philosopher-theologians in particular have reflected on their limited everyday lives and wondered whether there might not be something "more," something "beyond" this limited empirical human existence. The Greeks called this "Beyond" *apeiron*—the unlimited, limitless, unbounded, boundless, infinite. Their unanimity in agreeing *that* there is an *apeiron* was equaled only by their unanimity in disagreeing about *what* it is.

Nevertheless, from the very beginning of Greek and, we can peacefully say, human thought, the *apeiron* has preoccupied human beings, the "common man" in the street as well as the expert in the groves of academe.

Was St. Paul playing on this preoccupation when be preached about the "Unknown God," whose altar he had discovered in the Areopagus in Athens (Acts 17:23–34)? It is not necessarily fanciful to involve St. Paul in support of our contention that all people are religious in some way or other, that they believe in some sort of God. I say this not only because he says ". . . an Unknown God. Well, the God whom you already worship without knowing it. . . ." Here we must also keep in mind that the God whom Paul proclaims is significantly different from the ones generally professed by the Athenians. Indeed the difference between Paul's God and the Athenians' gods may very well have been considerably greater than the difference between Paul's God and those of modern, secularist, pragmatist "atheists." But I also think that another statement in St. Paul's discourse might support our understanding of religion as a universal human phenomenon: "Yet in fact he [the deity] is not far from any of us, since it is in him that we live, and move, and have our being (exist) . . . so that . . . all nations might seek the deity and, by feeling their way toward him, succeed in finding him." Here St. Paul is not proclaiming a simple, monistic pantheism—certainly not. But he is also not proclaiming a distant, remote God, totally other (Dt 30:11–14), separated from the world—"his children," as Paul calls all of us human beings—by a yawning, cavernous abyss. We do not "feel our way" toward God, as if there were any chance that we would or would not find this God. Because of the way in which God has created and graced the world, the outcome is not in doubt. This is not facile, supercilious optimism. Rather, "It states the fact that hope (in love) hopes that the real saving will of God is truly operative. . . . God's salvific will acts by causing it to be hoped for precisely as what is the incalculable. Because the salvific will wills a salvation which is God himself, he has made a creature to attain it."[14]

It is the God of this universal will whom all people seek. It is this God whom St. Paul proclaims as having been found by all people, even though and when they are not explicitly aware believers and worshipers. It is this God whom we explicit believers believe to have been revealed in Jesus Christ as Father-Son-Holy Spirit. It is this God of whose universal saving will for all humankind we believe the Church to be sacrament.

TRIUNE GOD

The God in whom the disciples of the risen Jesus, his many brothers and sisters (Rom 8:29) believe, is named Father, Son, Holy Spirit. Indeed, this triad can be taken as the proper name of God, not merely some general designation.[15] The religion which the disciples of Jesus practice is known by various names. Usually it is called Christian, but we should be careful of this short name. It would always be better to use Judeo-Christian, so that we would never forget our Jewish ancestry and heritage.[16] As Hans Urs von Balthasar has pointed out, when the Christian Church forgets its Jewish heritage, it inexorably tends to Gnosticism.[17] This is important, as we shall see later on, because Gnosticism essentially denies that the material world is the good creation of the good God. Hence, it is also a rejection of the sacramental communion between God and humanity. So, we would do well to emphasize that we are Judeo-Christians. A further specification of this Judeo-Christian religion is Catholic. Catholic is generally associated with Roman. It also legitimately refers to the Anglican and Orthodox interpretations or traditions of the Judeo-Christian religion insofar as these three can be and are distinguished from the Protestant traditions. This book is written within the Catholic tradition, but always keeping in mind the ecumenical dimensions and requirements of the catholic, that is, universal Judeo-Christian tradition. Within this Judeo-Christian tradition we tend to speak of religion concretely in terms of Church. Thus we speak of the Roman Catholic Church to identify a specific, definite way of being religious within the Judeo-Christian religious tradition. Within this specific tradition, we shall speak of God, of God's relationship with the world and of the Church as the sacrament of this relationship, which is regarded as saving. It is our contention that both salvation and the Church can be

understood only in relationship to and in the context of the triune God, the
Father-Son-Holy Spirit, who is the origin, the pattern and the end of all non-
Godly being.

It is generally agreed that the doctrine of God as Trinity does not play a
major role, at least explicitly, in the religious lives of Christians. Already in
1967 Karl Rahner spoke of "The Isolation of Trinitarian Doctrine in Piety and
Textbook Theology." He noted that, "despite their orthodox confession of
the Trinity, Christians are, in their practical life, almost mere 'monotheists'
. . . Should the doctrine of the Trinity have to be dropped as false, the major
part of religious literature could well remain virtually unchanged. . . . The
Christian's idea of the incarnation would not have to change at all if there were
no Trinity."[18] In a certain sense, this is a strange and unexpected state of affairs. After all, how often do Catholics, making the sign of the cross, remind
themselves prayerfully of the name of the Father, Son and Holy Spirit! And
how often do all Christians similarly remind themselves of the Trinity in the
doxology when they proclaim "Glory be to the Father and to the Son and to
the Holy Spirit, as it was in the beginning, is now and will be forever!" Nevertheless, there is widespread agreement with Rahner's evaluation. In fact, William Hill begins his comprehensive investigation of Trinitarian theology by
citing Rahner,[19] with whom he otherwise often disagrees. Robert Jenson begins his book: "It need not be argued that the Western church now little uses
or understands Christianity's heritage of trinitarian reflection and language."
He ends his book on a hardly more optimistic note: "Whether the Western
church can renew its trinitarianism, whether it can recover specifically Christian proclamation and faith, may well be doubted."[20] Jurgen Moltmann also
agrees with both Rahner's and Jenson's evaluation: "Whether God is one or
triune evidently makes as little difference to the doctrine of faith as it does to
ethics. Consequently the doctrine of the Trinity hardly occurs at all in modern
apologetic writings which aim to bring the Christian faith home to the modern
world again." He also emphasizes that "ever since Schleiermacher we have
been told that this doctrine 'cannot count as being the direct statement of the
devout personal consciousness' . . . since Kant that 'nothing whatsoever can
be gathered for practical purposes' from the doctrine of the Trinity."[21] On the
other hand, Raimondo Panikkar adds ecumenical urgency to the retrieval of
the doctrine of the Trinity within Christianity. He not only finds vestiges[22] and
hints of "the trinitarian conception of the Ultimate . . . within the several religious traditions." He also maintains that the Trinity is a privileged "meeting
[place] of the religions" of the world.[23]

Obviously we cannot give an extended treatment of Trinitarian theology
here. In addition to the books already mentioned, all of which are rather de-
manding, recourse can be had to theology textbooks, encyclopedias and a recent survey by Joseph Bracken, *What Are They Saying About the Trinity?*[24]
Here we shall mention only what is necessary for our precise purpose.

Although technical terms like Trinity, person, nature, hypostasis, etc. do not appear in the New Testament, the reality these terms try to describe does. The origin of the doctrine of the Trinity is the New Testament, which speaks of the *apeiron* as Father, Son, Holy Spirit.[25] The New Testament itself does not provide an explanation of how the one God can be simultaneously three persons. Admittedly, the New Testament does not use the word person to describe the three. But Father and Son are clearly personal terms, and Holy Spirit is also able to be thought of in terms of personality. In any case, we always use our best human words to speak about God. Person is certainly one of our best.

Very early in the Church's history theologians used the terms of philosophy to help "explain" their faith. Of course, God is essentially mystery. Therefore we shall never comprehend God, that is, achieve perfect and exhaustive knowledge about God. But this does not mean that we know nothing about God. It is just that, the more we know about God, the more we find that we know less than we thought. Every true knowledge about God necessarily reveals to us how little we do know. The more we know, the less we know. Nicholas of Cusa coined the famous phrase *docta ignorantia* (learned ignorance) to describe this state of affairs. Now, this is not intended to induce an inferiority complex in human beings. This situation is not so much that result of human ignorance as it is of the unsurpassable divine knowability.

So, human theology about God is not intended to explain away the divine mystery. It is, rather, as another favorite word of Nicholas has it, to unfold or explicate the presence of God in and through the creation. As God unfolded himself in creation, so does human thinking unfold this divine presence in symbols. This symbolic unfolding takes many forms. The form known as theology uses concepts and words. A prime source of such concepts and words is philosophy. That is why Christian theologians have "philosophized" about their faith—their religion, their Church—from the very beginning—not because they think that they will thus comprehend God, but because as human beings they must think and talk about their faith in God. In regard to Trinitarian theology, St. Augustine himself remarked that we speak of one essence and three persons "since they [many authoritative Latin writers] could find no better way to put into words what they understood without words. . . . When one inquires three of what, then the inadequacy of human language becomes manifest. The preferred expression is, however, three persons. This does not mean, of course, that thereby the truth is positively [completely, perfectly] expressed—only that it is not left completely in silence."[26]

This very imperfect talk of theologians about God has two goals—to unfold our experience, discovered and revealed, of God and to defend the truth of God's existence and nature against errors. The three major errors about the triune God are modalism, tritheism and subordinationism. They all appeared in the very first centuries of the Church's existence. All three destroy the triune God revealed and described in the New Testament. Modalism destroys the three persons in favor of the one nature. Tritheism destroys the one nature in favor of the three persons. In the first you get a God who is only one person, but plays three roles in salvation-history—a sort of one actor show. In the second you end up with polytheism—three gods instead of one three-personed God. Subordinationism destroys the divine communion by making either or both the Son and Holy Spirit inferior to the Father.

All of Trinitarian theology may be understood as the defense of the God Father-Son-Holy Spirit against these three "isms." In sports we often hear that the best defense is a good offense. Similarly, in theology one defends best by providing a positive explanation. William Hill has thought it possible to discern and classify five major positive approaches to the unfolding or explication of the Trinity in the present.[27] From the more than twenty examples he examines, we shall attend to only two.

The first is associated with St. Augustine and is called the psychological approach. It looks to the human person, its constitution and functions, for ideas and concepts which will enable us to understand, to talk about God as Father, Son, Holy Spirit—one divine nature, three divine persons. St. Augustine finds an analogy for the triune God in the human being, which is one personal self consisting of memory (mind, self-consciousness, self-presence), knowing and loving. There is one self, which is triply "act-ual." These three acts are neither identical nor separately independent from the self. Naturally, St. Augustine knew that this explanation (even his full explanation, which is, of course, much more elaborate than our oversimplified summary) did not explain the Trinity. But he hoped, nevertheless, that it would enable believers to talk about the Trinity correctly.

St. Augustine's psychological approach could be called an "inner way" of spirituality and theology. It has certainly been the dominant approach in Western Christianity. But there is also another and complementary approach, which can be traced back to Richard of St. Victor. It is sometimes called the social, societal or "intersubjective" approach.[28] In Book III of his work *On the Trinity,* Richard inquires about "what we should hold concerning the plurality of divine persons."[29] To "prove" that there are and must be three persons in the one true God, Richard has recourse to the divine goodness, which must be supreme goodness. But, as human consciousness and experience show, supreme goodness cannot be without charity. Charity requires another, a second person, to be the beloved. Self-love, good and necessary in itself, is nevertheless not charity. Since charity can only be between equals, creation cannot be the primary and original beloved of God the Creater. Hence, there is another divine person. But even two persons are not sufficient. This is because perfect, excellent charity is not and cannot be content with the love between the original lover and beloved. Charity inherently wishes the mutual love it originally experienced to be shared with a third. This is rooted in the dynamism of the good which is self-diffusive. Hence, the very nature of "charity is not only mutual love between two; it is fully shared love among three."[30]

Once again, Richard would be the first to admit that such reflective thought would not be able to prove the existence of the Trinity if God had not revealed it in and through Jesus. However, once this revelation has taken place, human beings, who are, after all, the image and likeness of the triune God, can find in their human experience analogates to help them think and talk about the God who has revealed himself in and to them. Attentive readers will notice that Augustine's approach could tend to modalism, Richard's to tritheism. Obviously, neither intended to nurture or encourage heresy. Each wanted to protect both the one divine nature and the three divine persons. They knew that such protection was important not only for God, but for the world created in the image and likeness of this triune God.[31] Here we have a splendid example of how good theory (orthodoxy) is necessarily also good practice (orthopraxis). Walter Kasper has this in mind when he emphasizes:

> The inner divine Trinity is, so to speak, the transcendental condition which makes possible salvation-history's self-communication of God in Jesus Christ through the Holy Spirit. It is nothing other than the logical exegesis of the proposition that "God is love" (1 Jn 4:8, 16).[32]

This is why Karl Rahner asserts that "the economic Trinity is the immanent Trinity and the immanent Trinity is the economic Trinity."[33] Here "economic" means salvation-historical, that is, the triune God who is revealed in Jesus as actively reconciling and saving the world (2 Cor 5:17–20). "Immanent" means the inner intimate life of God in himself. If the immanent and salvation-historical Trinity do not coincide, then the world which we believe God created and the salvation God is effecting are impossible. Consequently, not only would our understanding of God have been off, our world would be *kaput*—finished. Only if God is Father-Son-Holy Spirit is there creation and incarnation, grace and glory—in a word, salvation. The intense pastoral dimension of Rahner's theoretical systematic theology is nowhere more evident than in his insistence upon the identity of the immanent and salvation-historical Trinity. God-in-himself is truly God-in-us. The history of the world is truly the history of grace, indeed, but this is only because the one God is indeed triune.

TRIUNE COMMUNION AS PERICHORESIS

But how are we to understand this tri-une-ness of God? Being the hardy monotheists we are, we have the tendency to establish that there is *one* God. And this monotheism is not to be undervalued or taken lightly. Even polytheistic religions are not without a monotheistic dimension or tendency, in that they usually have a chief god or set of gods. There is a sort of God beyond the gods. There is usually also some sort of ordering among the many gods, so that, again, one god or one set of gods has a sort of primacy. There is, then, something like a *mon*-archy—a rule of one among the many gods. This concern for monotheism can unfortunately be reflective of and conducive to a monarchical and monistic totalitarianism. That is its shadow side. On the other hand, it can also reflect the desire to escape anarchy and chaos, which is the condition of plurality, of the many without a principle of order and unity. As James Collins has well noted, the problem of the one and the many is a classic and perennial problem of "the whole history of philosophy . . . of all periods."[34] This problem is not only metaphysical but also political. Indeed, we can say that it is not only philosophical in the sense of theoretical reflection. It is also practical, in the sense that it occurs in our everyday lives, both sacred and secular, civil and ecclesial. It is certainly, then, an important question in theology and religion. Against this background, the concern of Christianity to discern and preserve monotheism is quite understandable.

But the same consideration also reveals the necessity of attending properly to the dimension of plurality. For it is always a question of the one *and* the many. So, we revert to the question with which we began this section: How are we to understand this triuneness of God? As hardy monotheists, do we not have the tendency to establish the one nature of God—and then divide this one nature up into three parts? These three parts are then called persons and identified as Father-Son-Holy Spirit. In a sense, we have split personalities theologically—monotheists for a while and then polytheists (*tri*-theists) for a while. Of course we don't want to do this. We aren't usually reflectively aware that we are doing it. It is against this tendency or temptation that Rahner argues so vigorously in the article we have already cited several times, "The Oneness (Unicity) and Threeness of God in the Dialogue with Islam."[35] I repeat that there is a double significance to this insistence—theoretical and practical. Theoretically, if we divide the One God into Three pieces, even if we call these three pieces persons, we no longer have the God whom we believe to have been revealed to us in Jesus. Practically, if we don't have this God, we no longer have the world we believe to have been created, graced and saved by this God. The importance of God as Trinity cannot be exaggerated. If we may not divide, separate and apportion the original one divine nature into three divine persons, how are we to think about this tri-une-ness of God? First of all, we must make the considerable effort to think of God as *one* and *three* right away, right at the beginning. This does not mean that we have to understand it—certainly not in detail. All it means is that we shall develop a habit of always and immediately thinking *that,* reminding ourselves *that,* God is triune. This will help us to avoid the errors of modalism and tritheism in our subsequent more detailed reflection. Of course, and unfortunately, this is not a magic formula which, having been invoked, works automatically and forever. But it can be a helpful pedagogical exercise.

As we noted above, when Christian believers wanted to reflect systematically on their belief, that is, when they wanted to theologize, they had recourse to the concepts and categories of their culture, especially of philosophy. Sometimes helpful concepts lay right at hand. At other times considerable searching was necessary before the proper concept or category was found. The latter was the case when the theologians went looking for ways to describe the intensely intimate relationships of the God Father-Son-Holy Spirit. Finally, they did hit upon a term which expressed this intimate relationship as best human language could. It is most fitting that the term was used originally in Christology, to describe the intimacy of the divine and human in the one person of Jesus Christ. In regard to Christ, Christian believers and theologians had to face the same basic heretical tendencies they had to face in regard to God—reduction of the many to the one, and the division of the one into the many. The classic formulations came to be one nature, three persons for God; one person, two natures for Christ. Both of these Christian theological problems are instances of the more general problem of the one and the many, as we have seen.

In order to protect the intimate union of the divine and human natures in Jesus, theologians had to ward off heresies such as Nestorianism, monotheletism and monophysitism. These heresies destroyed the perfect communion of the divine and human in Jesus by destroying either the human or the divine. Of course, this was one way to solve the problem of how the human and divine could be two but still one in Jesus. Unfortunately, this kind of solution solves the problem only by eliminating the reality which is problematic. So, the question remained: How would theologians preserve the true identity of Jesus, the God man, recorded in the New Testament and solemnly proclaimed at the Council of Chalcedon? How could the language of theology correctly express Chalcedon's faith that in Jesus the perfect communion of the divine and human has been achieved? Jesus is simultaneously true (perfect) man and true (perfect) God—without, as Chalcedon insists, mixture, transformation, separation, division.[36]

As I said above, the theologians finally did settle upon a term which they thought truly expressed this perfect communion, this perfect presence of the human and the divine to one another in Jesus. The term is *perichoresis*.[37] The word was used first in regard to Jesus, but was also soon applied to the Trinity. In both cases it is intended to help us think and talk about the intimacy of the one and many in both Jesus and God. Originally I had the impression that this term came from the Greek verb to dance, to dance around with.[38] I then proceeded to explain its significance for Trinitarian theology on the basis of the symbolism of dancing. Although there are war dances, dancing tends to describe a happy state of being. People are pleased with one another and with the way "things are going." They respond to this state of affairs by dancing, either spontaneously in free form or ritually in established patterns. Their dancing is a sign that they are pleased with another, pleased to be with one another. It is, therefore, both a sign and means of their being together, their union, their communion. Applied to God as Trinity, as triune, this would mean that the Father, Son and Holy Spirit are so pleased with being God, and with being Father-Son-Holy Spirit, and with being with each other that their very being is "act-ual." Their intimate triune communion could, then, be theologically expressed in human terms as a dancing together—a perichoresis. Unfortunately, I learned that perichoresis has a different etymology.[39] Although the words look alike, perichoresis comes not from *perichoreuo* but *perichoreo*. Its original etymological meaning is, therefore, not to dance, but to go round about, to come round to, to come to in succession. In theology it acquires the meaning of to penetrate, interpenetrate, as the German translations indicate: *Ineinandersein; gegenseitige Durchdringung.* This is a good example of how theology transforms a word from its customary meaning into a precisely theological term.

Now, although my etymology was wrong, I still think my general explanation remains correct and pertinent. The one God is not triune, God is not Father-Son-Holy Spirit merely out of a dull sense of duty or because he has to be that way, and he is resigned to it. Rather, God's triuneness is the mode and expression of the very inner act-uality of God. God "bes" so intensely that the divine being cannot be just one—it must also be three. The very unity (and unicity) of God is precisely plurality, without ceasing to be unity. We can say, then, that precisely God's rejoicing in being divine, in being perfectly, fully, infinitely, requires and "results" in God's being triune. God can be no other way. This is important not only theoretically, but also pastorally. For it is precisely this rejoicing in being and being in communion (inwardly) that enables God to be not only Father-Son-Holy Spirit, but also Creator and Incarnate Son-Word-Savior. In the theandric Jesus, the hypostatic union of the divine and human, being is also communion, the communion of the human and the divine. This union is also a perichoresis—etymologically, intensely intimate presence of the human and the divine to and with and in one another; really, also the mutual and joyful pleasedness with one another, so that the being of Jesus is an "act-ual" rejoicing in which the human and divine dance with one another. To the Divine Dancing of the Trinity corresponds the Theandric Dancing of the Hypostatic Union. And therein also lies the origin of the Church as the sacrament of the salvation of this perichoresic triune God and his perichoresic biune Messiah, Jesus. Consequently the Church itself must be a communion, a perichoresis.

Before we proceed to a detailed consideration of the Church as communion, a few more remarks about perichoresis are in order.

The richness as well as the problematic of perichoresis as a theological term is illustrated by its Latin translation. Although the word perichoresis had been used theologically since Gregory of Nazianzen and Maximus the Confessor in Christology, and had become a technical theological term with John Damascene in both Christology and Trinitarian theology, its equivalent first appeared in Latin in the mid-twelfth century translation of Damascene's work. And then it received a very hesitant welcome.

Originally translated as *circumincessio,* it was also translated as *circuminsessio* in the thirteenth century. This development was apparently caused by a non-theological factor, namely a change in French diction, whereby "c" began to be pronounced as "s". Nevertheless, the double translation aptly illustrates the two emphases and tendencies of Trinitarian speculation. The dynamic approach which emphasizes the relationship of the three persons among themselves in the one divine nature as a going into (*Ineinandergehen*) and living in/into (*Ineinanderleben*) one another, prefers *circumincessio.* The static approach, which emphasizes these relationships as being or resting in one another (*Ineinandersein*), prefers *circuminsessio.* In either case, however, and as the single Greek word emphasizes, "in both Christological and Trinitarian systematic theology, perichoresis is the shortest formula to describe the doctrine of simultaneous Unity and Diversity."[40]

It likewise serves to remind us that all theological speculation about God Father-Son-Holy Spirit is primarily intended to preserve their personal diversity with the unity of the divine nature. As we have repeatedly emphasized, this has value not only for our understanding of the God revealed in Jesus, but also for the world created, graced and saved by this God.[41]

Kasper's contention that the inner Trinity is the transcendental condition of the world's salvation must not be restricted to salvation from sin, which we call redemption. It also applies to the "original" salvation from nothingness, which we call creation. In view of this, theologians have consistently looked for traces or footsteps of the divine Trinity in the divinely created world (*Vestigium Trinitatis*).[42]

All religions, including the biblical, emphasize that the world has been created and exists as the image and likeness of the Creator God. Michael Schmaus correctly notes: "If, then, God is necessarily trinitarian, being (*Sein*) itself must also be trinitarian in its deepest roots. Since all created being is participation in the divine being, this necessarily Trinitarian structure of being will also be reflected in some way [in creation]. . . . It would indeed be strange, were nothing of this to enter into human consciousness."[43] This does not mean, of course, that apart from the special divine revelation in Jesus, human beings would have been able to come to a knowledge of God as Father-Son-Holy Spirit on their own.[44] It does not mean that every triad in nature is an immediate and univocal signal of the divine triune transcendent. It does mean, however, that in the very being of the world the proper relationship of the one and the many is not suspicion and envy, rivalry and hostility. It is, rather, diversity in unity and unity in diversity. It is perichoresis, circumincessio, circuminsessio. Being itself is relation, relationship, relatedness. In a word, substantial being—real, true full being—is communion.

This understanding of being—this ontology—is a significant departure from classical Greek ontology, which emphasized that real being (substance) was precisely not relatedness but independence, not communion but monarchy. A consideration of the contrast between these two ontologies is the final preparation for our consideration of the Church as communion, sacrament and communication.

One of the most famous lines in all of philosophy is Aristotle's[45] statement that "there are several (many) senses in which a thing may be said to 'be'. . . ." He continues, "Now there are several senses in which a thing is said to be first; yet substance is first in every case. . . . For of the other categories none can exist independently, but only substance."[46] Further, "substance, in the truest and primary and most definite sense of the word, is that which is neither predicable of a subject nor present in a subject; for instance, the individual man or horse. . . . All substance appears to signify that which is individual. In the case of primary substance this is indisputably true. . . . All substance appears to signify that which is individual."[47] Other categories, or ways of being, are called "accidents." This term does not mean that they happened by chance, but that they are "incapable of existence apart from the said subject."[48] Accidents in this sense are quantity, quality, relation, place, time, position, state, action or affection. Of these accidents it can truly said that they "be," for they are not nothing. But it must also be said that they don't be really and truly, for their "be-ing" is very thin—phthsic, one might say. Of all the accidental modes of being, relation may well be the thinnest—the un-beingest.[49] If all accidents are unsubstantial, relation is the most unsubstantial.

Such abstract philosophical, theoretical considerations are not without their practical consequences. St. Thomas sums up the classical understanding of substance: "The name substance signifies an essence to which it belongs (is proper) to exist . . . on its own" (by or through itself: *per se*).[50] On the other hand, according to Aristotle, "Those terms, then are called relative, the nature of which is explained by reference to something else, the preposition 'of' or some other preposition being used to indicate the relation."[51] Since relation is really *pros ti,* that is, "towardness" or toward something, it cannot be substantially, cannot be a substance. Thus substantial, or real, true being is not dependent, it is independent. Other ways of being might depend on it, but it does not depend on anything else for its own being. In such a thought world, true being is very easily, even necessarily, equated with the singular, with *one.* In fact, much Greek philosophy regarded *many,* that is, plurality, diversity, as a deterioration of true being, which had to be *one.*[52]

This approach, which emphasizes the one-ness of being, moves very easily from non-dependence to independence to isolation, in which one is not only one as unique, but also as alone, solitary. Non-dependence becomes isolation. Anthropologically, this means that the ideal human being is the loner, someone on whom others can perhaps depend, but who depends on no one himself—the John Wayne image. When these loners are not basically benevolent, as are the characters usually played by John Wayne, society, indeed human beings as such, can hardly be thought of except as "the war of all against all; there is no . . . industry . . . no knowledge . . . no arts; no letters; no society; and worst of all, continual fear, and danger of violent death; and the life of man, solitary, poor, nasty, brutish, and short.''[53]

The ontology implicit in the doctrine of the triune God is quite different.[54] It is neither isolationist nor collectivist, but communional.[55] It both enables and requires human beings to live together freely, cooperatively, peacefully. The doctrine of the triune God discloses that ''to be really and truly'' is not to be independently, in isolation from, but to be relatedly, in relationship with. To be is to be with. The inner being of God as Father-Son-Holy Spirit enables and requires created being, which culminates in the theandric Jesus, who as man is the one mediator between the Godly and non-Godly (1 Tim 2:4–6), to be itself a communion. The world's origin is precisely in and through the divine Son and Logos (Jn 1:2–5, 9–12; Col 1:15–20). Hence, as creation, the world is already in communion with God. In the incarnation this communion is intensified and expanded. Jesus' very being is the communion of the divine communion with the human communion. Because it is precisely the Logos of God which makes the world possible and actual, and because it is precisely in the Logos that the human and divine communion is consummated, it can be truly said that the world itself is logical, logostic. It makes sense, it is meaningful.

The innermost meaning of Christ is that the human communion is not an independent, isolated, distant and therefore pale imitation of an equally independent and distant God. Rather, the communion being of the divine nature which allows the one divine nature to ''bubble up'' and ''foam over''[56] into the triune or three-personed God also allows this three-personed God to bubble over into creation and into intimate, joyous communion with its creation. And thus is also possible not only creation but also incarnation, not only humanity but Church (the body of Christ), not only knowledge but grace and glory.

To quote Ratzinger once more, the incarnation reveals, strangely enough, not God's limitation, but precisely God's unlimitedness. God is not a prisoner of eternity, hemmed in by the ''spiritual.''[57] Rather, we might say, God is as much at home in matter as in spirit, in history as much as in eternity, in the world of becoming as in the absolute of pure subsistence. Against the Gnostics and others, we can and must assert, therefore, that creation from nothing, creation without pre-existent raw material (*creatio ex nihilo sui et subjecti*), is neither a mistake nor a result of sin.[58] It does not establish an abyss between God and Man, between divine and human being. Finitude and materiality do not signify separation or alienation from God. Rather, they are the means whereby the communication and communion of God with the non-Godly take place. They are not dividers of man from God, but mediators of God with man.

Already the Old Testament emphasized that God's *wisdom* is manifested in the material creation, the world cosmos (Prov 3:19; Jb 38—39; Sir 42:15—43:34) and history (Jb 12:13; Is 31:12). It is worth noting that precisely the *wisdom* literature asserts that creation manifests the "logos-tic" triune God. Although much caution is due, it is possible to see in the Old Testament personification of Wisdom (Prov 8:22; Wis 7:22, with the Jerusalem Bible notes) a shadowy intimation of Christianity's three-personed God. Again, only with the full revelation in Jesus is this clearly perceived. But it is also clear that "already" in the Old Testament God had to be "thought" other than in merely monistic, monarchical, monotheistic categories.

The wisdom literature also offers support for our understanding of creation as already a joyful "perichoresis" between the divine communion and the human communion. Of God's wisdom, which will be fully revealed in Christ as the Incarnate Logos, Proverbs 8:31–32 says:

> I was by his [Yahweh's] side, a master craftsman, delighting him day after day, ever at play in his presence, at play, everywhere in his world, delighting to be with the sons of men.[59]

God's wise delight is clearly, then, to be with the creation. Creation indeed is divine delight. The relationship between the divine communion and the human communion, a perichoresis from the very beginning, becomes unsurpassably and irreversibly so in the hypostatically united theandric communion of Jesus—the Word-Wisdom of God incarnate in human nature and history.

It is perfectly legitimate, then, to seek out and rejoice in the *vestigia trinitatis* in this world and its history. For God has not been a reluctant or stingy Creator, but, as Dante said so well, a *lieto fattore*, a joyous, happy maker.[60] For this reason, Dante's humanity, finite and fallen, can also be happy: "Gladly do I grant myself indulgence for the occasion of my lot and it does not trouble me. . . . Yet here we repent not, but smile; not for the fault, which does not return to the memory, but for the power which ordained and saw."[61] The world is where the wise God dances and plays with his creatures. Certainly, then, one would expect traces and footsteps of this triune God not only in cosmic nature, but also human history. For both are the manifestation of the wise, "logos-tic" (therefore also symbolic, sacramental, sign-full) God. From the overflowing communion of God within, Father-Son-Holy Spirit (over-) flows the creation which is, and must become, communion, so that it is not only the ontological, but also behavioral image and likeness of God.

From the communion of the triune God comes the communion of the Church.

NOTES

1. For elaboration of this contention, see Robert Kress, "Religious Indifference—Definition and Criteria," *Concilium* 165 (May, 1983) 11–19; "Everyday Life a Spiritual Discipline," *Spiritual Discipline and Ultimate Reality,* ed. James Duerlinger (New York: Paragon, 1984) 13-42.

2. See Michael Nicolau and Joachim Salaverri, *Sacrae Theologiae Summa I* (Madrid: B.A.C., 1955) 64–75.

3. Thomas Aquinas, *Summa Theologiae,* II—II, q. 81, a. 1.

4. Wolfgang Riess, *Glaube als Konsens* (Muenchen: Koesel, 1979) 173–78.

5. See Robert Johann, *Building the Human* (New York: Herder and Herder, 1963) 15–17. Support for this position is provided by the decisions of some civil courts in the United States: Torcasso v. Watkins, 397 U.S. 488 (1961) at 495, n. 11; United States v. Seeger, 380 U.S. 193 (1965); Peter v. United States, 324 F. 2d 173 (9th Cir. 1963); Macmurray v. United States, 330 F. 2d 928 (9th Cir. 1964). In these decisions secular humanism, which explicitly denies the existence of the traditional, transcendent, personal God of theism, was discerned and decreed to be a religion. In this decision, the court did not pass judgment on the value, the truth and goodness, of secular humanism. It simply stated that the specific pattern of human behavior known as secular humanism corresponds sufficiently to traditional theistic religions to qualify for the same legal and social status enjoyed by those traditional religions. The court noted that it is possible to have an ultimate which is not spelled with an upper case "G" (God), but with a lower case "g" (god). In this sense, everybody has an ultimate—a god—however varied these ultimates, these gods might be understood. The Ninth Circuit Court of Appeals decided that "man thinking his highest, feeling his deepest and living his best" qualified for status as religious belief. Likewise, human belief in a "goodness" or even a "livingness" in the very heart of things is also acceptable as religious belief. Thus, from the sociological, anthropological, phenomenological point of view, "a given belief that is sincere and meaningful [which] occupies a place in the life of the possessor parallel to that filled by orthodox belief in God" can and must also be regarded as (a) religion. We must concede once again, of course, that such an approach to religion is not riskless. It can easily overlook the enormous differences among these religions and deities. On the other hand, this approach does have the enormous advantage of locating the human argument about the nature and meaning of human existence where it properly belongs—in religion. The human argument is not between religion and unreligion. It is between (among) religions. Crudely put, the argument is: Who has the best religion? Who has the best God? This argument can be conducted bellicosely or peacefully. In either case, however, it remains *the* human argument, the human quest.

Of course, this also makes it clear that religion as such is not only and necessarily good. In our approach, religion can be good or bad. The Germans speak of the essence or nature (*Wesen*) as well as the unnature or anti-essence (*Unwesen*) of religion. (Bernhard Welte, *Auf der Spur des Ewigen* [Freiburg: Herder, 1965] 279–296). By this they mean to indicate that, as the organization of life on the basis of ultimate insights and values, any given religion can be destructive as well as constructive. The insights can be true or false, the values good or bad. Whichever, however, human being is inescapably religious. Consequently, human history is inevitably an argument about the relative preference of any given concrete definite religion in regard to others. It need not be, therefore, imperialist to describe as religious people who explicity do not want to be religious. Our approach does not force anyone to belong to a certain religion. It only discloses that to refuse one religion is not to become un-religious; it is, rather, to become differently religious. Neither is it, as such, imperialistic to prefer one's religion to another. One can behave imperialistically in this regard. But comparison and preference in the face of variety seem to be inevitable and virtuous human behavior. Indeed, it is a dimension of the human quest for the truth, for ultimate meaning. St. Paul could well include such comparing and preferring in his description of human beings' "seeking the deity, feeling their way toward him" (Acts 17:27).

That some people would like to believe in God, even though they are very reluctant about the likelihood of God's existence, is amply attested among "atheistic" authors. Viteslav Gardavsky, *God Is Not Yet Dead* (Baltimore: Pelican, 1973); Max Horkheimer, *Die Sehnsucht nach dem ganz Anderen* (Hamburg: Furche, 1970).

6. Paul Tillich, *Christianity and the Encounter of the World Religions* (New York: Columbia Univ. Press, 1961) 4.

7. Huston Smith, *The Religions of Man* (New York: Harper and Row, 1965) 132–139.

8. Bernhard Stoeckle points out that the need (*Beduerftigkeit*) for redemption is universally present among human beings, even if they do not explicitly feel this need (*Beduerfnis*), "Erloesungsbedurftigkeit des Menschen und Vorauswirken der Erloesung," MS II, 1024–1039.

9. Louis Dupre, *The Other Dimension* (New York: Seabury, 1979) 329–356. Irving Fetscher, "State Socialist Ideology as Religion," *Christianity and Socialism*, eds. J.B. Metz and J.P. Jossua, Concilium (105) 85. See also A. Bohm, ed. *Haeresien der Zeit* (Freiburg: Herder, 1961), esp. 215–374.

10. Bernhard Casper, *Wesen und Grenzen der Religionskritik* (Wurzburg: Echter, 1974) 40.

11. Raimondo Panikkar, *Myth, Faith and Hermeneutics* (New York: Paulist, 1979) 408.

12. Alfred North Whitehead, *Religion in the Making* (New York: World, 1960) 16.

13. Karl Rahner, "Kirche und Atheismus," *Stimmen der Zeit,* 106 (1961) 3–13.

14. Karl Rahner, "Salvation," ET, 1504.

15. Robert Jenson, *The Triune Identity* (Philadelphia: Fortress, 1982) xii, 3, 112, 186.

16. Robert Kress, *Christian Roots* (Westminster, Md.: Christian Classics, 1978).

17. Hans Urs von Balthasar, *Martin Buber and Christianity* (London: Harvill, 1961) 108.

18. Karl Rahner, *The Trinity* (New York: Crossroad, 1974) 10–11. Later on Rahner resumed consideration of the Trinity, emphasizing that "the doctrine of the Trinity is neither appendix to nor mere attentuation of Christian monotheism, but, rather, its very radicalization" (ST, XIII, 139).

19. *The Three-Personed God* xi.

20. *The Triune Identity* ix, 186.

21. Jurgen Moltmann, *The Trinity and the Kingdom* (San Francisco: Harper and Row, 1981).

22. Ewert Cousins, "Raimondo Panikkar and the Christian Systematic Theology of the Future," *Cross Currents* 24 (Summer, 1979) 148.

23. Raimondo Panikkar, *The Trinity and the Religious Experience of Man* (Maryknoll: Orbis, 1973) vii-viii, 41–69; here, 43.

24. New York: Paulist, 1981

25. These names are not intended in a male sexist or chauvinist sense. That they are male or masculine terms is largely a matter of their historical and cultural context. Jenson's attempt to justify a preference of Father strikes me as both unnecessary and

contrived (*The Triune Identity* 10–16). God is not called Father because ''he'' is male. The bodilessness of God eliminates any such consideration. God is called Father because, analogously, both the human and the divine Father enable life or being to be, which otherwise, on its own, would not be. In the Judeo-Christian tradition there have been strong *bio-cultural* reasons for the preference of Father rather than Mother to describe this divine creative activity. Likewise, ''Son'' applied to the Logos, Jesus and us does not designate maleness. Its contrast is not with daughter, but with orphan or outsider. It designates full membership in the family, full identification with the family. It does not designate sexual identity. On this, and especially on God as Mother, see Robert Kress, *Whither Womankind* (St. Meinrad: Abbey, 1976; now Westminster, Md.: Christian Classics).

26. *De Trinitate V,* 9, n. 10; see also VIII, 4, nn. 7–9 (PL 42, 918, 939–941).

27. *The Three-personed God* 81–238.

28. Ewert Cousins, ''A Theology of Interpersonal Relations,'' *Thought* 45 (1970) 59.

29. *De Trinitate,* PL 196. Book III has been newly translated in Grover Zinn, *Richard of St. Victor* (New York: Paulist, 1979) 371–397; here 373.

30. Zinn, ''Introduction,'' 48. He summarizes Richard's argument on pages 46–48.

31. Some consequences of excessive or monistic and monarchical monotheism are summarized by Moltmann (191–203). However, a certain caution would not be misplaced in regard to his remarks, since the church order so dear to his heart tends to be a romantic personalist communion instead of a sacramental ontology communion.

32. *Jesus der Christus* (Mainz: Grunewald, 1975) 218.

33. *The Trinity* 22, 34; ST, XIII, 139.

34. *A History of Modern European Philosophy* (Milwaukee: Bruce, 1954) 10.

35. ST, XIII, 129–147.

36. The Council of Chalcedon (451) proclaimed: ''We teach that one and the same Christ, the Son, the Lord, the Only-Begotten is to be recognized in two natures—unmixed, untransformed (asugchutos, atrepto—against Monophysitism), unseparated, undivided (adiairretos, achoristos—against Nestorianism) whereby the difference of the natures in consequence of the unification was never abrogated, but the peculiarity of each of the two natures remained preserved'' (D 148; DS 301). This translation is from Ludwig Ott, *Fundamentals of Catholic Dogma* (Dublin: Mercier, 1955) 145. In Aloys Grillmeier, *Christ in Christian Tradition* (New York: Sheed and Ward, 1965) 481, the adverbs are translated without confusion, without change, without division, without separation.

37. Michael Schmaus, *Perichorese,* LTK 8, 274–276.

38. Robert Kress, ''The Church Communio: Trinity and Incarnation as the Foundations of Ecclesiology,'' *The Jurist* 36, 1/2 (1976) 140.

39. Yves Congar, ''Autonomie et pouvoir central dans l'Eglise vus par la theologie catholique,'' *Irenikon,* L111/3 (1980) 291–313. I wish to thank my colleague, Professor Doctor Father Patrick Granfield, for calling this article to my attention. I am encouraged to proceed as I have in the present text, although my original etymological basis cannot be sustained. Etymology is, after all, and fortunately, not everything. Even more encouraging however, is the fact that, although Congar felt obliged to note the errant etymology, he did not think that it invalidated my arguments.

40. Michael Schmaus, ''Perichorese,'' LTK, 6, 276. I have wondered whether

the Greek language's ability to combine a plural (neuter) subject with a singular verb might have been exploited by Christian theologians in regard to Trinitarian theology. Heraclitus' famous dictum, panta rei, could be translated "all things flows," although the standard translations read "everything flows" (Philip Wheelwright, *Heraclitus* [New York: Atheneum, 1964; fragment 20] 29). Granted that the divine persons are not neuter (but neither are they masculine or feminine), could not this Greek grammatical usage, as Greek vocabulary has been, be adapted by Christian theology to express the plurality of persons, the singularity of nature in God? I found neither grounds for denial nor examples of exercise in Nigel Turner, *A Grammar of New Testament Greek,* III (Edinburgh: Clark, 1963) 21–28; Maxmilian Zerwick and Joseph Smith, *Biblical Greek* (Rome: Pontifical Biblical Institute, 1963) I–8; F. Blass and A. Debrunne, *A Greek Grammar of the New Testament,* tr. and ed. Robert Funk (Chicago: University of Chicago Press, 1961) 1–4, 36, 73–79. On the Pre-New Testament Greek usage, Herbert Weir Smyth, *Greek Grammar* (Cambridge: Oxford University Press, 1956) 264.

41. A point also strongly urged by Jurgen Moltmann, *The Trinity and the Kingdom* XIV, 151–159; 191–221.

42. Eberhard Juengel, *The Doctrine of the Trinity* (Grand Rapids, Mich.: Eerdmans, 1976) 5–14. This interpretation and paraphrase of Karl Barth's Trinitarian theology (viii) unfortunately shares and reflects what has been called Barth's "Hypertheism" (Leo Scheffczyk, *Gott-loser Gottesglaube?* [Regensburg: Habbel, 1974] 190, 193) as well as his "Christomonism" (Gerhard Hasel, *Old Testament Theology* [Grand Rapids, Mich.: Eerdmans, 1975, rev. ed.] 106, 111). Like Barth, Juengel "fears that the teaching of *Vestigium Trinitatis* concerns—probably against the intention of its discoverers—'a genuine *analogia entis*' (8; also xvi)." This fear of the *analogia entis,* which discerns a similarity, however much greater the dissimilarity, in divine and human being (DS 804), severely hampers Juengel's attempt to ground the "encounter between God and man" in "the movement of God's being" (xx, xxi). This fear is also the likely basis for Juengel's extraordinary and unusual use and interpretation of the philosophical concept of "becoming" *(Werden).* Distrust of the *analogia entis* seems inevitably to lead to nominalism (see Moltmann 52–55, 196) and voluntarism (Juengel 68–82; Moltmann 99, where the divine "decision" is so emphasized). In such an approach, it is inevitable that recourse will be had, must be had, to a God of love, whose love is able to save, even universally, although the being-full and power-full dimensions of this God and divine love are so neglected that it is no longer evident how such love can effectively love and save (Moltmann, 151–157); on Juengel, see Leo O'Donovan, "The Mystery of God as History of Love: Eberhard Juengel's Doctrine of God," *Theological Studies* 42 (1981) 265–271: In *Gott als Geheimnis,* God's dominion is so subordinated to God's love that it can be spoken of only as the power of love; love has only love with which to defend itself" (270). A similar problem is evident in Jenson, *The Triune Identity,* who prefers "event" (176–184) to Juengel's "Becoming," but who nevertheless also runs headlong into metaphysics and the ontological question (181). Since the event-God is also, and must be, "enduring reality," how is this event related to being? What is its status in being? And then does analogy once more, and inevitably, raise its head, beautiful or ugly, depending on one's viewpoint (184).

43. "Trinitaet," H t G, I, 713.

44. According to St. Thomas Aquinas, and Christian theology generally, the *vestigia trinitatis* can be discerned and appreciated fully only after the Trinity has been revealed (*"trinitate posita"*; ST, I, q. 32, a. 1). Indeed, only after, but what critics tend to overlook is the conviction that the triune Trinity is truly imaged in the creation. The *vestigia* are not first placed by what is called supernatural revelation. The relationship between the creator and the creation is so positive that, even though they are not readily discerned, the vestigia are there from the very beginning. The unity in diversity and diversity in unity which is operative and expressed in the Trinity is also present in the nature of the created world, although it is still seeking its full realization, and actualization, which are possible only in and through the special revelation and elevation (the *theiosis*) of God's grace. As Karl Rahner speaks of a "suchende Christologie" (seeking, searching, questing Christology) (with William Thuesing, *Christologie—systematisch und exegetisch* [Freiburg: Herder, 1972] 60; ST, XIII, 174, 225), so may we also speak of a *suchende Trinitaetstheologie.* This would be one dimension of the total program and process of triune gracing and divinization proclaimed in the New Testament (2 Pet 1:4). This "searching" means that so-called nature of the natural order has been so created by God that it is open to ever and ever greater being—even greater participation in life, the nature, the goods of God, if God so chooses to share. As supernatural elevation correlates to created natural capacity, so does the supernatural revelation of the triune God correlate to the natural capacity to receive. Since this triune God is Logos, so must its creation, grace and salvation also be logical (that is, "logos-tic"; Joseph Ratzinger, *Einfuehrung in das Christentum* [Munich: Kosel, 1968] 37:53, 103–124). In this "logos-tic" creation, salvation must also include consciousness and knowledge of the precisely saving God, who is triune. This knowledge should be natural as well as supernatural. As in all such human discovery and revelation of God (Avery Dulles, "Revelation and discovery," *Theology and Discovery,* ed. William Kelly [Milwaukee: Marquette University Press, 1980] 1–29), the natural and supernatural are not identical and do not produce identical results. But neither are they equivocal, rivalrous or hostile. They are, rather, coordinated and correlated. Indeed, in their own way, they also enjoy a perichoresis. Hence, the doctrine of the *Vestigium Trinitatis* is not to be regarded as a trivial bagatelle. It is, rather, one more illustration of the truth that God has created a world precisely so that God himself can be its salvation. The saving God being triune, the saved world must also be triune—in its own proper way. The world's *vestigia trinitatis,* then, are neither human invention nor human hybris. They are, rather, as is all, the gift of the divine triune source of all being.

45. I have used the edition of Richard McKeon, *The Basic Works of Aristotle* (New York: Random House, 1941).

46. *Metaphysics* VII 1 (10,28,2,10,31).

47. *Categories* V (2a 11; 3,6,10).

48. *Categories,* II (1a 23).

49. Similar considerations can be found in Juengel, *The Doctrine of the Trinity* 89–93.

50. ST, I, q. 3, a. 5, ad 1.

51. *Categories* VII (6b 6–8).

52. Parmenides remains the prototypical representative of this approach. See the texts and commentary of Philip Wheelwright, *The Presocratics* (New York: Odyssey, 1966) 91–105.

53. Thomas Hobbes, *Leviathan,* ed. M. Oakeshott (Oxford: Blackwell, 1946) I, 13; p. 82.

54. Ratzinger *(Einfuehrung 112)* emphasizes that in contrast to the God of the Greek philosophers, who is essentially independent and pure thought, the God of Christianity is precisely characterized by the category of relation and is, as thought, love.

55. For those who find Marxist and socialist models helpful and attractive in developing theological models, especially for God and Church, and society, caution in regard to the difference between societal and socialist, between communional and collectivist, can hardly be exaggerated.

56. I realize that such words are not customary theological terms. They may seem too figurative, even too earthy. They are intended to give more graphic meaning to the word "act-ual" I have used earlier, to counter the minimalist interpretations of being as merely not-nothing. In any case, Juengel speaks of God as *ueberstroemendes Sein* (overflowing being: *Gott als Geheimnis der Welt* [Tuebingen: Mohr, 1977] 302). In language more befitting Bavarian and Munich theology, Schmaus notes that "the divine nature is of such a frothy, over-foaming fullness [of being] that it can be adequately described only as a threefold I" *(von einer so ueberschaeumende Fuelle;* H t G, I, 698).

57. *Einfuehrung* 229.

58. Eric Voegelin, *Science, Politics and Gnosticism* (Chicago: Regnery 1968). Hans Jonas, *The Gnostic Religion* (Boston: Beacon, 1963) and *Philosophical Essays* (Englewood Cliffs: Prentice-Hall, 1974) 263–348. Creation ex nihilo does not, as Paul Tong would have it, "chisel an infinite gap between God and man. This yawning abyss can be bridged only by another action of God: redemption, the process whereby God and man gradually work out their reconciliation." Paul Tong, "A Study of Thematic Differences between Eastern and Western Religious Thought," *Journal of Ecumenical Studies X* (1973) 347. Rather, as Oliver Lacombe has emphasized, "the doctrine of creation *ex nihilo* . . . is the sole adequate safeguard of divine transcendence and at the same time the secure assurance of the reality and value of the creature who has come into existence by the command of the First Love." Oliver Lacombe, *Existence de l'homme* (Bruges: Desclee, 1951) 140. It is only this doctrine that enables the utter perichoresis of the divine and human, for it eliminates any other possible intermediate agency such as the Platonic demiurge or the archons and emanations of Gnosticism and Neoplatonism. One might legitimately say that *creatio ex nihilo* is demonstrated and required by the unique, sole mediatorship of precisely "the man Jesus" in 1 Timothy 2:4–6.

59. Hinduism has a doctrine that the world is *lila,* God's play. Huston Smith, *The Religions of Man* (New York: Harper and Row, 1958) 84. Under Karl Rahner's direction, at the University of Munich, a doctoral dissertation was written on this topic: Bettina Baeumer, *Schoepfung als Spiel. Der Begriff lila im Hinduismus, seine philosophische und theologische Deutung.*

60. Dante, *The Divine Comedy* (The Carlyle-Wicksteed Translation. New York: Random House Modern Library, 1950); *Purgatorio* xvi, 19

61. *Paradiso* IX, 34, 103–105. On this, see Robert Kress, "Cosmos and Conscience in the History of Religious Imagination," *The Pedagogy of God's Image,* ed. Robert Masson (Chico, Cal.: Scholars Press, 1981) 198–202.

62. On the perichoresis of indicative and imperative statements about Christian being and life, a favorite Pauline theme, see Rudolf Schnackenburg, *The Moral Teaching of the New Testament* (New York: Herder and Herder, 1965) 342. Rudolf Bultmann, *Theology of the New Testament* (London: SCM, 1965) I, 330–333.

2

THE CHURCH AS COMMUNION

THE CHURCH OF THE TRINITY

We must always keep in mind that the true founder, foundation and origin of the Church is God, indeed, the triune God. This is important because historical conditions have often led theology to focus on the historical origin of the Church so strongly that its divine origin is neglected. However, very early (140–155) in the Church's history we were provided with a graphic statement of the pre-historical, divine origin of the Church:

> Brethren, a revelation was made to me in my sleep by an exceedingly beautiful young man, who said: "Who, do you think, is the elderly lady from whom you took the book?" "The Sibyl," I said. "No," he said, "you are mistaken." "Who is she then?" I said. "The Church," he said. "Why is she elderly?" I asked. "Because she was created before all things," he said, "For this reason she is elderly and for Her sake the world was erected."[1]

This text reinforces our understanding that the Church is really the world from a certain viewpoint, in a certain condition. We shall examine the many meanings of the word Church in detail later on. For now it suffices to know that there has always been a universalist dynamism in the Judeo-Christian tradition and that this dynamism continued in the Church, however, clouded over or implicit it may have sometimes been. Hermas' text emphasizes that the world is really the Church, which, as we have seen, is the sacrament of God's saving will in the world. Sacrament means that something is both the cause and the sign of the effective presence of God's grace in the world. God's grace is always a share or participation in God's life and being. God's life and being, as we have seen, is triune perichoresis. It is communication and communion. All theology of the Trinity and Christ and the Church can be seen as the attempt to understand such New Testament texts as the following.

The Father and I are one. . . .
Then you will know for sure
that the Father is in me
and I am in the Father (Jn 10:30–38).

Do you not believe
that I am in the Father
and the Father is in me?
You must believe me when I say
that I am in the Father
and the Father is in me (Jn 14:10–11).

Father,
may they be one in us,
as you are in me
and I am in you,
so that the world may believe
it was you who sent me.
I have given them the glory you gave to me,
that they may be one
as we are one.
With me in them and you in me, may they be so completely one . . .
(Jn 17:21–23).

What we have seen and heard
we are telling you
so that you too may be in union with us
as we are in union with the Father
and with his Son Jesus Christ
(1 Jn 1:3).

If the Church is the sacrament of the divine salvation, then it must also be the sacrament of the divine triune perichoresis or communion. That the early Church was at least implicitly aware of this is evidenced by its emphasis that the salvation-historical (economic) Trinity is the immanent Trinity.

Cyprian describes the Church as the "De unitate Patris et Filii et Spiritus Sancti plebs adunata" (A people brought into unity by the unity of the Father, Son and Holy Spirit").[2] This idea was taken up by Vatican II (*The Church* 4). Cyprian elaborates, emphasizing that ecclesial unity is thoroughly rooted in the triune *unity of God:*

Our Lord says: I and the Father are one; and again, of Father, Son and Holy Spirit it is written: And the three are One. Does anyone think then that this oneness, which derives from the stability of God and is welded together after the celestial pattern, can be sundered in the Church and divided by the clash of discordant wills?[3]

Tertullian speaks trenchantly of this Trinitarian source of the Church's existence and nature, especially insofar as it is in the Holy Spirit:

> For the Church is itself, properly and principally, the Spirit Himself,
> in whom there is a trinity of one divinity, Father, Son and Holy
> Spirit. He unites in one congregation that Church which the Lord
> said consists of three persons. And so, from this time on, any num-
> ber of persons at all, joined in this faith, is recognized as the Church
> by Him who founded and consecrated it.[4]

Thus the most profound source of unity among the various and many individual members and among the various and many local Churches is not an
abstract principle of similarity or the desire of human beings for companion-
ship. It is, rather, the triune unity of God, who is the Church's original founder
and source. Unfortunately, Tertullian did not stay true to this divine origin of
the Church. His rigorism led him to Montanism. He had forgotten that this divine Spirit of unity was also the divine power for the forgiveness of sins (Lk
24:47–49 with Acts 1:4–8; 2:1–4, 14–41). How could it have been otherwise, since this Holy Spirit is the ''other Paraclete'' (Jn 14:16) sent by Jesus,
who is himself the friend of sinners (Mt 11:19; Lk 7:34). The divine communion is such that it is neither defeated nor put off by sinful human communion.
We shall return to this theme later on.

For now our consideration is the divine communion in the human communion. One instance of this divine-human perichoresis is Jesus Christ. Truly
divine and truly human, Jesus is described as the hypostatic union because in
him the communion of the divine and human is perfect. However, this communion is not limited to him. As the Holy Spirit, the Power of God in the
world, overshadowed one human being in Nazareth, Mary (Lk 1:26–38), to
bring forth Jesus as the unique union of the divine and human, so did the same
powerful Holy Spirit overshadow many human beings in Jerusalem to bring
forth the Church as the universal union of the human and divine (Acts 2). In
the hypostatic union of Jesus the divine-human communion can say ''I''; in
the ecclesial union of the Holy Spirit, the human-divine communion can say
''We.''[5]

Traditionally, theology and piety have distributed the divine-human communion variously among the three persons of God. Thus, the Father creates
the world and enters into the covenant with Abraham (already with Noah, and
even with Adam, in one sense), Moses and David. The Fatherhood of God is
not to be understood in a sexist manner. As we noted earlier, God is not called
Father because God is male. God is Father because God is the source of being.
The source of being precisely as Father emphasizes the personal dimension of
creation. The world's origin is not blind fate. It springs from neither polytheistic caprice nor monistic necessity. As the creation of the personal, paternal
God, created and especially human being is precisely gift. As within the Trinity all possible patriarchalism is eliminated by the divine perichoresic communion, so is all patriarchalism within the world (and Church) without

foundation in the Fatherhood of God. For the very same reasons that God can be called Father, God can also be called Mother.[6]

The gift-communion ontology already present in creation is continued in the incarnation of this Father's Word-Son. We could also say "enworldment" or "historification." In the Son, God truly becomes part of world history.[7] The theandric communion begun in the creation is revealed to be without limits on the part of God. God's *philanthropy,* the divine humanity and kindness (Tit 3:4), is not restricted to disparate benevolent deeds. Rather, God's philanthropy *is* God's very own self.[8] If God the Father is the beginning of salvation-history (the communion of the triune God with humanity), then the incarnate Son is the historical culmination, once-for-allness and irreversibility of this salvation. The risen Jesus placed in human history (not only in God's will) and proved once for all that God can and will overcome not only the original threat of nothingness (in creation), but also the secondary threat of hamartiological (sin induced) nothingness (in redemption).

If the Father is the beginning and the Son is the culmination of salvation-history, then the Holy Spirit is its universalization. Theologians are often reproached with neglecting or slighting the Holy Spirit.[9] To some extent this reproach is justified. However, we must recall the perichoresis of Father, Son and Holy Spirit, both in regard to the one divine nature and to one another. Hence, to understand anything about the three-personed God is to have understood something about Father, Son and Holy Spirit. Otherwise they would not be three persons in *one* God, and there would be no perichoresis. Furthermore, Jesus himself described the Holy Spirit, whom he was to mission and who would thus be his (Christ's) mission, as "another Paraclete" (Jn 14:16). Also, the New Testament text does provide more theologizable material about Jesus than either Father or Holy Spirit. Finally, we must also recall that salvation-history is history.[10] As such, it need not reveal Father, Son and Holy Spirit "equally" at all times and in all places. The ecclesiological principle of diversity in unity and unity in diversity[11] can also apply chronologically to the revelation and discovery of God. The history of the world after Pentecost is truly the history of the Holy Spirit, in whose powerful communion we come to appreciate and understand better Jesus' God, Father-Son-Holy Spirit, who is with us "always, yes, to the end of time" (Mt 28:20). The special dimension of salvation-history accorded to the Holy Spirit is its unlimitedness. This attribute does coincide well with the Spirit "who blows wherever it pleases. . . . You cannot tell where it comes from or where it is going" (Jn 3:8). The Holy Spirit universalizes God's paternal and maternal power and filial truth-love in the world. The Holy Spirit is the one who frees true spiritual worship from all confinements, whether in human cities or natural places (Jn 4:21). The unlimitedness of the Holy Spirit enables God's good news and grace to go into the very heart of the world and to its very ends (Rom 5:5 with Acts 1:8).

The divine triune communion, then, has truly entered into communion with the human communion which is its creation. We can legitimately speak of not only the divine origin of the Church in the one God. We can also speak of the triune origin of the Church in the Triune God. As the unoriginate origin of all being, the Father is the theo-ontological origin of the Church; as incarnate God born in and into the world, Jesus the Son is the theo-historical origin; as missioned, empowering other Paraclete in history, the Holy Spirit is the theo-societal origin. All together, the three-personed God is the transcendent *apeiron* become (Jn 1:14) immanent in the cosmos' salvation-history.

Communion is, then, a most apt term to describe the participation of the non-Godly in the Godly. In the course of history, this communion has enjoyed many titles. In the Christian tradition the dominant title has been Church. Whatever the title, and however many, they all have but one intention—to help us understand the communion of God with humankind.

I have diligently avoided the word definition. The reality of the Church is so rich that it doesn't submit to definition very well.[12] Consequently, theologians customarily have recourse to more or less elaborate descriptions, in which they try to include as many identifying and demarcating elements of the Church as they can. The problem is complicated by the existence of diverse ecclesiologies—already in the New Testament[13] and certainly in later theological history. Recently Raymond Brown has sketched three different ecclesiologies, which he entitles Blueprint, Erector-Set and In-Between, and shown how they influence one's appreciation of the Church as well as one's approach to problem solving in the Church.[14] An important discussion of ecclesiological diversity has been offered by Avery Dulles in his *Models of the Church*.[15] A special value of this approach is its inherent caution that, while one understanding of the church may be perfectly legitimate, it is not perfectly sufficient by itself. Another advantage of this model approach is that it allows for expansion, as a subsequent article by Dulles has shown.[16]

Vatican II's response to the problem of defining the Church was to invoke "various figures of speech" and "images," especially flock, vineyard, temple, spouse (*The Church* 6). These are not "mere metaphors," which in no way represent the reality of the Church. Rather, recognizing the ultimate mystery of God and therefore of God's union with creation, these and other figures of speech convey aspects of this unspeakable communion. The Council was in good company, the New Testament, where Paul Minear has discovered "more than eighty separate analogies" and ninety-six major and minor images. Nevertheless, there is a unity in all this diversity, for, "as a matter of fact, each major image points toward a perception of the character of the Church that agrees, to an amazing degree, with the perceptions produced by other images."[17] As we move from the consideration of the divine triune communion to the earthly ecclesial communion, it is good to emphasize this indefinability of the Church. For any definition or description, however good and helpful, will always be partial. Should any try to be all-sufficient by itself, it would in that very moment, become false. By its claim to exclusivity, it would have automatically eliminated other necessary descriptions. This applies even to the Church as communion, to which we shall now proceed.

The word "communion" comes from the Latin *communio*, which comes from the Greek word *koinonia*. We are most familiar with it in reference to "Holy Communion" in the Eucharist. Its basic meaning is union with, although it does not as such specify the members of the union, its origin, purpose, conditions. Etymologically, it comes from the Latin: either *cum moenus*, a defensive installation such as a camp or fortress, or *cum munus*, a common task, duty, undertaking. In either case, the point is that many (diverse) people make their own proper contribution to one and the same activity. As usual, however, and as Yves Congar has explained, the etymological explanation is not sufficient.

> However, the word also has an ecclesial meaning which surpasses its etymological signification. It translates the Greek word Koinonia, which was already present in classical literature (for example, in Aristotle's analysis of friendship), but which became a favorite word of Christian writers, especially of St. Paul. In a general sense Koinonia means that one shares in something with others. Its fundamental Christian meaning designates the community of the faithful with Christ, hence their common participation in Christian "goods"; the faith, the body and blood of Christ (1 Corinthians 10:16), the Spirit (2 Corinthians 13:13), and, finally, the community which the Christians constitute on the basis of all these things: In that they are in community with God they are also in communion with one another (see 1 John 1:3,6). Thus the communio is seen to be constituted by the Christian life in its fullest sense. It can be subjectively more or less intensive since there are multiple elements which one can more or less actively possess, but it is in and of itself indivisible. One is either *in communione* or one is not. Consequently in Christian usage the term Koinonein, communicare, is used in an absolute sense: in the Roman canon we speak of the "Communicantes."[18]

It may be asked also, as Raymond Brown notes, "whether *koinonia* does not have a Semitic antecedent in *yahad*, 'community, oneness,' which is once more a Dead Sea Scroll self-designation. . . . These parallels confirm the thesis that the initial Christian self-understanding was in terms of Israel, and then there was a sense of oneness or unity from the beginning."[19]

Communion is clearly a rich and complicated term. As Jerome Hamer has pointed out, it can be applied to the Church, if this richness is respected. Communion designates a way of life, a network of relationships among local churches and also among individual Christians. Applied to the Church, it designates both communion between God and humankind and within humankind. The Church itself enjoys a twofold communion: between the life of grace and the means of grace and among the diversely gifted and hierarchically ordered members.[20]

In the ancient Church, a synonym for communion was peace. In fact, they often appeared together as a doublet. Indeed, sometimes "peace" alone indicated the community, the communion of saints, the Church.[21] This equivalence of peace is significant for our considerations. According to St. Paul, "Christ . . . is the peace between us [Jews and Gentiles], and has made the two into one and broken down the barriers which used to keep them apart, actually destroying in his person the hostility . . . to create one single new man in himself out of the two of them and by restoring peace . . . to unite them both in a single body and reconcile them with God. In his own person . . . he came to bring the good news of peace, peace to you who were far away and peace to those who were near at hand. Through him, both of us have in the one Spirit our way to come to the Father" (Eph 2:13–18).[22] This peace, which happens in Jesus, is communion—of God with man and of humans among themselves. This peace does not cease when the earthly ministry of Jesus ceases. Rather, in the Holy Spirit he has given us a lasting *way* to the Father. Not only is Jesus "the Way, the Truth and the Life" (Jn 14:6); so is the Church, according to St. Paul: "It is according to the way which they describe as a sect that I worship the God of my ancestors . . ." (Acts 24:14; also 9:2; 16:17; 18:25–26; 19:9, 23; 22:4; 24:22). This passage from Ephesians locates ecclesial communion precisely in the triune communion. Since we have already discussed the origin of the Church-communion in the triune communion of God and in God's creational communion with the non-Godly, we can now proceed to its historical origin in Jesus. Then we shall discuss the nature and meaning of this ecclesial communion as it has developed during the actual history of the Church.

JESUS: FOUNDER AND FOUNDATION

The problem of Jesus as "founder of the Church" runs parallel to the problem of the "Jesus of history." Since the growth and development of literary and historical criticism of the biblical text, the use of isolated, individual proof texts for particular doctrines has been seen to be questionable. This critical approach has also alerted us to the danger of retrojecting our concepts and categories, legitimate in themselves, into a past culture where such concepts and categories were not indigenous. A corollary of this is that we must be careful about the very questions we ask. What is very important to us today may not have been important to them then. This does not mean, of course, that we can ask and know nothing of the past, but only that we must be alert and careful.

A prime example of this is our present topic, Jesus as founder of the Church. A much agitated question among theologians and exegetes has been, "Did Jesus found a Church, at all"?[23] Two preliminary questions must be answered before this one can be answered. First, how does one define Church? Second, how does one define founding a Church? Answers given to the original question not infrequently indicate that too little attention was paid to these two preliminary ones. As we noted earlier, Church is a polyvalent term. It can apply to all of salvation-history or to various stages within that history.[24] To state that Jesus either founded or did not found a Church depends on how one defines Church.

Perhaps even more to the point is the precise content of the concept "to found" a Church. Here we recall that in the Christian context, Church and religion can be regarded as equivalents. Consequently, the admonition of the sociologist of religion, Joachim Wach, cannot be overvalued: ". . . the difficulties involved in making generalizations about the sociological effect of the activities of the great founders of religion becomes apparent. . . . What, then, are the distinctive features of the founders? It is significant that this term does not denote any intrinsic quality or activity of the personality but refers to the historical and sociological effect of his charisma. As is well known, none of the great founders intended to 'found a religion.' They were, each in his own way, deeply concerned with following out an experience which became decisive in their lives and which determined their own attitudes toward God, toward the world, and toward men.' "[25] For G. van der Leeuw, the "founder, in the first place, is primarily a witness to revelation: he has seen, or has heard, something." Founders are also "prophets . . . teachers . . . theologians . . . reformers . . . examples, [and] when, finally, they devote their entire existence to foundation, they are called mediators."[26]

Had these "definitions" of religious founder been kept in mind, many of the disputes about the founding of the Church by Jesus could have been avoided. One would not have had to have recourse to Hans Küng's distinction between "the pre-Easter Jesus, who, during his lifetime, did not found a Church, [but] who did lay the foundations for the appearance of a post-Easter Church. . . . There is Church only from the beginning of the resurrection-faith. . . . Consequently, the Church has its origin not simply in the intention of and the commissioning by the pre-Easter Jesus, but in the entire Christ-event."[27] Later on Küng is even more direct: "This all means: In his lifetime Jesus *founded no Church*. . . . The 'Church,' in the sense of a special community separated from Israel, is univocally a *post-Easter entity*. . . . Therefore, Jesus is *not* that which one commonly understands as a *founder of a religion* or church" (Küng's emphases).[28] Of course, Küng rather begs the question in the second explanation. Whatever may or may not have been Jesus' intention in regard to a possible Church, he and his followers clearly remained within Israel and Judaism during his lifetime. Küng's statements can be appreciated as a reaction to—and against—the apologetic approaches dominant in the Latin theology manuals prior to Vatican II. However, his own explanations frequently display as little sophistication as did the manuals.[29]

These manuals did themselves and theology a disservice by their vocabulary. They delight in using words like *instituere, constituere, conferre, potestatem tradere, jurisdictio* and *primatus* when they speak of the origin of the Church in Jesus' life and mission, that is, when they speak of Jesus founding the Church. They complicate their mischief by immediately proceeding to describe the Church in terms of primacy, hierarchy and supreme power.[30] Now, such terms have legitimate meanings and places in ecclesiology. But in regard to both the history and the significance of the Church, these words represent later, and secondary, elements. Furthermore, words like institute and constitute tend, by their very selves, to emphasize one dimension of the Christian and ecclesial reality to the detriment of the rest. In the distinction between *vie* (life) and *structure* (institution, structure), so dear to Yves Congar, the manuals' favorite words emphasize not life, which is primary, but structure, which is undeniably necessary and important, but also secondary.[31] In this distinction life refers to grace, structure to the means of grace. From our preceding considerations about the triune origin of the Church, it is clear that, however Jesus would have gone about it historically, his primary concern would have been the sharing of the divine life with humans. His primary concern would have been the theandric communion, and all else would have been secondary and contingent upon its effectiveness in enabling this communion. Jesus is founder of the Church primarily because and insofar as he is "the throne of grace" which we confidently approach (Heb 4:16).

To expect or require Jesus to have called a Constitutional Convention, to have written a Declaration of Independence and a Constitution, complete with a Bill of Rights, is as unreal as it is unnecessary. As Aelred Cody has noted, "The Church does have Jesus as its founder, though not in a strictly juridical sense." In any case, "The brute fact of an institution's 'canonical erection' tells us little about that institution's purpose and meaning. In this respect, the real question of importance is whether or not the Church in its development is faithful to the purpose and mission which Jesus proclaimed to his disciples." According to Cody, the proper phrasing of the question is this: "What did Jesus himself do toward founding the Church and its institutions, and what arose rather in the Christian community after his resurrection and ascension? In those things which arose or were shaped in the Christian community after Christ's exaltation, is there continuity with the mission of Jesus on earth?"[32] Those who deny any connection between Jesus and the post-Easter Church and who speak of an original Church-less Christianity, whether charismatic or eschatological, are few and far between today.[33] Even Josef Blank, "minimalist" in so many respects, suggests a way in which Jesus can be considered to have founded the Church, although he obviously takes no delight in this terminology. "The thesis that Jesus founded the Church says too much and too little. Too much, in that it is not historically verifiable; too little, in that it accords too much value and weight to the factor (reality) Church, and thereby minimalizes the lasting mutual connection (feedback) with the person and work of Jesus."[34] Blank is typically frightened by the possibilities of "ecclesial triumphalism" and "narcissistic pre-occupation" (306, 307). Likewise typically, he finds such temptations and tendencies preeminently in the "institutional" Church, where it must unfortunately be conceded that it certainly has flourished. However, only the most romantically naive and ideologically straitened would assert that only the Church precisely as institutional and hierarchial has been triumphalist and narcissistic.[35] Apart from this, Blank suggests that "the Gospels show us not so much the historical Jesus as founder of the Church, but rather the Church in development (as happening) among the disciples and within the discipleship of Jesus" (306). Blank emphasizes that this is not to be undervalued or minimized in contrast to a later, explicit, developed ecclesiology. It helps us understand that "Church is nothing other than the discipleship of Jesus, whose purpose and meaning is (very) essentially to spread the message of Jesus' person and work" (305). Obviously, although Blank feels compelled to dwell on it, the post-Easter separation of the Church from Israel was not and need not have been Jesus' precise and original intention. He could still have been, and be, the Church's founder.

Most recently Gerhard Lohfink has summed up the present state of the question in seven points (all emphases his):

1. Jesus never had the intention to found a new *religious community* (religion).
2. Neither did Jesus have the intention to establish a *holy-remnant-community* or a *separate community* in Israel.
3. Rather, Jesus addressed *all of Israel* (Israel as a whole), without excluding any group or class of the Jewish people.
4. This mission to all of Israel is continued in the mission of the primitive (apostolic) community, which understands itself as the *eschatological* people of God, in which all of Israel is to be gathered together in belief in Jesus and his message.
5. In the origin of the societal and theological phenomenon "Church" a decisive role is played by the factual, historical, contingent denial (rejection) of Jesus by the greater part of Israel. In today's sense of the term, "Church" first comes into existence in the believing part of Israel.
6. The origin of the Church is, then, not to be located so one-sidedly in discrete, fixed, explicit foundational acts by the earthly or risen Christ. The Church originated in a *process,* which was, of course, immediately connected with the preaching and praxis of Jesus.
7. This whole and highly complicated process is the *work of God,* who is creating his eschatological people through Jesus Christ and the Holy Spirit.[36]

This summary has special value for our consideration of the Church as communion for several reasons. It does emphasize, at the very end, that the best, first, primary and unsurpassable answer to the question "Who founded the Church?" is God. Even the historical Jesus is "only" the sacrament of this founding, saving God. Second, the summary also emphasizes the universality of Jesus' mission and consequently of the Church's mission, indeed, of the Church itself. Finally, this mission is the preparation of the world for the in-breaking reign and kingdom of God. The reign and kingdom of God is Jesus' preferred expression for what we have been calling the theandric communion of the triune God with humankind.[37]

It is in Jesus' preaching of this reign and kingdom of God *and* the response of Israel thereto that the origin and founding of the historical Church is to be located. Some still like to locate it in "the crisis of the delayed parousia [which] found its solution in the historifying of the Church and the de-eschatologizing of the faith."[38] However, whatever may have been the case with the imminent eschatological expectations of Jesus and his disciples, Jesus' inability to convince even the majority of his co-religionists of the truth of his understanding of God and the divine rule/kingdom forced him to live his life and conduct his mission differently than if all Israel (his originally intended audience) had accepted his preaching and converted. The origin of the Church is, then, precisely in the understanding of God preached by Jesus, its reception by some of Jesus' contemporaries, its rejection by others. Thus, Jesus would be the founder of the Church.

Even this assertion is problematic, for, as van der Leeuw has noted, for any given religion "there are infinitely many founders. . . ."[39] This is historically true of Christianity. Although it is somewhat oversimplified, it is not wrong to say that Christianity originated in a dispute between Jesus and others about the meaning of what Jesus' Christian disciples came to call the Old Testament.[40] The Church originated in these disciples, expanded with later Jewish and Gentile converts and is now the tradition (1 Cor 15:1–4; handing on) and memory (1 Cor 11:25; Lk 22:19) of Christ alive in time and space until the eschatological fulfillment of theandric history in the glorious parousia of *the* theandric person, Christ, when the heavens and the earth will become new, as the celestial city (Jerusalem), and humanity will become the new celestial spouse (Rev 21–22).

Gerhard Lohfink does not want to use the word "found" to describe the origin of the Church in the person and mission of Christ. Nevertheless, his description of the *process* (the new code or buzz word, apparently) of the formation of the Church amounts to a founding by Jesus, unless one wishes to insist that only that which is solemnly constitutional, juridical and ritual qualifies as founding. Lohfink sketches the origination of the Church, the "way of God" (Acts 18:26), in the writings of Luke:

1. This way begins in the Old Testament.

2. A second stage is the revival movement of John the Baptist.

3. The missionary activity of Jesus, gathering together all Israel, is the third stage. Insofar as only some respond to Jesus' initiative, his disciples become the representation (representative, vicar) of the true Israel and thus the pre-formation of the future Church. Luke emphasizes the continuity of Jesus' community in and as the true Israel. The selection and mission of the Twelve (apostles) is very important ecclesiologically. As Twelve they represent Israel as a whole, and it is to all Israel that they are sent. Jesus' movement is not sectarian.

4. The fourth stage on the way to Church is constituted by the Easter appearances of the risen Lord, who becomes part of the reign and kingdom of God to be preached.

5. The fifth and most important stage begins with Pentecost. The community of Jesus' disciples receives the Holy Spirit. Through their preaching the mass of Jews, always basically on Jesus' side, gathers around the apostles. Nevertheless, some still do not believe.

6. This Jewish failure to believe leads into the beginning of Gentile belief as the sixth and final stage in the formation of the Church. Only thus is the prophecy of Amos (9:11–12), cited by James at the Council of Jerusalem, fulfilled:

> After that I shall return and rebuild the fallen house of David; I shall rebuild it from its ruins and restore it. Then the rest of mankind, all the pagans who are consecrated to my name, will look for the Lord, says the Lord, who made this known so long ago (Acts 15:16–18).

In this context it is clear, as Lohfink notes, that to ask whether and when Jesus founded the Church is itself a questionable question. For this reason we have emphasized that the primary and original origin of the Church is the triune God. Thus, we can answer the question "Who founded or instituted the Church?" with a one-word answer: God. On the other hand, historically the word Church appears precisely in regard to the community of believers flowing from the person and mission of the historical Jesus.[41] Its relative infrequency in the Gospels is not a diriment impediment to relating it to Jesus. Were we to use only the words of Jesus himself, our vocabulary would be quite limited. Furthermore, since other writings of the New Testament are older or as old as the written Gospels, only pristinism would want to eliminate the word Church from the personal and missionary narrative of Jesus and restrict it to post-Easter theology. Sufficient awareness to the polyvalency of the term should permit us to describe Jesus as the founder of the Church and his preaching, healing and gathering ministry of holiness as the foundation of the Church.

IMPLICIT AND EXPLICIT FOUNDATION

Before we look at this ministry, to discern its implicit Church founding words and actions, we must at least quickly survey its Old Testament or Jewish context. As St. Thomas emphasizes, "Ignorance of this mystery [God's plan of salvation for Israel, even blind] could be dangerous for us."[42] Here we can only briefly summarize the saving history of Israel.[43] We shall select certain "most important" items for consideration, insofar as these items played a significant role in the public preaching and mission of Jesus. We shall be in good company, of course—the Gospels. They also narrate only certain items, the ones that most highlight the precise nature and understanding of Jesus. Even the Gospel genealogies are interesting in this regard.

Selective as both are, each has its own point to make. In order to place the person and mission of Jesus, Matthew traces his generation back to Abraham (1:1–17). As usual, Luke is artier. He does not stop even with Adam. He goes all the way back to God's very own self. Although the evangelists themselves have different purposes in mind, fortunately both serve ours.

Together they emphasize this—if we wish to understand and appreciate Jesus, we can't start with Jesus the public preacher. Indeed, we can't start with Jesus as baby, even should we go all the way back to his conception. We must start with Jesus' ancestors, their history and their religion. Thus, we should start with Abraham. But Luke knew that even this was not enough. Granted that Jesus was thoroughly Jewish (Gal 4:1–4), he is nonetheless not Savior of the Jews alone, but of all humanity (1 Tim 2:4–6) and creation (Rom 8:18–25; 9–11). Therefore, one cannot stop with Abraham, the father of the Jews (Rom 4:1–25; Gal 3:6–9; Jn 8:31–59). We must go all the way to Adam and Eve, father and mother of all the living (Gen 1:26–29; 3:20). However, as we have emphasized—and Luke would certainly have been pleased with us—if we really want to understand the Church and Jesus its founder, we can't even stop at Adam. Neither Jewish history nor human nature is enough. No, we must go all the way back to God. For only in God is there sufficient reason for our existence as humans and Christians.

In regard to Jesus, it is especially important to begin with God. God is not only the source of Jesus' person and mission, in an altogether unique way. God is also the subject of Jesus' preaching and the object of his mission. Ultimately, Jesus will rest the case for the truth of his mission not only on the orthodoxy of his doctrine, and the probity of his life, but precisely on his personal, ontological relationship with God. Certainly, then, one must begin any consideration of Jesus with God. We have already done this sufficiently for our purpose. Now we can proceed to the mission and preaching of Jesus.

In the long run, it is precisely about God, the nature and meaning of God, and God's relationship with the world that Jesus preached and argued. Sometimes this preaching and arguing focused directly on God. At other times its immediate topics were significant people, ideas and institutions in the history of Israel. Especially Abraham, Moses and David, but also Adam, Noah, Jonah, Solomon, and Jacob are subjects of Jesus' preaching and arguments with his fellow Jews. In fact, it is possible to read the first twelve chapters of John's Gospel as an argument about the superiority, in fact, the uniqueness (Jn 10:1,8,29) of Jesus in the salvation-history of God's triune communion with humanity and creation. Jesus also preaches and argues about religious ideas, practices and institutions such as the promise, the covenant, the law (torah), holiness and the means of holiness, the temple, ritual sacrifice, alms, "church" dues, "church" office, the sabbath. The sabbath was an especially neuralgic point. Basically, Jesus observed the sabbath (Mk 6:2, Lk 4:16,31). On the other hand, Jesus refused to accede to the "hypocritical" interpretations of the Pharisees about the requirements of the sabbath rest (Mt 12:1; Mk 2:23; Lk 6:1; 13:10;14:1; Jn 5:9; 7:22; 9:14). However, Jesus claimed superiority not only over his contemporary Jewish co-religionists. When he claimed to be "master (Lord) of the sabbath" (Mt 12:8), he implicitly claimed superiority over Moses, who was considered to have "given you the law" (Jn 7:19). Of course, the point of Jesus' assertions was not his self-aggrandizement nor was it the denigration of Judaism (hence, the contrast between Jesus and other Jews provides no basis for anti-semitism). Jesus' sole purpose was to preserve and promote the communion between God and creation. This is the meaning of his proclamation, "The sabbath was made for man, not man for the sabbath" (Mk 2:27). What had been given as a gift to be enjoyed, a mode of human participation in the divine nature, a special stage in the human communion with God, had been moralized into a burden. As elsewhere, Jesus' sole concern was the theandric communion.

It is the same in regard to Abraham (Jn 8:31–59). The case that Jesus makes is not against Abraham, but against a certain understanding of Abraham which does not encourage God's communion with the whole world through Abraham (Gen 12:1–3), but imprisons God's communion, limiting it to certain peoples and places. Of course, Jesus does not claim to be doing this on his own. Rather, he does what he does and says what he says only because this is what he sees and hears God his Father doing (Jn 5:38; 7:19; 8:38; 12:49). In fact, whoever sees Jesus sees the Father (Jn 14:8–13).

Nowhere is this claim of Jesus more graphically put than in his defense of his conduct, especially his eating with outcasts and sinners: "The tax collectors and the sinners were all seeking his company to hear what he had to say, and the Pharisees and scribes complained. This man, they said, welcomes sinners and [even] eats with them" (Lk 15: 1–3). As we shall see later, Jesus' meals with others, especially sinners, is a crucial element in his founding the Church. Of course, how could it be otherwise for the incarnate theandric communion of the divine communion. For now, though, this Gospel passage is important for us because it emphasizes that God's merciful will to save will not be put off. To rebut the Pharisees' charges that he cannot be a holy person, a true prophet, because of the company he keeps, Jesus tells three parables. The

Jerusalem Bible subtitles this chapter "The Three Parables of God's Mercy." That is not wrong, but it is also not all right either. The emphasis is precisely on God's *nature*. Mercy is not one act or attribute among many others. Mercy is not something God does sometimes. Rather, God's very nature, his perfection itself, is mercy and compassion (Lk 6:36; Mt 5:43–48).

W.F. Albright translates Matthew 5:48 "Be true, just as your heavenly Father is true." His commentary indicates that true being is merciful being. "A rabbinic commentary (TB, Shabbath 133b), quoting a first century A.D. authority, paraphrases this as: 'Be like him. As he is gracious and merciful, so be you gracious and merciful.' The Greek word *teleios* in the context does not refer to moral perfection, but truth, sincerity (cf. Deut 18:13). . . . It does not here have the later Greek meaning of being 'totally free of imperfection,' which is the meaning found in both the King James and the Revised Standard Version."[44]

Nor is God reluctantly or penuriously merciful. Rather, God's mercy takes the initiative. That is the precise point these three parables make. This point is somewhat obscured by the titles we have given these parables—the lost sheep, the lost coin, the lost (or prodigal) son. In reality, the focus is not on the object lost, but on the person seeking—the shepherd, the woman, the father. These represent Jesus' heavenly Father, of whom Jesus is the sacrament in the world. The reason that Jesus must be among sinners is because that is where his Father is. The entire Old Testament is a history of this holy God's initiative, searching out sinners—not to execute them but to forgive them and recall them to participation in the divine communion (Ez 18:23, 32; 33:11).[45] This initiative is especially obscured in some presentations of the third parable. Too often emphasis is placed on verse 20: "While he was still a long way off, his father saw him and was moved with pity. He ran to the boy. . . ." This verse emphasizes the enthusiasm of God's mercy, but not its initiative. The divine initiative is described much earlier in the parable, in verse 17: "Then he came to his senses and said, How many of my father's paid servants have more. . . . I will leave this place and go to my father. . . ." The Father's role does not begin when the lost son is already underway. The son is able to be underway only because the Father has already been active—in the lost son's memory. This parable is a good illustration of our contention that the Gospels can be read as arguments between Jesus and other Jews about the meaning of the Jewish religious tradition, especially about God, God's nature and God's relationship to the world. Of course, Jesus did more than just preach argumentatively. He did many other things too. We shall now survey these other activities to see how they imply the founding of the Church.

Those who are reluctant to speak of Jesus founding a/the Church are fond of emphasizing that Jesus spends his time preaching the reign and kingdom of God, not placing juridical, constitutional acts. There is, of course, some value in such a contention. On the other hand, Jesus would have been an extraordinarily unusual and odd preacher, had he not preached to people.[46] One may well have a message, one which one thinks extraordinarily important, but what is a message without an audience? Normally a preacher has to seek out an audience. This is especially true in the case of a wandering charismatic preacher, as Jesus apparently was.[47] In the very act of preaching, an organizational element and dimension is inevitable—and natural. Of course, one does not move from such an organizational dimension to the Holy Roman Catholic Church, or any churches as they exist today, in one bound. But it is important to note that societal arrangement and organization is not something that needs to be supernaturally revealed or fall ready-made from heaven.[48] Organization, order, and the means of orderliness are inherent in human nature and being itself. (Indeed, if we take the doctrine of the Trinity seriously, we have to say the same thing about the divine nature and being.) Hence, if Jesus, his message and his mission are not going to be inhuman or anti-human, his very preaching will entail some organization in the call and formation of his listeners who will become his followers and disciples.

We must also recall that Jesus did not preach in a vacuum. He preached and gathered disciples in a particular historical and cultural context. The dominant element in this context was the Jewish religion, then well over a thousand years old. It had become a sophisticated, highly organized, at least in certain ways, but nevertheless pluralist socio-religious phenomenon. We have already seen some of the elements in this religious complex. Other factors at the time of Jesus were also crucially (I use this term on purpose) important. Most striking was the Roman occupation. For Jewish sensibilities this dominion and domination by an alien power was not only social, economic, political and psychological. It was also, and primarily, religious. Not only certain excesses of Roman policy and practice, but the very presence of the Roman Empire in the Holy Land, ruling the chosen people, was a religious affront to Yahweh, sole Lord of the universe in general and of this people in particular. Such an alien presence was a ready source of morally sinful temptations as well as of ritual, cultic impurity.

In response to this alien, unclean presence as well as to the theoretical interpretation and practical implementation of the torah, various religious groups had arisen within Judaism. If we eliminate the negative and pejorative overtones of the terms, we could call these groups sects or denominations within the larger Judaism.[49] At the same time we should note that these groups were not totally free of the negative tendencies associated with sectarianism. Nevertheless, their basic intent was to provide legitimate and effective ways of being Jewish. The four best known were the Pharisees, Sadducees, Essenes and Zealots.

The Pharisees have gotten an especially bad press among Christians.[50] This began already in the Gospels. At the time of their final composition, the other Jewish groups had been mostly eliminated by the Romans. The Pharisees were almost the only Jewish survivors, certainly the dominant group. When the Gospel writers wanted to point up the difference between Jesus' interpretation of the torah, Judaism, and God and that of the Jews who did not accept Jesus' interpretation, it was usually the Pharisees who provided the contrast. On the other hand, of all the groups in contemporary Judaism, Jesus probably most resembled the Pharisees, although he stood more in the prophetic tradition; the Pharisees were more in the Ezra tradition, emphasizing the law and the book. Furthermore, not only Jesus criticized the Pharisees. They were accused by the Sadducees and Essenes of being both too strict and too lenient in their interpretation of the law. The most serious accusation against them was that they had erected a wall or fence around the law. This wall consisted of their oral interpretation of the written law. It was intended to help and further the practice of the law. However, it was so detailed and so severe that it did not promote but rather demoted observation of the law by the masses of people.

It did not make the law accessible to the people. It prevented the people from gaining access to the law. On these grounds Jesus was especially intense in his censure of the Pharisees: "You . . . shut up the kingdom of heaven in men's faces, neither going in yourselves, nor allowing others to go in who want to. . . . They tie up heavy burdens and lay them on men's shoulders, but will not lift a finger to move them" (Mt 23:1–32). W.F. Albright and C.S. Mann offer an interesting interpretation of Jesus' condemnation of this legalism as hypocrisy, and of the Pharisees and scribes as hypocrites.[51] Hypocrite is a misleading translation of *hupokritai/hupokrites,* because the American word now means two-faced—people who play a part or act a role which is at variance with their own convictions and life. Such a meaning does not fit well with either the lifestyle of the Pharisees or their condemnation by Jesus. According to Albright and Mann, the term really "denotes an overscrupulous, pettifogging con-cern with the minutiae of law" (cxii). Hence, "it was not that these people were consciously acting a part which did not correspond to their own inner convictions, but that they were parading their own scrupulousness in public. This is the reverse side of casuistry: not merely an attempt to legislate for all possible contingencies, but setting up a self-conscious example, and thus bringing the service of God into contempt" (cxxi). "Legal hair splitting made the law less and less an expression of man's responsive loyalty to God and God's gracious gift to his people" (cxxii). The law had become increasingly burdensome because of and in the Pharisees' interpretation. Even worse, their oral interpretation had come to enjoy dignity and authority similar to that of the written law. When Jesus said "You have heard it said, but I say. . . ." he was referring not to the torah, but to the Pharisaic (and other contemporary interpretations) of the law, which, after all, he had come not to destroy, but to fulfill (Mt 5:17). Jesus' chief objection to the Pharisees was that their interpretation of the law was elitist. The communion of God and man which the law was supposed to promote was restricted and ruptured precisely by the Pharisees' legalistic interpretation. Even the name Pharisees would have agitated Jesus, although they thought of themselves in terms of brotherhood or community.[52] The Pharisees wanted to be the true Israel and lead all

Israel to true righteousness, to true service and worship of the true God. In this intention they would have found in Jesus an ally, and he one in them. However, their actual approach and practice to God and religion were elitist and separatist. Jesus, the sacrament of the God who wishes to save *all* people, could hardly have acquiesced in the Pharisaic interpretation of God and torah.

Unlike the Pharisees who were lay people, both Sadducees and Essenes claimed priestly status. The Sadducees are frequently identified with the Establishment—aristocratic, wealthy, landowners, patrician. With due caution, this description can be accepted. The Sadducees regarded themselves as "guardians of tradition,"[53] a term and concept we shall apply to the Church later on. The Sadducees cultivated a strictly literal interpretation of the torah and developed their own penal code, which was very strict. Like the Pharisees, the Sadducees remained within Judaism, although they, too, were a closed and restricted group. They would, therefore, have been liable to the same criticism by Jesus. Insofar as they denied the resurrection (Mk 12:18), they were liable to even further criticism. In both cases they denigrated the power of the one living God to enter into full saving communion with the non-Godly. Their interpretation of God and God's salvation was too narrow for Jesus to have accepted them.

Until recently when the Dead Sea Scrolls were discovered, very little was known about the Essenes. In many ways they were the most elitist and separatist of all the Jewish groups. They claimed to be the true descendants of the true priest Zadok. They found the corruption of Israel, even Jerusalem, its temple and Sadducaic priesthood, entirely too much. They fled even the Holy City and separated themselves from their sinful and unclean fellow religionists to form the "true Israel." Among the Essenes, the Old Testament "holy remnant" was transformed into a holy elite; emphasis on human performance tended to overshadow the gift-ness of God's graciousness. Humankind was divided into the "sons of light" and the "sons of darkness." This division was not salvation-historical, based on the conduct of the people involved. It was predestinational-anthropological, based on an eternal divine decree, according to which some human beings are good, some evil. Historical life only reveals; it does not constitute who is good, who is evil. Practically, this discernment of spirits was made on the basis of membership in the Essene community. There was a certain fanaticism in the Essene concept of God and holiness, emphasizing, as it did, the God who loves and hates. Holiness meant loving and hating, in the manner and imitation of God.

> Everyone who wishes to join the community must pledge . . . to love all the children of light . . . and to hate all the children of darkness, each according to the measure of his guilt, which God will ultimately requite. And these are the regulations of conduct for every man that would seek the inner vision in these times, touching what he is to love and what he is to hate. He is to bear unremitting hatred

toward all men of ill repute, and to be minded to keep in seclusion from them.[54]

Obviously, such an approach to God and God's relation to the world could not have been acceptable to Jesus. Whether Jesus had direct contact with the Essenes is disputed. In Matthew's account of Jesus' interpretation of the law, there may be an indication that Jesus was at least familiar with Essene doctrine if not the Essenes themselves:

You have heard that it was said: You must love your neighbor and hate your enemy. But I say this to you: love your enemies and pray for those who persecute you (5:43).

Exhaustive searches of the Old Testament have not been able to find a text exhorting hatred of one's enemies. This has led some to the conclusion that "the second part of this commandment is not, and could not, be found thus formulated in the law. It is the brusque expression of a language (the original Aramaic) which has few half-tones and is equivalent to 'There is less obligation to love one's enemy'(cf. Lk 14:26 with its parallel Mt 10:37)."[55] Such explanations are not really satisfying. The words "You have heard that it was said" are not merely random words. They are, rather, "a technical formula pointing to a juridical or legal formulation to which Jesus contrasts his own law or command. Hence it is not a sufficient occasion for Jesus to have made this statement to point out that the Jews factually hated their enemies. Only a legal formulation as prescript or command will suffice. The only such command found so far is in Qumran (1 QS1, 10; 9, 21). The following conclusion is, therefore, legitimate. Jesus did indeed have knowledge of the Qumran interpretation of the law, from which he decidedly distanced himself."[56] Jesus further distanced himself from Qumran and Essene understandings in regard to their clericalism and ritualism (Lk 10:29–37; Mk 7:14–23). The crucial difference between Jesus and the Essenes lay in their contrasting, in fact, conflicting understandings of God's holiness. For the Essenes, God's holiness involved absolute intolerance and rejection of anything imperfect, unholy. On the other hand, for Jesus it is precisely the divine holiness that enables and requires God to search out the fallen, the sinful, the imperfect. As the sacrament of this holy God, Jesus is also "the Holy One of God" (Mk 1:24). Consequently his place is among the fallen, the sinful, the sick, for it is precisely they who need the care of the holy theandric physician and healer (Mt 9:10–13). This dimension of the divine holiness the Essenes had failed to understand. The divine holiness is communion, not excommunication.

The final major group of Jews was known as the Zealots. They were radical revolutionaries, bent on the expulsion of the Romans from Israel. The Zealots could perhaps be best described as guerrilla fighters. Small in number, they could hardly hope to win a head-on confrontation with Roman military forces. When they did try, they were not only defeated, they were exterminated. Suffused with intensely apocalyptic, eschatological hopes, they hoped for a direct divine intervention which would enable their military efforts to overcome Roman military superiority. Once the Romans had been evicted, Israel would become a theocracy and the divine rule and kingdom permanently established. Jesus would not have been acceptable to the Zealots, although they shared a certain expectation of the imminent in-breaking of God's reign and kingdom.

Their zeal for God's reign and kingdom may have been equally intense. Their understanding of it and the means to "erect" it, however, was considerably different. A few years ago an English scholar, S.G.F. Brandon, launched a concerted effort to prove that Jesus was a revolutionary—to no avail.[57] More recent attempts by political and liberation theologians to portray Jesus in terms of a radical social critic and social reformer do not succeed much better. It is not that Jesus was not concerned with the poor and with social, economic and political oppression. On the other hand, Jesus clearly offered nothing that even vaguely approaches a theory and program for positive social, economic, and political justice. As John L. McKenzie has emphasized, "I will admit that Jesus gave me no instructions on how to become involved in politics and employ them as means for his purposes. That leaves me, I think, much in the same position as the fact that Jesus left me no instructions on how to invest my savings (of which I have a meager amount). . . ."[58] Then as now, a long journey must be made from the preaching of Jesus to the just social order. Reconciliation, love of neighbor, love of friend and enemy, tolerance of failure and compassion for the failer—these and all the other religious admonitions of Jesus do not automatically and easily transfer into "holy" and just social institutions. The long journey is through the theoretical disciplines of the social sciences and the implementation of effective economic, business, and political measures. About these Jesus said little. In fact, he could be deemed to have avoided the issue. When he was directly confronted with the relationship of religious faith and public policy, he replied, "Very well, give back to Caesar what belongs to Caesar—and to God what belongs to God" (Mt 22:15–22). As such, religious leaders and practitioners as well as theologians have no specific competence in discerning and implementing social, economic and political institutions and structures that will produce a just and wholesome society. Knowledge of and skills in the social sciences and applied disciplines are not in striking evidence among them.[59] For this reason, the Church today, as was Jesus then, must be aware of the limited role it can play in the direct arrangement of society. The temptation to Zealotism did not die forever in 115. On the other hand, the Church must also be aware that this awareness can easily lend to a caution which amounts to identification with and support of any given existing society.

Since pacifism describes not only non-violence, but a complex ideology (in the good sense) of social behavior nowadays, it is better not used to describe Jesus and the early Church.[60] On the other hand, violence did not enjoy a good reputation with Jesus. In this matter the difference between Jesus and the Zealots would have been great. However, the difficulty we have been describing remains: How does one implement an ontology of communion in the social, political and economic institutions of society? To this question the world still awaits the answer. From the Jesus recorded in the New Testament we have received no blueprint, no program. In this he also differed from the Zealots.

But most of all, he differed from the Zealots because their approach to the reign/kingdom of God was decidedly uncommunional. This was their fundamental error, which expressed itself concretely in their identification of their particular political program with the reign/kingdom of God. My emphasis on the Church as communion admittedly runs the risk of being too "theoretical," too far removed from the nitty-gritty of practical life. However, I think this danger is less dangerous than the zelotic danger of identifying the Church with particular socio-economic-political programs—especially when these are not necessarily all that practical and pragmatic themselves, most especially when their provenance is a religious passion for social justice.

It was within the complex context we have just described that Jesus preached, gathered his disciples, fulfilled his mission and ministry. Unless Jesus was a complete simpleton and romantic, he would certainly have undertaken not only to call and assemble followers, but also to organize and arrange them so that his preaching might be as effective as possible. This does not mean, of course, that Jesus had first to acquire an MBA from the Harvard Business School. It means only that he would have taken the ordinary, common sense measures available to his contemporaries and thus to him. Granted that Jesus was more of a wandering, itinerant, charismatic preacher than a sedentary, fixed local teacher, the Gospel accounts still reveal his public ministry to have been planned, at least to some extent, and not purely spontaneous and free-lance. There was a pattern to it, as there was a pattern within his disciples.[61] There was a large crowd of disciples (Lk 6:17; 19:37; Jn 6:60), within which there were articulations into twelve (Mt 10:2–4; Mk 3:16–19; Lk 6:13–16; Jn 6: 67; Acts 1:13; 1 Cor 15;5), three (Mt 17:1–8; Mk 2:8; Lk 9:28–36), seventy-two (Lk 10:1,17) and even one, the beloved disciple (Jn 13:23; 18:15; 19:26; 20:2; 21:7, 20). Within the discipleship of Jesus, the Twelve play (or plays—here again we might involve the Greek grammar of a plural subject with a singular verb) a significant role.[62] This role is both symbolic and practical. Symbolically the Twelve (apostles, as they were later called) represented the twelve tribes of Israel and symbolized Jesus' mission to the whole nation or people of Israel. Thus Jesus clearly demonstrated his claim to be *the Messiah* (Jn 10:1–21) and rejected any and all sectarian restriction. Practically, the Twelve were also commissioned to preach as missionaries (Mk 3:13–21; Mk 6:30–44; Jn 6:1–15; especially Lk 9:10–17).[63]

In Mark's description of the selection of the Twelve, we have a classical summary of the foundation and nature of the Church: "He now went up into the hills and summoned those he wanted. So they came to him and he appointed twelve; they were to be his companions and to be sent out to preach, with power to cast out devils" (3:13–15). The Church consists of the call of Jesus and the response of people. When this happens, we speak of disciples. Within the discipleship there is not elitist and sectarian exclusivism, but articulation, so that not everyone does exactly what everyone else does. Nevertheless, all must do in their own way what discipleship as such entails: first of all, to *be with* Jesus; then, to make Jesus present in the world, as we would say nowadays, or, in an earlier vocabulary, to preach (the positive promotion of theandric communion) and to cast out devils (exorcise; the negative destruction of the hindrances to this communion).

In the mission of Jesus and his dealings with his disciples, preaching and exorcism were performed not only by spoken words, but also by ritual and symbolic actions (Jn 9:17; 12:1–19; 13:1–20). Of all Jesus' ritual and symbolic actions, the most important were his meals, especially those with sinners, most especially the Last Supper. So important were these meals that one famous Catholic exegete has felt himself able to say that "the essence of Christianity is *sunesthienai*—to eat with one another."[64] The general symbolism of the meal is widely acknowledged.[65] The Judeo-Christian tradition has emphasized this in its description of the communion between God and man as a heavenly banquet. Consequently, it is most fitting that Jesus, as the sacrament of theandric communion, should eat with even sinners, thus reconciling them with the communion his heavenly Father has always wanted with creation.

During the course of Jesus' preaching, it became clear to him that his success would be limited. Not all of Israel would respond to his call to metanoia. For the time being, the theandric communion would remain partial. One speaks of the Galilean crisis, when "many of his disciples left him and stopped going with him." The Twelve remained, however, for they continued to think/believe that Jesus had "the message of eternal life . . . was the Holy One of God" (Jn 6:66–71). Jesus continued to preach and do his good works. Henceforth, however, he would direct his attention to a smaller group of disciples, whom he would instruct in regard to the likelihood, fact, and meaning of his death for the communion reign/kingdom of God which he had preached and continued to preach (Mk 10:35; 14:25; Lk 9:22, 31, 51; 22:16).[66] Would Jesus have used the figure of the suffering servant of Yahweh from the prophet Isaiah in this preparation?[67]

The preparation of the disciples for continued discipleship after the death of Jesus would have culminated in the Last Supper. In that real and symbolic meal, Jesus provided the disciples with a most special and specific means of preserving and promoting his memory, his very life (body *and* blood), among them, the true disciples, the true Israel, however small a remnant, and thus among all peoples.[68] In this ecclesial (Church founding) meal, Jesus continued the foundation and nature of the Church which he had begun early in Mark's Gospel (3:13–19). As we saw there, Church means, above all, to *be with* Jesus; then to preach the good news and to exorcise evil. In the Eucharist, Jesus gave not only a spoken word, not only a ritual, symbolic action to keep his memory alive—he gave his very self. In the Last Supper's Eucharist and Calvary's cross, the daily sacrifice of Jesus' total self-reference and dedication to God and God's reign/kingdom achieved its most intense expression, symbolically and really.

That this total (pure) sacrifice was totally acceptable to God was revealed in the resurrection of Jesus from the dead. As Jesus learned in his appearances to his disciples (Mk 16:1–15; Lk 24:1–43; Jn 20:1–29) and as St. Paul learned in Athens, people tend to be a bit skeptical about "rising from the dead" (Acts 17:32). However, a teaching of St. Thomas Aquinas hints that nothing should have been more obvious than that Jesus should rise (be raised) from the dead. A favorite Scripture for St. Thomas was Wisdom 1:13–15; "Death was not God's doing; he takes no pleasure in the extinction of the living. To be—for this he created all." Inspired by this text, St. Thomas emphasized that created things do not have the power of self-annihilation within themselves, so intense is their ontological relationship with the triune, divine *apeiron*. St. Thomas thought that, by virtue of the infinite divine power, God could destroy finite creatures. However, by virtue of the divine wisdom God would and could not destroy the creation he had made to begin with.[69] This sapiential interpretation of God's creative and preserving nature is reinforced and intensified by Jesus' revelation that God's very perfection is compassion (Lk 6:36) and love (Jn 3:15; 1 Jn 4:8–17). Hence, as implausible as the resurrection of Jesus (and us, as his many brothers and sisters; Rom 8:29) may be from one point of view (ours), it is just as plausible from another (God's).

In view of this, the mission of "another Paraclete . . . the Holy Spirit . . . who will teach you everything and remind you of all I have said to you" (Jn 14:16, 26) was not just another kindness on the part of Jesus. It was a necessary stage in the triune divine communion's communion with humanity, another necessary stage in the history of salvation. It is one more sign of the totality of the triune God's commitment to theandric communion, of the divine philanthropy, of the divine friendship for humanity. For this reason I think the difficult term paraclete,[70] sometimes translated as advocate, helper, intercessor, is best translated as friend. According to Congar, "The Eastern anaphoras, that of St. Serapion, for example, delight in calling upon God under the lovely name of 'Friend of men.' "[71] So do the Christian mystics.[72] Are they being presumptuous? Is this one more instance of human *hybris*? The answer is a resounding *no*! The relationship of Adam-Eve with Yahweh in the garden could easily and certainly be described as friendly. Furthermore, in Exodus 33:11 we read that "Yahweh would speak with Moses face to face, as a man speaks to a friend." The wisdom literature insists that the divine wisdom "makes them [holy souls] friends of God" (Wis 7:27, 14). In the New Testament this Incarnate Wisdom-Word insists on being "the friend of sinners" (Mt 11:19; Lk 7:35). St. Paul exhorts us "to treat each other in the same friendly way as Christ treated you" (Rom 15:7). If the Holy Spirit is in perichoresis with the friendly Father and the friendly Son, and if this Holy Spirit is "another paraclete of the Christic" Friend of sinners, then it is certainly most fitting that this Holy Spirit, sent to enliven, instruct and empower Jesus' disciples to be his living memory in the world, be called or named "(another) friend" of humanity.

It is not fanciful to suggest that Pentecost is the event and feast of God's unlimited Christly friendship for the world in and through the Holy Spirit. As soon as they had been empowered by the Holy Spirit, "Peter stood up with the Eleven and addressed them in a loud voice." He quoted the prophet Joel (3:1–5): "In the days to come—it is the Lord who speaks—I will pour out my spirit on all mankind . . . sons and daughters . . . young men . . . old men. . . . Even on slaves, men and women, in those days, I will pour out my spirit . . ." (Acts 2:14–21). This declaration follows the speaking in foreign languages, which "devout men living in Jerusalem from every nation under heaven" were able to recognize and understand (2:1–13). This is usually explained in reference to the tower of Babel, where "Yahweh confused the language of the whole earth" (Gen 11:9). This confusion would, then, have been undone on Pentecost and the unity and "common language" of humanity would have been restored. Although such a symbolic interpretation is not unattractive, it does have its drawbacks. Another interpretation has been suggested by Jacob Kremer. He states flatly, "The Bible offers no grounds for the widespread assumption that the Pentecost miracle must be interpreted in regard to the confusion of tongues in Genesis 11."[73] On the basis of striking parallels in contemporary Jewish and rabbinic literature, literary analysis of Acts 2, the parallel between the torah and the Spirit as gifts of God, and the date of Pentecost, Kremer suggests that Luke's account of Pentecost is framed in terms of the Sinai tradition, not the tower of Babel narrative. Jewish tradition had emphasized that the proclamation of the torah on Sinai had been made in the various languages of the world, to emphasize the universal validity of the torah. The point of Luke's description of the Pentecost event is, then, the universal (worldwide) validity of the Gospel, proclaimed henceforth not by the historical Jesus but by the disciples-apostles of the risen Jesus in the power of the Holy Spirit. "In the proclamation of the apostles—Pentecost is the beginning and simultaneously the expression of that which happened in the primitive Church—the Holy Spirit gives testimony on behalf of Christ (Acts 5:32). In the final analysis, however, it is the *voice* (language, tongue: *echos, phone*) and the speaking (*lalein heterais glossais*) of the Lord in heaven which calls all men to repentance and faith through the languages of the apostles. Coming as they do from the worldwide diaspora, these Jews vicariously represent all men" (70).

The universal friendship of God for man, which is rooted in the triune communion of God and which became a part of human history in the Incarnate Word, was assured universality (catholicity) through the Pentecostal outpouring of the Holy Spirit. Many theologians have been correct, then, when they placed the birth of the Church in this universal outpouring of the Holy Spirit on Pentecost. Others, like St. Augustine, were also correct when they suggested that the Church was born when the side of Christ was pierced and blood and water, representing the sacraments (baptism and Eucharist) and the Church, flowed forth (Jn 19:34).[74] Hermas the Shepherd was also correct when he suggested that the Church was born even before the world was created. All these are founding or foundational acts of the Church. We are also correct when we emphasize that Jesus founded the Church during his earthly ministry when, by his preaching and exorcising, he called forth people to follow him as his disciples, whom he commissioned to carry on his own mission in various ways. Jesus' resurrection reveals the everlasting validity of his earthly mission; the coming of his Holy Spirit reveals and empowers the mission of Jesus' disciples to keep his memory alive throughout the whole world.

In addition to this implicit Church founding process, Jesus is also reported to have acted in ways which are more or less explicitly Church founding. We shall describe these briefly, for they only make slightly more definite and concrete the foundational process implicit in the entire mission and public life of Jesus.

The first of these is an exorcism recounted by both Luke (11:14–22) and Matthew (12:22–29); it is also recounted by Mark (3:22–27), but his version is not pertinent to our purpose. In this scene Jesus has cast out a devil. He was accused of being in cahoots with Beelzebul, and only thus able to exorcise. He responded by referring his ability to the "finger of God" in Luke (see Ex 8:15 and Ps 8:3), the "Spirit of God" in Matthew. This is already very interesting, since one would really expect Luke to have "Spirit" and Matthew to have "finger" in their respective accounts. The whole scene is paradigmatic of Jesus' mission. There is an eschatological urgency in regard to the reign/kingdom of God which is experienced not collectively, but individually (Jesus and the "possessed" person).[75] The critical verse is the claim: "But if it is through the finger (Spirit) of God that I cast out devils, then know that the kingdom of God has overtaken you" (Lk 11:20; Mt 11:28). The critical question is how closely Jesus associated this reign/kingdom of God with not only his mission, but his very person. This question spontaneously calls forth the equally debated question about Jesus' perception of this kingdom as already present, only future, or some combination of already-not yet.[76]

Whatever may have been the case with Jesus' present-future orientation, scenes like the Beelzebul exorcism clearly show him to have had a unique self-understanding. The self-awareness of Jesus portrayed in the Gospels both requires and reflects those Johannine statements about the perichoresis of Father (God) and Son (for example, 3:11, 32–34; 5:19; 8:28). Jesus distinguished himself from all rabbis, prophets and teachers of wisdom in the total identification of his person and his preaching. His proclamation that through his exorcisms the reign and kingdom is revealed to be present in the world in his very own person was singular.

This unique self-concept of Jesus was such that it transformed the prevailing contemporary Jewish apocalyptic eschatology. No longer was the emphasis to be on the still outstanding judgment of God. No longer was the reign/kingdom of God still to be awaited. No, it was already present in the world, present within humanity. As David Flusser points out, "He (Jesus) is the only ancient Jew known to us who not only announced that one stood at the approach, on the border of the Final Age, but simultaneously that the new Age of Salvation had already begun."[77]

As Walter Kasper says, "The unheard of claim of the earthly Jesus leads immediately over to the statement of the fourth Gospel, 'The Father and I are one' (Jn 10:30)."[78] Thus we are led to the question about Jesus' relationship to God. Christians certainly thought him to be the presence of God in the world (Jn 1:14; Heb 1:1–4). Did Jesus himself? Although Jesus may not have termed himself God directly and immediately, this is no great lack. As Ernst Fuchs has pointed out, "Such a claim—to be the Son of God, or the Son of Man, having come or still coming, or any of the various dogmatic Christological titles—is no longer necessary. Taken in themselves, all such claims assert not more but really less than Jesus' own behavior and action."[79] This behavior/action of Jesus is the expression of his consciousness, which is itself the expression of his being. From these expressions (sacrament-like) we come to the conclusion that in the person of Jesus the reign-kingdom of God has definitively entered into human history. In our preferred terms, Jesus' unique self-understanding demonstrates that the communion of the divine with the human is already a reality. Later on, the Church, having meditated this state of affairs, will directly declare that in Jesus the divine was substantially present, hypostatically united with the human. This theandric communion was and is for all people. Thus, Jesus is God's "absolute act/deed . . . event of salvation,"[80] in which the theandric communion becomes irreversibly and ineradicably present in the history of the world.

Explicitly as well as implicitly, then, Jesus can and must be seen to be the foundation of the Church, ontologically as well as historically. As the body of Christ and temple of the Holy Spirit, the Church is and wants to be the sacrament of God's salvation for the whole world. This salvation is communion of the non-Godly, the human, with the divine, God. Jesus is precisely this, and not only for himself, but precisely *for* others.[81] He is this for others not in mere velleity or general benevolence, but in effective power.[82] Jesus has been this, of course, for all eternity in the inner life of God, for all history is the created communication of God's life. It is in, by and through him that there is creation at all. As we have emphasized all along, this divine communication has not been stingy, but overflowingly generous. In Christ this divine generosity became irreversible in the very history of the world. It is this irreversible victory of God's grace that is manifested variously in the words and events of Jesus' life. And it is these words and events which are the founding events of the Church, as Jesus' person is the foundation. The Church, we need to recall continuously, is not primarily the institution, not even the means of grace. It is primarily the body of Christ, the temple of this Christ's Spirit—altogether, the communion of God with man.

In itself, this communion-Church does not require a division within humanity. Likewise, it did not of itself require a division within Judaism. That it did in fact *occasion* a division is not to be credited to its account, but to that of the unbelievers. Factually, in history, the Church may be said to have come into existence precisely with the refusal of (some of) the Jews to accept Jesus and the willingness of the Gentiles to accept him. But this division is neither required by the very nature of the communion-Church, nor is it a permanent feature, as St. Paul emphasizes in the Epistle to Romans (9–11). Hence, for the Church as the communion of the divine with the human to exist, the refusal of Israel was not necessary. If this is so, then the refusal of Israel was also not necessary for the entrance of the Gentiles into the discipleship of Jesus and hence into his Church. What the unbelief of Israel amounts to is not even primarily the blindness of the Jews or their enmity (Rom 11:25–32). It is, rather, a negative cipher of God's invincible will to save. For God transforms Israel's disobedience into the means of salvation for both Jews and pagans (Rom 11:30–32). The Church is, then, an interim solution. But even as such it is the sacrament of the final solution, namely the merciful communion of God with all humankind (Rom 11:32).

Thus we are brought once more to the truth that the saving triune God is the Church's true and original founder. Is Luke perhaps hinting at this when he describes the origin of the Lord's Prayer? In Matthew's Gospel Jesus takes the initiative in teaching this prayer to his disciples. But Luke places the initiative in a petition by "one of his disciples [who] said, 'Lord teach us to pray, just as John taught his disciples' " (11:1). Noteworthy for us is the context "just as John taught his disciples." We have not dealt with the disciples of John the Baptist as one of the groups which Jesus confronted in his preaching. We do know that they also offered an interpretation of the torah which some preferred to Jesus' (Jn 1:6–8, 15, 19–34). John appears to have been a bit more aggressive in ferreting out sin and proclaiming its punishment (Mt 3:1–12). His understanding of God's perfection as compassion may not have been as intense as Jesus'. But such a comparison is not our purpose here. What interests us is that John's disciples had their own, proper, distinctive prayer, which revealed and reinforced their self-concept and identity. In contrast, Jesus' disciples seem, according to Luke's account, to have had an identity crisis. They did not have their own prayer. Therefore they did not have an adequate means of identifying themselves, of distinguishing themselves from others. So Jesus gave them their own prayer, which served as their insignia (Thomas Aquinas, as we shall see, speaks of the sacraments as the insignia of the Church). Once again, this prayer peculiar to the disciples did not make Jesus into or reveal him to have been a separatist, a sectarian all along. Indeed, only shortly before the text we are now discussing, Jesus had emphasized that "anyone who is not against you is for you" (Lk 9:50). What the proper prayer does indicate is that Jesus was aware of what he was doing. He was aware that he had certain followers. His disciples constituted an empirically discernible and describable social entity. Although he preached to all, he did not just preach in general—for the simple reason that one can't. It is impossible. Rather, as an intelligent, capable person, Jesus dealt with definite people in concrete situations. He made provisions for those who were in fact his disciples, both when he could more or less realistically hope that *all* would be, and also when he had realistically to accept that *not* all would be. These provisions for a *de facto* limited discipleship can be understood as acts whereby Jesus founded the Church which *de facto* came into existence—already during his lifetime. Although Jesus trusted in God's providence unconditionally (Lk 12:22–32), he did not thereby cease to be the wise and prudent householder or "man of affairs" (Lk 7:48–49; 12:54–59; Mt 24:43—25:30). When Jesus realized that the response to his call to repent and believe the good news would not be universally affirmative, he would have had two options. He could have despaired and given up all hope for the universal salvation of which he was the preacher (and sacrament, as we now know). But we know that he did not take that route, however sorely tempted he might have been (Mt 23:37–39). The other option was to prepare his disciples for the future which could realistically be expected. This he did, and in so doing laid the foundation of that which would eventually be called his Church.

Has any verse in the New Testament evoked more controversy and commentary than the one where Jesus promised to build his Church on Simon Peter (Mt 16:18)?[83] Was Matthew anything but sheerly brilliant in the immediate juxtaposition of Jesus' prophecy of his passion-death to this promise (Mt 16:21–23)? I think, though, many of us would have found it more "logical" to place the prophecy before the promise. For the Church, as it actually happened in the context of unbelief and belief, was an interim solution, compared to how it would have happened in a context of belief, had all Israel responded positively to Jesus. Would it not have been more logical to have placed the recognition of failure before the promise of the means of survival in spite of the failure? Perhaps, but such a logic might also misunderstand the mysterious ways of the divine wisdom which simply overwhelms our feeble minds (Rom 11:33–36). It would certainly misunderstand the actual history of salvation. This history has been through and through a history of God's gracious gift-giving and equally the history of God's initiative. At no time does God first react to someone else's initiative—and certainly not to sin. God is always out in front, way ahead of the obstacles that sinful human beings try to put in the way of the divine will and plan to save all. I have often wondered whether the greatest sin might not be the fascination with sin, the preoccupation with sin,

which characterizes so many of us, even Christians who should know better
(Lk 5:1–11, esp. 10). Although its advocates did not intend it so, how presumptuous the theory that God became human because man sinned, that without human sin there would have been no incarnation. In one sense that has to
be the greatest hybris of all. I sometimes wonder whether this fascination with
sin is not a desperate attempt to feel important. If our sins can "make" God
do something, then we can't be entirely unimportant. We would actually have
accomplished something!

    Unfortunately for this kind of pomp and posturing, and fortunately for all
of us, such pretensions were laid to rest long ago. That even fratricide has been
anticipated and contained by God, was already and clearly understood by the
ancients, our forebears in faith: "I am Joseph . . . your brother whom you
sold into Egypt. But now, do not grieve, do not reproach yourselves for having
sold me here, since God sent me before you, to preserve your lives. . . . God
sent me before you to make sure that your race would have survivors in the
land and to save your lives, many lives at that. So it was not you who sent me
here but God. . ." (Gen 45:1–8).

    I think that we can apply this text to the events of Matthew 16:16–23.
However unacceptable the unbelief of some of Jesus' co-religionists, it was
not their unbelief which caused the Church to come into existence. It was,
rather, the saving God of Jesus. It was this God who enabled the disciples,
"the apostles and prophets [to be the] foundations of a building [the Church]
God's household . . . one holy temple in the Lord [of which] Christ Jesus himself [is] its main cornerstone" (Eph 2:20), whose divinely granted insuperable
perpetuity and invincibility is shared and represented in a particular manner by
Simon Peter, the rock. (Here we should recall van der Leeuw's theory of the
many founders.) Of course, Simon Peter's particular role was hardly intended
to develop into hierocratic papalism and monarchical privilege.[84] It was intended to support the brothers and sisters in belief in Jesus, in perseverance in
preaching this Jesus[85] and his preaching, and in exorcising evil from the world
(Lk 22:32). How much grief the failure of Simon Peter and his "successors in
office" have caused the faith-full, the faith-less and the wavering need not be
detailed here.[86] One cannot, however, avoid wondering how much of the dispute about the text of Matthew 16:16–19 has been caused not by the text itself,
but by those who invoked that text and ignored the juxtaposed one (16:21–28)
which required even of the primatial, rock-like Peter the crucial following of
Christ.[87] However, even the sinfulness of the holy Church does not corrupt the
Church, which in one sense can be said to have been born in the betrayal and
desertion of Jesus by not only Judas, but also, and even, by the Rock (Simon
Peter). Here, though, God has once again anticipated failing, falling, sinning
humankind—even apostolic humankind. So, Jesus had already prayed for Simon's conversion and recovery well before he had even sinned (Lk 22:32).

    We should, then, not locate the origin, birth or founding of the Church in
the sin of the world or the sin of Israel or the sin of Judas or the sin of Simon

Peter the Rock. The origin is, rather, in the saving will of the triune God who enters into communion with finite, even falling and fallen humanity. In Jesus this communion becomes embedded in the very history of humanity. In the Holy Spirit this communion is spatially and temporally universalized. As Jesus is the embodiment of God-Son-Word, so is the Church the embodiment of the Holy Spirit. This Church is one body with many members who have different en-Spirited gifts and missions in the continuation and consummation of salvation-history. One of these gifts is a special, strengthening ministry of universal unity and communion, both effectively and symbolically. Because of this ministry Simon Peter the Rock has been called the servant of the servants of God. Even when inadequately and sinfully exercised, this Petrine ministry, given to the Church by Jesus, is for the sake of "the kingdom of heaven" (Mt 16:19). Heaven is the primordial symbol for the home of God. The God of Jesus, and therefore of Simon Peter, is Father-Son-Holy Spirit—the triune God whose very nature is communion. As Jesus, so also is the Church the sacrament of this communion. In this sacrament-communion Church it is most fitting that there be a rock-firm center strengthening all the brothers and sisters in communion with one another and with the triune God. The Petrine ministry is not to be a peak pyramidally above, but a center communionally within. Matthew 16:16–19 need not be a problem for the Church as the sacrament of God's communion with humankind. In fact, it is one more, and explicit, element in the process whereby Jesus, the perfect communion of the human and divine, provided for the preservation and promotion of this theandric communion from Jerusalem to the very ends of the earth after his passage to the saving Father, whose historical, inner-worldly sacrament Jesus was and the Church is.

Given all this, we can now propose a "definition." The Church is the sacramentally endowed and socially articulated people who accept Jesus as the definitive revelation and actualization of the triune communion with the non-Godly, and who promote this theandric communion through the various empowering gifts they have received from the Holy Spirit. More succinctly, the Church is the communion of believers who exist as the sacrament of Christ who is the sacrament of God, who is the communion of Father, Son, and Holy Spirit.

THE NATURE OF THE CHURCH

Obviously, something as rich in being as this sacramental communion of the triune God with the creation, with humankind, can never be exhaustively explained. In all honesty, we find that very unexhaustive explanations can themselves be quite exhausting. This difficulty of definition has, as we have already emphasized, led the Church and its theologians to talk about the Church in images, metaphors and figures of speech. Some of these are more

figurative, others more conceptual. Because the Church and its theology are
historical, different images and concepts play different roles at different times
and places. As we have also noted, for various reasons communion and sacrament did not play major roles in ecclesiology for centuries.[88] Of late they
have been revived.

We have emphasized the complementarity of these two terms. Communion emphasizes the intimate relatedness and relationship of being as being
with, both in the triune divine Creator and the cosmic, human creation. Sacrament (or symbol) emphasizes the Logos quality of this communion—its un-
derstandability, intelligence and intelligibility, its expressibility. Being is not
merely ontic communion, it is ontological communion. In God, and in God's
created image and likeness, being not only is, it is with; it is not only with, it
is significatively with. Being knows and is known precisely insofar as it
"bes" at all. Consequently we say that being, again both creating and created,
makes sense; it holds together; it is meaningful.

In the factual history of Christianity, the communion between the invisible divine and the visible human has been designated especially by the term
"sacrament." For various historical reasons, the word sacrament has come to
be restricted almost exclusively to the seven sacraments: baptism, confirmation, Eucharist, penance, anointing of the sick, matrimony, holy orders. Although this restriction was not all bad, it was certainly also not all good.
Walter Kasper was correct when he insisted: "Above all, we must relinquish
our fixation on the precisely 'seven sacraments' and begin to emphasize more
the sacramental dimension and signfulness of the entire Christian life. This
would require a creative and relevant renewal of the sacramentals. Only if the
whole of human and Christian life is sacramental, are the precisely full and
perfect [seven] sacraments meaningful."[89] We shall examine the sacraments
in detail in the next chapter. Here we shall mention only that which is necessary for a consideration of precisely the Church as sacrament.

Piet Smulders correctly points out: "Although the term sacrament appears hardly at all in the New Testament in regard to the Church and only ex-
tremely rarely in the patristic period, there is probably no expression more
fitting to characterize the primeval conception of the Church in its totality than
the category of the sacramental."[90] He regards sacrament as the key word in
the Church's new awareness of itself, which is founded in a sacramental economy of salvation, itself rooted in the incarnation. To speak of the Church as
sacrament immediately recalls the theology of Jesus as sacrament. According
to Otto Semmelroth, the Church conceptualized as mystical body leads to and
requires speaking of the Church as sacrament.

This is because sacrament emphasizes the positive correlation between
the visible and invisible, the human and the divine, sign and grace. Sacrament
is the best means to avoid the two paradigmatic ecclesiological errors which
Pius XII pointed out in his encyclical on the Church as the mystical body: false
naturalism, which regards the Church as merely a physical-biological or

moral-organizational unity, and false mysticism, which emphasizes the supernatural, graced sharing in Christ's life to such an extent that the members of the Church lose their personal identities and are subsumed or fused into a new kind of spiritual person.[91] The first error destroys the supernatural, the second the natural. True Christianity always tries to preserve and promote both the human and the divine, the visible and the invisible in the greatest possible communion.

If both fission and fusion in the Church itself and in the theology of the Church are to be avoided, a general hermeneutical principle capable of sustaining all their elements in unity must be discovered. Semmelroth finds this principle in the concept "sacrament."

> This truth of the Church as primal and/or original sacrament (Ursakrament) does not signify just one more conceptualization of the Church among many others. It is, rather, a reflection on the supernatural ontology which is contained in the statements of revelation about the nature or constitution of the Church. To speak of the Church as sacrament is to describe the relationships which obtain among the various individual partial dimensions of the Church, especially between its metaempirical divine interior reality and its societal human exterior reality. For it belongs to the essence of sacrament . . . that in it a complex of realities which are interior and exterior, divine and human are united with one another in a relationship of sign and signified and simultaneously cause and effect.[92]

This understanding of sacrament was eventually captured in very brief formulas—one could almost say mottos or slogans—such as those used by the Council of Trent. Sacrament is "the visible form (figure, shape, *Gestalt*) of invisible grace" (Ds 1639); "The sacraments contain and confer the grace which they signify" (DS 1606). Obviously, such a definition brings to mind first of all Christ himself. As we have seen, in Jesus the divine and the human are perfectly united, for the sake of others, so that Jesus could truly say "To have seen me is to have seen the Father" (Jn 14:9). Jesus is both cause and sign of God's grace in the world, elevating and fulfilling God's original and gracious signful self-communication in creation. For this reason, Karl Rahner has delighted in emphasizing repeatedly that

> our order, in that it is the order of Christ, bears with its very own self a quasi-sacramental quality or characteristic. In our order, all grace is the grace of Christ, and thus all grace shares the characteristic of him who is its source and origin. Christ is truly the fount of grace insofar as he is the incarnate word of God. All grace, therefore, proceeds not only from the metahistorical will of the transcendent God, but also from him who, as incarnate in the history of the world and

humanity, occupies a certain place and definite time, and thus re-
deems the world and grants grace in his "body," indeed in his
"flesh," which is weak and subject to death. Hence, the grace of
Christ is always "historical" . . . and at least in this sense "sacramental," that is, dependent on an historical and "visible" fact,
without which it would neither exist nor be conferred. This "sacramentality" of grace is also the reason why grace is also necessarily
"ecclesial."[93]

For this reason all grace tends toward the Church; all grace has an inner
dynamism to be incorporated and expressed in the Church. In this, the Church
and Christ are utterly similar—the grace of God's saving will visibly expresses
itself in the world in Christ and the Church. Or, Christ and the Church are the
visibly, sensibly perceptible manifestations of God's will for saving communion with the non-Godly. Rahner continues, saying that the Church can be described as the *sacramentum in essendo*—sacrament in being—and the seven
sacraments, in the stricter sense, as the *actus secundus et quidem ex essentia
necessarius, sacramentum in agendo*—the second act [of this sacrament in
being] and essentially necessary, that is, sacrament in act.

Henri de Lubac summed all this up very nicely: "The Church is a mystery, that is, a sacrament. . . . Here below it is the sacrament of Jesus Christ,
as Jesus Christ himself is for us, in his humanity, the sacrament of God."[94]
Here de Lubac is playing on a famous statement of St. Augustine that "there
is no other mystery (sacrament) than Christ."[95] To speak of the Church and
Christ as sacrament is, then, only to be faithful to the "incarnational principle," as it is called. According to this principle, the created material cosmos
is not evil, anti-godly or divisive. It is, rather, the image and likeness of God
as well as the means ("cause") whereby God communes with the non-Godly.
This incarnational principle achieves various degrees of intensity in human
history, which is thereby essentially salvation history. Although not all the
"incarnations" of God's communion with the non-Godly are equally intense,
they are nonetheless all equally sacramental.

To emphasize that the Church is sacrament is to detract from neither the
seven sacraments as special and privileged sacramental actions nor from Jesus
as the altogether unique original sacrament. It is, rather, to rediscover and retrieve one of the Judeo-Christian ontology's most important universal hermeneutical principles. The sacramentality of all created and graced being. For
this reason, Congar[96] and Semmelroth are correct in emphasizing that sacrament is not just one more image or concept or definition of Church among
many other equally satisfactory ones. Sacramentality describes, rather, the ontology (the way being "bes") implicit in the Judeo-Christian revelation, history and tradition.

Hence, all of reality is sacramental, the means and sign of God's communication with the non-Godly. To distinguish among the various stages and intensities of this sacramental communion, the Germans have distinguished *Ursakrament, Grundsakrament* and *Sakrament.* In German "Ur" means and emphasizes origin, first, primordial. Although it is often translated as original, I think originary or originating might be better. Original, both by virtue of its pronunciation and excessive usage, does not have the emphatic character of the German "Ur." I have sometimes resorted to spelling it origin-al and pronouncing it accordingly. In any case, "Ur" emphasizes something as the beginning, source and model of what follows. "Grund" is much like the English "ground." It also means source, but is not as strong as "Ur." It is frequently translated as fundamental. This usage is not, of course, univocally clear. However, one looks in vain for absolutely and perfectly clear and distinct terms. In fact, both "Grund" and "Ur" were used interchangeably to describe Christ and Church. In view of theological developments associated with Vatican II, Rahner made the following observation and recommendation.

> Clearly, the concept of "sacrament" can be considered egalitarianly leveling only if it is used exclusively in a univocal-horizontal manner and reduced to some purely formal characteristics. If, however, one also considers its origin and history, then one can conclude that the appearance of Jesus Christ was itself sacrament, that the Church as a whole is sacrament in the sense of a salvationally effective sign. Since Vatican II, a conceptual clarification seems to have been achieved and deserves to be observed for the sake of a more pertinent and encompassing understanding of sacrament in general and of the concrete sacraments in particular. According to this clarification, Jesus is to be described as the *Ursakrament,* the Church as the *Grundsakrament.* This usage will make the derivative character of the Church as sacrament clear. As Jesus is foundational (*grundlegend*) for the Church as sacrament, so is the Church in its turn foundational for the individual sacraments celebrated in the Church. Until recently, these individual sacraments were exclusively, and often in strict isolation from one another, the sole object of sacramental theology.[97]

Rahner has observed this terminology in his later writings.[98] As I noted above, it is not absolute in German, and in English it is even less binding. However, it is worth observing, precisely because it forcefully illustrates the relationships among Jesus as the origin-al, primordial sacrament, in reference to which the Church is not original, but derivative. However, this same derivative Church-sacrament is fundamental in regard to the seven sacraments (and sacramentals) which are derivative in regard to both the Church and, through the Church, to Christ. The historically incarnate Christ is the sacrament of the

Logos who in turn is the sacrament (symbol, word, Logos) of the Father. The theology of the Church as sacrament inevitably leads us back to the Trinity. Striking confirmation of this "inevitability" is offered by this fact:

> The members of the official Dialogue Commission between the Roman Catholic and Byzantine Orthodox Churches . . . resolved to pursue their ecclesiological dialogue by a discussion of the sacraments that would relate the mysteries of the Church very closely to the mystery of the Blessed Trinity. If it seems somewhat odd to take the Trinity as the *starting point* of the . . . dialogue . . . this may perhaps remind us that ecclesiology has always at its heart something mysterious, that is, something that partakes of the ultimately mysterious life of God.[99]

It could not be otherwise, of course, since the Church, like Christ himself, is the signified and signifying communion of the divine, itself significative communion, with the human. All of this is summed up in Vatican II's statement that the Church is the sacrament of salvation.

Sacrament is a term that is apt to avoid both the false naturalism and mysticism we mentioned earlier. It keeps the natural and supernatural in communion without denaturing either of them or Christ or the believers who are members of his body. The terminology suggested above will also help any "future ecclesiology [avoid] describing the Church, in an undifferentiated way as the 'continuation' of the incarnation. It will proceed on the basis of the analogy between these two distinct but unseparated mysteries."[100]

In the Church as sacrament meet the analogy of being given in the creation and the analogy of faith given in the incarnation. The communion of "God and man" is not only present there, it is also symbolized there. As we shall see in the next chapter, the seven sacraments and all sacramentals are the many sacramental acts of the one Church-sacrament, whereby its general ontological sacramentality achieves even more definite and concrete signfulness in human society and history. The Church is the sacrament of salvation not only for those who are already explicit members, but also for those who share in the theandric communion without explicit awareness of its Christic foundation. As we have seen, the Christian tradition has been able to relate the Church not only to Christ, but also to Abel, even Adam. Indeed, as Hermas reminded us, the Church is the reason there is creation at all. As Christ is the sacrament of God's universal saving will, so also is the Church, in its own way. For this reason Karl Rahner has developed the theory known as anonymous Christianity.[101] This is not a venal attempt to shore up Church membership rolls in an age of declining numbers. Nor is it an ill disguised totalitarianist attempt to make people Christians against their will and own lights. It is, rather, a theory to explain how the universal transcendent divine saving will can be operative universally in history. It fits very well with the sacramental ontology which we have been proposing. It fits very well with the theology of Christ and Church as the sacraments of God's eternal, universal and always operative saving will. In such a view, the always present offer of invisible divine grace achieves visibility in various ways throughout human history (Heb 1:1–4). Special and unique ways are Christ and the Church, but they are not the only ways and signs of the divine communion with humanity. It is often said that Rahner's theory of anonymous Christianity is a blatant consequence of his explicit Christology. That is true, of course. But it is also equally, and perhaps more to the point, to emphasize that Rahner's explicit Christology is only possible within the context of this creational, sacramental, communion ontology, whereby the created cosmos does not establish an abyss between God and man, but is the signful means of the communion of God with the creation.

For this reason, ecclesiological usage of "sacrament" is not a subsequent and derivative abstraction from the theology of the seven sacraments. Rather, the ecclesiological usage enjoys both historical and systematic precedence. And this is also the case precisely because not even the Church is the *Ur*—the origin-al, primordial—sacrament. Christ is. Christ himself is, only because he is the Son-Word of the divine triune communion, of which creation is already the incipient sacrament, which peaks in the incarnation and resurrection and "then" spreads to all in the Church, the sacrament of God Father-Son-Holy Spirit, Savior of the whole world.

This universal sacrament of salvation—St. Augustine calls the Church the *mundus reconciliatus,* the reconciled world—must now be explained further.[102] We shall briefly examine some of the preferred "names" of the Church, to highlight the specific insights each contributes to our understanding of the Church. Among all the titles of the Church, people of God and mystical body of Christ have been dominant in this century. We shall begin with these and then proceed to others, keeping in mind at all times that no single image, conceptualization or definition is ever sufficient to describe the Church adequately.

PEOPLE OF GOD

It is likely that people of God was the preferred image at Vatican II and has been ever since. This is somewhat strange, since people of God has not enjoyed consistent favor among theologians throughout the Church's history.[103] Even more interesting is the fact that Pope Pius XII issued his encyclical on the Church as the mystical body of Christ in 1943. The encyclical strongly and expressly asserted that the most fitting definition of the Church is mystical body. However, just three years earlier a German theologian had published a book in which he rejected mystical body as the preferred title and suggested people of God as the primary and best definition.[104] Events seem to have borne out his contention, which, admittedly, was overstated. Again, it is not a matter of accepting people of God and rejecting mystical body as fitting descriptions of the Church. Especially these two descriptions are to be kept in tandem as mutually complementary. Both attempt to highlight certain dimensions of the disciples of Jesus Christ in their communion with the triune God, Jesus and one another, insofar as they are an identifiable group of people located in and moving through various ages and cultures of world history. The historical cultural context also implies that even the same term can have varying emphases at different times and in different places.

In one sense, people of God was intended less to counterbalance the Church conceived as the mystical body than as the hierarchical perfect society (*societas perfecta*),[105] that is, the Church conceived in a parallel manner to the civil state. The "perfect society" approach had been nurtured in opposition to the Protestant tendency to deny the institutional dimension of the Church and to the increasingly secularized and laicized European states' tendency to claim authority over the Church. Throughout European history, the Church, precisely as institution, was not infrequently in combat with the state or nation, again precisely as institutional. The ultimate root of this was the approval of the Church as a legitimate and then favored (official) religion by Emperor Constantine. The resulting mutual "incorporation" of Church and state eventually gave birth to Caesaropapism and rivalries between Pope and emperor for control of the whole society. Such rivalries emphasized precisely the structural, institutional elements and dimensions of the Church. Particular emphasis was given to the hierarchical structure and office of the Church. An unfortunate consequence of this was the division of the Church into two classes, the clerical, priestly hierarchy and the simple faithful. This ecclesial division was reflected in theology and became so intense that Yves Congar described the resultant ecclesiology as hierarchology. A great advantage of the Church as the people of God is that it does not emphasize the Church as a stratified or class or hierarchical structure, but as popular communion. We shall examine this particular contribution of people of God to ecclesiology further in Chapter 4.

The original and primary emphasis of the Church as people of God is not even found in the word "people." This particular definition of the Church emphasizes precisely the Godliness of the people in question. They are God's possession—God is their origin, their sustainer, their goal. Indeed, properly taken, God is their owner, they are God's choice, chosen possession (segullah) or "property" (Deut 7:6). This Godliness gives the people their identity and dignity. It establishes them in being. That this is so, even after the fall and in the context of sin, is emphasized by Hosea: "I will love Unloved, I will say to No-People-of-Mine, 'You are my people,' and they will answer, 'You are my God' (2:24–25)."

This theme is taken up in the New Testament and applied to the "new" people of God, whose identity is also explicitly related to Jesus Christ. Paul even applies it to the pagans who have been saved by the patient God's mercy in Jesus (Rom 9:25). Peter uses it to emphasize the dignity and identity of Christians who, though scattered, form the one "spiritual house" which is the Church, "a chosen race, a royal priesthood, a consecrated nation, a people set apart" (1 Pet 2:4–10). People of God emphasizes that the Church really belongs to God, both in its origin and in its history, even when this history has become sinful. Such emphasis, of course, is not intended to encourage sin or indifference. Its goal is to console and encourage the people, who are the Church, to persevere in avoiding evil and doing good, in making their lives "spiritual sacrifices . . . acceptable to God." This text also emphasizes the common dignity of all believers. In this context, Vatican II speaks of "a true equality with regard to the dignity and to the activity common to all the faithful for the building up of the body of Christ" (*The Church* 32). Thus, even though the primary purpose of people of God is to emphasize the Church's communion with God, it also simultaneously emphasizes the communion of the Church within itself.

The origin of the people, which is the Church, in the God of the Old and New Testaments can hardly be exaggerated. This divine personal origin prevents us from being the accidents of chance, the mistake of inept deities, the playthings of blind fate. Rather, from the very beginning our being is personal communion and communication or dialogue with God.

We are thus led to another insight provided by people of God, namely the Church's history and universality. According to Vatican II, "Israel, according to the flesh, which wandered as an exile in the desert, was already called the Church of God (2 Esd 13:1; cf Num 20:4; Deut 23:1). . . . While it transcends all limits of time and race, the Church is destined to extend to all regions of the earth and to enter into the history of mankind" (*The Church* 9). Here we are reminded of the various meanings that the term Church can have, and the people of God too. Expansive terms like these can, unfortunately, deteriorate into chaotic equivocity. On the other hand, our best human words are all complicated and not restricted to one, simple meaning. Some theologians think that people of God can refer to the whole of humanity, others do not.[106] I would be in favor of such extension. Christian theology speaks of salvation history as universal and particular. Universal means that the whole of humanity and its entire history is meant for salvation and thus the whole world shares in the saving grace of the universal divine saving will. On the other hand, within this universal salvation-history there is a particular history which is salvational in a special way. This special history serves as a sacrament—the sign and means/cause—for universal salvation history. Given the intimate connection between creation and incarnation, we would certainly not want to restrict people of God exclusively to the historically special, sacramental people of God. We need recall only Hermas, who told us that the Church is even older than the world. If people of God can legitimately refer to the whole of humanity, it would help mightily to keep us explicitly aware of this universal or cosmic dimension of salvation and of the Church as the sacrament of this salvation. It would aid in avoiding that ecclesiocentrism we remarked earlier. Without sacramental awareness, we can easily allow the relationship between the divine and the human to be diluted, their communion to become very thin. If we think sacramentally, we shall continually be reminded that the Church, the special history of salvation, is really the outward and visible sign of the inward and invisible communion of the God whose people the whole world is—and is to become.

BODY OF CHRIST

The second image or definition of the Church requires sacramental thinking to protect itself from the opposite error. Body of Christ emphasizes the communion of the Church's members, the people of God, with Christ so intensely that they could easily lose their human identity and be osmosed into some kind of biological-mystical Christo-organism. In the 1940's, theologians felt compelled to warn against what they called a Christomonism. This false opinion described the union of Christ and his members in such a way that they seemed to have been absorbed into Christ. There was no longer a union of the two, the human and the divine, into one body. There was only a one—a mixture of the divine and human in which neither the divine nor the human as such continued to exist. Nowhere else is the parallel between Christological and ecclesiological heresies more evident. Here as there, sacrament is a term apt to designate the greatest possible communion of the divine with the human, without the one being absorbed by the other. The analogy between the theandric communion in Jesus and in the Church both enables and requires each to be called sacrament. As additional terminology is needed to distinguish the various instances of sacrament, so is additional terminology needed to distinguish the various instances of body of Christ. This need led to the practice of describing the Church as the "mystical body of Christ."

The word "mystical" is intended to distinguish—not separate—the Church as the body of Christ from the Eucharistic body of Jesus in the sacrament of the Lord's Supper and the historical body of Jesus in Galilee and Judea.[107] Separation or indistinction in regard to these "Three Bodies," which are really only the one Jesus Christ in different modes of existence and stages of history, is catastrophic. It is, indeed, the destruction of Christianity. According to Joseph Ratzinger, this is why any definitions of the Church must include reference to this threefold body of Christ: "When primitive Christianity calls itself Church, it understands itself thoroughly as the new people of God, as the eschatological Israel, which receives its unity from the glorified Lord and which actualizes itself in the community assembly in which the glorified Lord makes himself present and unites himself with this community through his Word and the communal sharing of the Eucharistic meal."[108] Thus N.A.

Dahl's assertion is right on target: ["The difference is that the concept of the Church in the Old Testament was exhaustively expressed by the term people of Yahweh, while the Church of the New Testament is the people of God only in that it is simultaneously the body of Christ and the temple of the Holy Spirit."[109] Because the Church is so complex, the adjective "mystical" can serve a good purpose. It can remind us that the Church is not merely a natural body, whether physical or moral-organizational. It can remind us that the Church is a higher body, a body of grace, a society of faith, a fellowship of faith, hope and charity. On the other hand, mystical has its own dangers. It can easily give the impression of vague, hazy, other-worldly, not in the sense of supernatural but in the sense of anti-this-worldly, unreal. But such an unreal body is precisely what the Church does not want to be. To prevent this, the Church as (mystical) body of Christ should always be kept in tandem with the Church as people of God.

Like people of God, body of Christ can further describe the Church in various ways. The earlier Pauline epistles are concerned with the local church as the body of Christ, the later ones with the universal Church. Both emphasize the Church as sacramental communion. According to Heinrich Schlier, "The chief interest of Romans and 1 Corinthians is that the local church is one body (of Christ) from many members, that is, it is a charismatic organism."[110] In the later epistles (Colossians and Ephesians) the emphasis is the communion of the body of Christ with its head, who is also Christ. There is no contradiction between these emphases. As Schlier concludes, "Only when the Church is understood as both the charismatic organism and the cosmos of Christ is the ecclesiological description of the Church as body of Christ fully present." As body of Christ, the Church is revealed to be a liturgical community, for it is essentially a Eucharistic community—one which celebrates the memory of Christ by eating and drinking the bread and wine become his body and blood, thereby becoming the very body of Christ. To describe the Church as a liturgical community is not to restrict it to the sanctuary or temple. As we shall see in the next chapter, all of graced creation is already liturgy. This cosmic liturgy is celebrated in a special way in the sacramental liturgy.

The body of Christ is an effective way to understand and develop theologically Jesus' Last Supper statement, "I am the true vine, and my Father is the vinedresser" (Jn 15:1). In both cases, there is communion of many members or branches in one life. The source of the communion is the Creator God-Father, the "place" of the communion is Jesus, the Incarnate Word, henceforth part of this bodily cosmos and its history. In the same chapter, Jesus promises the Spirit of truth, who will come from the Father and who, together with the friends-disciples of Jesus, will become worldwide witnesses of Jesus, because they have been with him from the beginning (Jn 15:15, 16–27). The end of Jesus' public life is a promise that its beginning will be continued: recall Mark 3:13–19, where Jesus called disciples to be with him and to be sent out to exorcise evil and preach the good news. The Church is not only the vineyard and vine of the Father, the body of the Incarnate Son; it is also the temple of the Holy Spirit.

TEMPLE OF THE HOLY SPIRIT

"Your body, you know, is the temple of the Holy Spirit, who is in you since you received him from God" (1 Cor 6:19). Earlier in the same epistle, St. Paul had asked, "Do you not know that you are God's temple and that God dwells in you? God's temple is holy, and that temple you are" (3:16–17). Of course, the New Testament also understands Jesus to be the temple: "Jesus answered, 'Destroy this temple, and in three days I will raise it up.' . . . He was speaking of the temple that was his body" (Jn 2:19–22). As we have seen, there is a universalist dynamism in the Judeo-Christian tradition. This universalism is present in the Church and is expressed variously in the various images and definitions of the Church. Hence, Jesus as true temple must also have universal dimensions.[111] St. Paul insinuates as much in his development of the Adam-Christ parallel (Rom 5:12–21; 1 Cor 15:20–22, 44–49). As Adam is the first man, in whom the whole human race is contained and represented, so is Jesus, as the second Adam, the ultimate man, in whom redeemed and elevated humanity is contained and represented. Using contemporary images of the body as an all-comprehending spatial reality, St. Paul describes Jesus as a sort of cosmic body or man (Eph 1:23; 4:13; Col 1:19; 2:9) in whom the whole created and redeemed universe is contained and represented.[112] This is already seminally so; in the future it will be purely and simply so. In the meanwhile, all Christian living and mission is for "building up the body of Christ . . . until we become the perfect man, fully mature with the fullness of Christ himself" (Eph 4:12–13).

In order to become this cosmic temple, Jesus had to delocalize the temple as the place where God's true presence and worship was reserved. In Greek the word for temple (*temenos*) comes from the word to cut out/off, to excise. It signifies a special place cut out from the world and reserved for the encounter with and worship of the deity.[113] Jesus delocalized "temple-ness" by transforming the temple into his body, which, as the body of the second Adam, is really the cosmos (humanity graced).

He had said as much to the Samaritan woman at the well: "But the hour will come—in fact it is here already—when you will worship the Father neither on this mountain nor in Jerusalem . . . [but] in spirit and truth" (Jn 4:21–24). One must not take this statement to advocate the abolition of public, ritual worship in favor of purely private, interior, invisible worship in the deep recesses of the individual's own heart. As Raymond Brown points out, "in spirit and truth" might be a hendiadys, really meaning in the Spirit of truth (see Jn 17:17–19, where Jesus promises to send the Spirit of truth).[114] This fits well with the event of Pentecost, when the Holy Spirit (of truth) was poured out on the disciples, who constitute the Church as the body of Christ and thus as the sacrament of universal salvation. Henceforward, the "temple" will no longer be a particular place geographically. Rather, the Church, both as a special people and as graced humanity, will be the "special place" where God is truly encountered and worshiped. The temple is no longer geographical or architectural. It is humanity, created and graced in the Logos Incarnate, which becomes the body of this Incarnate Logos and his Holy Spirit. Again, the Trinitarian origin of the Church is quite evident. Nevertheless, it is most fitting that this new temple-body of Christ be described as the temple of the Holy Spirit, for precisely the Holy Spirit is especially connected with the unlimitedness and universality of salvation of the people of God.

Again we see that the various images of the Church are not mutually exclusive, but mutually inclusive. They complement and perfect each other as, one might dare to say, the divine Father, Son and Holy Spirit themselves do. This is fitting, of course, since the Church is the sacrament of this triune God.

As we remarked earlier, the Holy Spirit frequently comes up short in theology. This also obtains in ecclesiology. To redress this deficiency, we would do well to heed the theologians of Eastern Christianity. According to Ignatius Ziade, the Maronite bishop of Beirut, "the period of the Church in the history of salvation is called the economy of the Spirit by the Fathers."[115] It is possible to speak of the Church as the body of the Holy Spirit, as long as we understand that the union of the Holy Spirit with all of human being is not hypostatic, like that of the Word with one human nature. In all likelihood, history dictates that the term "incarnation" should be reserved to the Logos become human. However, we must also be alert lest the divine union with humanity in the Holy Spirit become tenuous and phthsic, precisely because of our efforts to preserve the uniqueness of this communion in the Incarnate Word.

A helpful approach has been developed by Heribert Muhlen. According to him, the Church can be thought of as "one mystical person," that is, one person (the Holy Spirit) in many persons (Christ and the members of his body). Such an approach preserves the parallel between the missions and embodiments of the Word and the Spirit in the world, while at the same time avoiding their equation: The Son of God appears in the human body of Jesus Christ. "The Spirit of God achieves this visibility in that he reveals himself in the visible bodiliness of the Church and in the various gifts of grace which become visible in the public life of the Church community."[116]

Again, it is obvious that the Church is a sacramental and therefore visible communion. The invisible grace of God becomes visible in the human members of the Church. As the people of God form the body of Christ, the Church is the visible and local realization and manifestation of the saving will of God. This does not mean that the Church no longer needs church buildings. It means, rather, that these buildings, where the people of God assembles to celebrate its being already and to become existentially even further the body of

Christ, are themselves temples of *the* temple of God's Holy Spirit. In other ecclesiological terms, church buildings are sacraments of the Sacrament: both
Ur (origin-al—Christ) and *Grund* (fundamental—Church).

The Holy Spirit has also been called the soul of the Church, because it is
from the Holy Spirit that the Church receives its life and identity. The life of
this Church is not dull and monochromatic. It is, rather, exuberant and filled
with variety, for its ensouling Spirit is the source of many and diverse gifts.
We shall see more of this in Chapter 4. Here we note it only to reinforce our
understanding of the Church as a communion in which the many are neither
chaotic nor anarchic, but orderly and united, as befits the Creator God's image
and likeness, become body and temple of the divine in cosmic history.

The Church is, then, a communion of Spirit-ually engifted persons with
one another in and through the union of the Holy Spirit with them. Consequently this "Spirit-ual" communion is also the communion of the human
with the divine. The being and identity of the Church as a communion of persons is achieved by the one person of the Holy Spirit, who, of course, is always in communion with the Father and the Son. As the perichoresic
communion of Father, Son, and Holy Spirit does not suppress them as persons, so does the ecclesial communion of persons in the Holy Spirit not suppress them. The Church, especially as the Temple of the Holy Spirit, is a
"*we,*" constituted by the Holy Spirit and the disciples of Jesus.[117] Therefore,
the "apostles and elders, our brothers," were being neither presumptuous nor
supercilious when they proclaimed the solution to the Church's first great crisis with these words: "It has been decided by the Holy Spirit and ourselves
. . ." (Acts 15:22–28). A better description of the Church than the Holy Spirit
and ourselves would be hard to find. This communion is sacramental, for it
has a twofold visibility: one in the very being, the membership, of the Church;
the other in the variety of gifts manifest in the many missions and ministries of
the members, in both sacred and secular spheres. Thus, the Church as the temple of the Holy Spirit is truly the sacrament of salvation for all humankind.

SPOUSE

It is not impossible that the intimate union of members and Holy Spirit in
the Church as temple of the Holy Spirit could lead to a problem like the Christomonism in the Church as body of Christ. So much emphasis could be placed
on the indwelling *one* Holy Spirit and the resulting communion of life among
the members that they would lose their personal identity and, once again, be
osmosed into a strange spiritualistic entity. As we have seen, this should not
happen, for the indwelling of the Holy Spirit established the Church precisely
as a "*we.*" There is another classical image of the Church which insures the
identity of the members of the Church against such an osmosis.

The Church is also described as the bride or spouse of God or Christ.[118]

This manner of speaking originated with the prophet Hosea. He spoke of Yahweh as the husband, Israel as the bride. This comparison, as such, has no sexist overtones or implications. It is true that divine God is spoken of in male terms, human Israel in female. This usage provides absolutely no basis for invidious evaluations of the relative dignity of male and female human beings. This image emphasizes that the relationship between God and humanity, between Jesus and the Church, is not merely a business relationship. It is not even a professional or client centered relationship. One could even say that it is not primarily a therapeutic relationship, although it is in fact supremely therapeutic. This image also informs us that the relationship between the divine and human surpasses the relationships of ordinary acquaintances and everyday living. Our relationship with God is, rather, like what we hope the most personal and intimate of relationships will be—marriage. As humanity's spouse, God is not like those males of whom Peggy Lee has sung so plaintively: "He was a good man as good men go, and as good men go, he went." No, God is the utterly faithful spouse. No trial marriage for him, no weekend and vacation liaisons. Furthermore, God's spousing is not content with the bare minimum of a legalistic and juridical fulfillment of duty, "for he is all compassion and tenderness . . . rich in graciousness" (Jl 2:13). It is this theandric intensity and intimacy that the spousal image of God-humanity, Jesus-Church emphasizes.

It is, furthermore, of exceedingly great value to note that this image originated in a context of sin. The narrative of Hosea is not entirely clear. It is clear, however, that Hosea, representing Yahweh, is to espouse a fallen woman, a harlot, representing unfaithful Israel (and, through Israel, fallen humankind). Through this loving espousal the fallen woman is redeemed and healed. Through this espousal Israel (humanity), which was formerly Unloved and No-People-of-Mine, becomes Beloved and People-of-Mine. Although God had been sorely tempted to refuse forgiveness and reject his people, to cease being their God, the divine holiness, precisely as divine, is not able to act thus. As the entire Judeo-Christian tradition attests, it is precisely divine holiness which does not reject failure and sin and which is not corrupted or undone by human failure. Rather, divine holiness pursues sinners, embraces them and thus heals (saves) them.

In addition to its emphasis on the personal intimacy of God's relation with finite humanity, the spousal image also emphasizes the perdurance of divine love for even fallen humanity. The theandric communion is not undone by human fault. Even sin and guilt are able to be overcome by the divine holiness. Jesus, the friend of sinners, is even able and willing to die for sinful humanity, for his Church, while it was still sinful, a sinful spouse, in order that it might become the "glorious bride, with no speck or wrinkle or anything like that, holy and faultless" (Rom 5:6–10 with Eph 5:25–27). The other paraclete whom Jesus sends is not only the spirit of truth, but also the power of God for the forgiveness of sin (Lk 24:47–49 with Acts 1:1–8; 2:1–41). The entire Ju-

deo-Christian tradition is eloquent testimony that God Father-Son-Holy Spirit
is the utterly faithful spouse, not only patient and long-suffering,[119] but also
powerful to forgive and heal faltering and failing humanity on its way to become the "beautiful bride" in the "new Jerusalem," "the new heavens and
earth," the new humanity, where "God will make his home among them; they
shall be his people, and he will be their God; his name is God-with-them"
(Rev 21—22). In this heavenly city there will be neither suffering nor tears,
neither lamp nor sun, for the divine communion with the human communion
will have become perfect. God will truly "be all in all" (1 Cor 15:28).

This is the message of all the classical images and descriptions of the
Church. Especially when all are taken together, these images emphasize that
the Church, which comes ultimately from God-Father-Son-Holy Spirit, which
is founded historically by Jesus the Incarnate Word-Son, and which is cosmi-
cally and humanly universalized in the Holy Spirit, is truly the sacramental
communion of the creating God with created humankind. Two other definitions of the Church, rooted deeply and explicitly in the New Testament, are
also critical for a proper appreciation, theoretical and practical, of the Church.
Unfortunately, "memory of Christ" and "tradition of Christ" are usually not
included, certainly not emphasized, in customary ecclesiologies.

MEMORY OF CHRIST

At the Last Supper Jesus explicitly instructed and enabled us to be his
memory. St. Luke and St. Paul emphasized the Eucharist as the "memorial of
me" (Lk 22:19). "Therefore until the Lord comes every time you eat this
bread and drink this cup, you are proclaiming the . . . Lord" (1 Cor 11:27).
St. John focused on the service of the brothers and sisters, symbolized in the
washing of the disciples' feet: "I have given you an example so that you may
copy what I have done for you" (Jn 13:15). As this copy of Christ (not a xerox
duplication, of course), the Church keeps his memory alive in the world. Even
more, the Church *is* this memory. All that it does, liturgy, ethics, social action, has one purpose and one norm—to be in such a way that people are able
to encounter Christ in *us, the Church*.

The Eucharist does have a special role to play in the Church's being the
memory of Christ.[120] It, more than anything else, definitely identifies the
Church as the memory of Christ. The sign-full-ness of the Eucharist is the
most explicit insignia, as St. Thomas would say, of the faith of Christ. But it
is not the only one, and not always the most effective or important. As Rahner
points out[121]

The Church's union with Christ's sacrifice could and can be manifested and achieved in other ways as well as in the sign of the eucharistic celebration. Indeed, in certain circumstances it can only be

convincingly demonstrated in other signs—in acts of charity to relieve urgent need, in devout prayer, etc. Nevertheless the celebration of the Eucharist was established for the Church as the constitutive sign of its union with the Lord who gives his life for the life of the world.

Although the Eucharistic celebration enjoys primacy as the signful memory of Christ, it is neither absolutely sufficient nor exclusively preeminent. We can at least imagine a conflict where a sacramental celebration and another virtuous act would have to take place at exactly the same time: "For example, the only time one could help Christ in a poor person would be precisely at the moment when the only Mass available was being celebrated. In this case, of course, the greater, more unselfish act of love is to be chosen, even if it would be 'only' a spiritual communion in the act of loving one's neighbor."[122] For emphasis, we can place this scene on Sunday! Such a conflict is highly unlikely. But it does make a point—however privileged the Eucharist may be in the Christian memory, it does not nullify other elements of this tradition.

As the memory of Christ, the Church is also clearly sacramental communion. For this reason it is important not to understand memory as merely intellectual recall on the part of individual human beings. As we saw, the Church is sacrament in being. Applied to the Church as memory of Christ, this means that the very existence of the Church as a society of people in general, and also as the liturgical assembly here and now, is the memory of Christ. This memory in being is put into action in the many and various acts of the Church. Of all these actions, the Eucharist enjoys special, even unique status, because of its uniquely close and explicit relationship with Jesus.

Recently Johannes Baptist Metz has introduced memory into his political and practical fundamental theology as a key category. He likes to emphasize the memory of Christ as a dangerous memory in current society and cultures.[123] Most recently he has focused on the Eucharist: "The Lord's Supper of Christians as Anticipatory Sign of an Anthropological Revolution."[124] I do not find Metz's more recent writings very helpful in relating the memory of Christ, whether historical person or Church, to the contemporary world. However, his attempt to retrieve and develop memory in general, the Eucharistic memory in particular, as effective ecclesiological categories is worth noting. His attempt is also instructive in that it illustrates that conceptual retrieval and passionate concern do not suffice to enable the memory of Christ to be effectively present and operative in the real world.[125]

In the section on Jesus as founder of the Church, we noted that, unless Jesus were simply an utter romantic, he had to take normal practical procedures to insure that his preaching be heard. The memory of Jesus should remind the contemporary Church of the same necessity. As the official Church of special salvation history, the Church has no special competence in secular affairs. Nevertheless, it must use all the knowledge and skills cultivated by the secular world to keep the memory of Jesus effectively alive in all the dimensions of the modern world. As the memory of Jesus, the Church can be indifferent to no human phenomenon or problem. Otherwise, it would not be true to its founder.

The Eucharistic dimensions and connotations of the Church as memory of Christ clearly reveal the Church to be a sacramental communion. The Eucharistic celebration of this memory can also reinforce the Church's awareness of its pilgrim and provisional status. It is not the reign and kingdom of God purely and simply. It has not yet reached its celestial consummation. As the memory of Christ, it proclaims the death and resurrection of the Lord until he comes, especially every time it eats and drinks the Eucharistic bread and wine (1 Cor 11:26). As the memory of Christ, especially Eucharistically, the Church is also the new covenant (11:25), which is the perfection of the covenants of the Old Testament and creation, which were themselves already the sacramental communion of the divine and human.

TRADITION OF CHRIST

The connection between memory and tradition is patent. And thus we are brought to our final definition or description of the Church—the tradition of Christ. This also has roots in the New Testament. In the First Epistle to the Corinthians St. Paul illustrates the idea of tradition perfectly when he says, "For this is what I received from the Lord, and in turn passed on to you" (11:23) and, "For I delivered to you as of first importance what I also received" (15:3). Tradition describes what Jesus received from his Father, what he gave to his immediate disciples, and what these disciples in turn gave to later ones. We are the latest, but not the last, to participate in this "handing on." What do we receive and hand on? Jesus.

This is clearly stated in the first quote above, for what Paul received there was the Eucharist. Jesus is the mediation of God's eternal, transcendent saving will in history. At one time he mediated through his historical body. Now he mediates this same incarnate saving will through his mystical and eucharistic body.

Since the Protestant Reformation Catholic and Protestant theology has tended to oppose Gospel and tradition, as if they were mutual enemies. This debate has two sources. The first is the history of the Church. The handing on or tradition of the Gospel has in fact been obscured by finite and fallible Christians. The second is Luther's pessimistic view of history[126] and his equally pessimistic tendency to focus on particular traditions and pious practices which were often suspect, so that for him "*traditio* came to be equated with *abusus.*"[127]

However, tradition does not have to be equated with abuse, nor history with decline. As Yves Congar has pointed out, "A tradition is an inestimable benefit. It means not to start from zero. It is to be rich from the very beginning. . . . A tradition is to the intellectual life what fraternity or brotherhood . . . is to the heart."[128] For the Judeo-Christian tradition, as we have seen, tradition starts with neither Jesus nor Abraham nor even Adam. It really starts with the triune God, whose very being, as communion, is already a handing on and over. This handing on is continued in the creation, whose peak is the saving incarnation, in which God gives (hands over/passes on) "his only Son, so that everyone who believes in him may not be lost but may have eternal life" (Jn 3:16). The same verb is at the base of this text and 1 Corinthians 11:23 and 15:1–4. Handing on or over need not be abusive betrayal, treason. It can be and is the means whereby the Godly communion is shared with the non-Godly, not only in the beginning, but throughout history.

Tradition is not properly contrasted with Gospel. In fact, tradition is the mode of the Gospel's good news achieving presence through time and space. As a contemporary Lutheran scholar, Krister Stendahl, notes, there is a legitimate sense in which

> the Church lives "sola traditione" ["by tradition alone" instead of the customary Lutheran "by Scripture alone"]. . . . But as a historically adequate statement, in the light of contemporary biblical studies it is an obvious statement, a platitude. It is obvious that on this analysis, Scripture *is* tradition, a special kind of tradition or it is better to say, it is not a special *kind* of tradition, but it is a special *amount* of tradition set apart in a special way.[129]

The Church as tradition emphasizes our continuity with the historical Jesus. The Creed reminds us of this. In it we profess our belief in the Apostolic Church. This Church of the apostles is our mediator to Christ. That is why we must be so patient with the "official" Church, as inadequate and sinful as it may be. It is our connection with the real Jesus of history, who is our connection with the transcendent *apeiron,* the triune God. This is also the import of apostolic succession, as it is called. The apostles and their hierarchical successors are not lords over our faith, but guardians of the tradition. Not only they, of course—we are all guardians and bearers of this tradition. But they play a special, ministerial and therefore subordinate, role in this tradition. More of this in Chapter 4.

Some years ago, Marshall McLuhan attracted much attention when he contended that "the medium is the message." This is a perfect description of the Church as tradition—the whole tradition, not just the hierarchy, not just the Bible, not even just the sacraments. All these elements are important, but their importance must not obscure the importance of the people, the faith-ful members of the Church. The *we* of the Church, the Holy Spirit and the people, are the tradition. The handing on of the good news, the Gospel of Jesus who is "with us always to the end of time," has been entrusted to us.[130] *We* must "make disciples of all the nations" (Mt 28:18–20).

Church as the tradition of Christ also emphasizes the sacramental communion which is the heart and essence of the entire Judeo-Christian revelation and tradition. Jesus Christ is, after all, *the* sacrament of God's salvation. Once Jesus has appeared, his preservation (memory) and promulgation (tradition) are the most important dimensions of human and Christian being. Because he thought the Galatian Christians had failed in this regard, Paul was especially incensed with them (Gal 1:6–3:5). The uniqueness of Jesus does not mean that everything else is worthless and evil. It does mean that, since everything is and is saved through the Word Incarnate, the memory and tradition of this Jesus Christ are the very stuff of human history. To neglect to hand on this Jesus would be to deprive history of its God-willed fulfillment. The absence of the tradition of Christ would truly be abuse, for tradition is the mode of the Christ's effective presence in the world after his ascension to the Father. By virtue of his ascension to the right hand of the Father, Jesus does not terminate the theandric communion, but insures that it will ultimately succeed. For the risen Jesus is the first born of many brothers and sisters (Rom 8:29) who already enjoy theandric communion in and through the other paraclete and await the consummation of earthly ecclesial in the celestial communion of the new city of God, the heavenly Jerusalem. As the tradition of Christ, the Church recalls the communion of God with man in the past, enjoys it in the present and makes it available to the future. As such, it is truly the fundamental sacrament of Christ, the origin-al sacrament of God and God's salvation.

CHURCH: THE LORD'S CONVOCATION

After all this, it might seem strange that we have not yet considered the origin and meaning of the word Church itself. I have delayed on purpose. It is important to keep in mind, as we have so often noted, that no one word is sufficient to describe the rich reality of the Church. Furthermore, a word which is used so much, as is Church, soon comes to be so taken for granted that it can lose much of its value. Finally, the word Church is not the transliteration of the original Greek word for Church, *ekklesia*. The Romance languages did transliterate the Greek and its Latin counterpart, *ecclesia*. Hence, Church is *Chiesa* in Italian, *Eglise* in French, *Iglesia* in Spanish, *Igreja* in Portugese. Etymologically, this term means to call forth, to call out of. It comes to mean community, assembly, the community assembled before (in the presence of) God. The English word "Church" comes from the Greek *kuriakon*. It means literally "Lordly" or "belonging to the Lord." In German this is *Kirche,* in Dutch *Kerk,* in Scots *Kirk.* Together the Greek and English words describe very well what the Church is—the community or assembly called together by and belonging to the Lord.

In the Greek translation of the Old Testament, *ekklesia* usually translates *Qahal,* and *sunagoge* (synagogue) usually translates *edah.* However, in both religious and secular use, both terms mean much the same, with some minor differences in emphasis: assembly, gathering, community, group. It should be noted, however, that *ekklesia* was the preferred term for the political city states of Greece, while *sunagoge* was the preferred term for the religious community and its meeting place among the Jews.[131] It is most likely that the early Christians chose *ekklesia* as their self-designation, because it would more effectively distinguish them from the Jews and the Jewish synagogue.[132] There is a significant difference between the Greek and Jewish (and consequently the Christian) assemblies. In contrast to the Greek, which excluded women and children, the Jewish and Christian assemblies included them. This difference is not without value for various questions about women's status and role in the Church today. An even greater difference is that the Greek males came together to determine a course of action, while the Jewish people assembled to hear what *God* had determined and to say Amen thereto.[133] For Israel the Sinai assembly and proclamation was evermore the ideal, although Israel did not always live up to this ideal purely and perfectly. As founded by and in the preaching of the dead and the resurrected Christ, the Christian *ekklesia* claimed to be the eschatological fulfillment of the Sinai *ekklesia.* This fulfillment happened and happens only in and through the Holy Spirit, the other paraclete of Jesus. The Church's origin, its founding, is incarnational and pneumatological as well as paternal and maternal (God-Father-Mother).

The Christian *ekklesia* of the triune God is actualized in various ways. The New Testament describes the Christian communion with the same term, *ekklesia,* whether it is a question of the domestic, local, particular (regional) or universal Church. All in all, *Ekklesia* is a most fitting term to describe that sacramental communion whose history we have traced all the way back to the triune God. The application of the term *ekklesia* to the historical, empirical Christian communities-community is an excellent example of the principle we have mentioned previously—unity in diversity and diversity in unity. The real communion of the disciples of Jesus, bearing his memory and tradition in various assemblies throughout time and space, to the very ends of the earth and the very end of time, is illustrated very well by the Acts of the Apostles, which speaks of the Church and the churches without hesitation, and without explanation too, it might be added.

By doing this, the Acts of Apostles gives practical witness to the ecclesiological realization of the Trinitarian and Christological ontology, namely the perichoresis of the one and the many, of the human and the divine. Thus the Christic communion is present in the local and universal Church just as the divine communion is present in the Father, Son and Holy Spirit, and as the theandric communion is present in the God-man, Jesus. The same word *ekklesia,* is used without hesitation for both the local as well as the universal Church, and it is used with equal ease in the singular and plural. Given the importance of this fact, it will be neither awry nor otiose to trace this ecclesiological perichoresis of the local and universal Church in the Acts of the Apostles in some detail.

Originally *ekklesia* would have referred to the Mother Church of all, the Church of Jerusalem (Acts 8:1). This is also indicated by the first occurrence of the term in Acts, namely 5:11. In 8:3 it is still the Church (singular) which Saul persecutes. However, this persecution will soon cause a condition to exist which will make the plural usage of *ekklesia* unavoidable, namely the flight of the persecuted Christians from Jerusalem and their dispersal "to the country districts of Judea and Samaria" (8:1). This geographical and sociological fact creates a demand for a theological insight and understanding. How can the one Church be one in many places? The solution is perhaps hinted at in a significant textual variant in Acts 9:31, where the Western and Antiochene texts have the plural, churches, the Alexandrian text the singular, Church:

> The churches throughout Judaea, Galilee and Samaria were now left
> in peace, building themselves up, living in the fear of the Lord, and
> filled with the consolation of the Holy Spirit.

In Acts, 11:26 the local and singular Church is emphasized, and there is no longer merely a church at/of Jerusalem, but a church at/of Antioch. Also noteworthy is the fact that at this first explicitly denominated church outside Jerusalem, the believers who make up the church(-es) are first called Christians. In passing, we may note here a good indication of the necessity and value of the local, particular, non-universal, Church (originally in Jerusalem the local and universal, the singular and plural Church would have simply coincided). Only here are the Christians able to achieve a sufficiently elevated degree of self-awareness, so that they are able to discern who they really are, namely Christians.

Persecution, this time by Herod, also plays a role in the next occurrence of the term Church. In 12:1, 5 the term can refer to either or both the local and universal Church. However, the next reference (13:1) is clearly local, "the church at Antioch." The same local church is clearly meant in Acts 14:27, where simple identification is made between disciples and church, an indication of the ideal pattern of church and churches. As soon as Paul and Barnabas return to the local church at Antioch, they report to that church "all that God had done" elsewhere; that is, in the other local churches and, therefore eventually in the universal Church.

A more fitting introduction to chapter 15, which describes the first conflict between the "universal" Church (here represented by Judea and Jerusalem) and local churches, could hardly be found. Throughout the history of the

Church the tension between the one and the many, between unity and diversity, between regional and central has been one of the most severe problems. It is a sort of negative consolation to know that even the ''golden age'' of the primitive Church was not spared.[134] This fact can help disabuse us of the illusion that at some time or other there was a perfect correspondence of theandric ecclesial perichoresis to the divine Trinitarian perichoresis. The pilgrim Church has always been the simultaneously sinful and holy Church.[135] Therefore its reflection (image and likeness) of the divine perichoresic nature has been and always will be approximate. Luke's description of the Council of Jerusalem offers us good instructions on both local-universal Church ecclesiology and problem solving in the Church.

Its problem was twofold. First, the role the traditional Mosaic law was to play in the new Christian *ekklesia* had to be determined. In order to solve this problem, the new *ekklesia* had to discover or invent a method or policy of problem solving. Such a policy did not have to precede the actual solution of the Mosaic law problem. It could be articulated in the very solution of this problem. By this time the Church had already become local, regional and central. Thus even then the problem of equating or confusing the central Church with the universal Church and even with Church itself *simpliciter* has arisen.

The policy actually achieved was one of accommodation. The freedom given the Church by Jesus was substantially secured, while the sensibilities of some members of the Church were simultaneously respected. The method was the interaction of all the involved parties. Acts 15:1–29 indicates that the solution was reached by the cooperation of the local, regional, and central (universal) churches. These churches were represented by Paul and Barnabas, certain members of the Pharisees' party, the apostles (as the successors of the Twelve) and elders, Peter, Barnabas and Paul again, James, the apostles and elders again, delegates (Barsabbas and Silas), the whole church (of Jerusalem, which as the ''mother church'' enjoyed special significance in relation to the universal Church) and last, but not least, the Holy Spirit. A better model of ✱convocation, of collegial decision making, can hardly be imagined, or one more distant from unilateral and monarchical fiat which came to be the dominant model of decision making later in Church history. The proceedings in Jerusalem narrated by Luke (Acts 15) are a splendid illustration of the Church as communion of believers among themselves in and with the Holy Spirit.

Acts 15:2–4 clearly reveals the *one* Church to be present in both Antioch and Jerusalem. The Christian communities in both places are described simply, almost laconically, as Church—with no indication even hinted of the later ecclesiological problems which will so exercise the minds of ecclesiastics and theologians alike. The resonances of Church as assembly, meeting, reunion are clearly present in these verses, as in verse 30 of the same chapter, where, instead of *ekklesia* which we would expect, we encounter *plethos,* multitude. Again the ideal relationship between the *one* Church and the many churches is illustrated—there is an immediate sharing and communication of what has happened, in the Holy Spirit (Acts 15:28), in the Church beyond a given local church. In the last verse of chapter 15 the plural "churches" is used without hesitation or elaboration. In this same vein, a most interesting remark is made in 16:5: "So the churches grew strong in the faith, as well as growing daily in numbers." This verse is interesting not only because of the plural, but also because the Church is stated to be both present, but also in a state of growth. The Church is both "fully" present (it is the Church), but also not yet "fully" realized, actualized, consummated. This provides the foundation for that Pauline practice of stating the same truth in both the indicative and imperative. What is already must also nevertheless still become that which it is.[136] The Church, both locally and universally, is still growing, still abuilding.

Later on Paul will "send for the elders of the church of Ephesus" (Acts 20:17). Not only for its mention of the local church, but even more so for its mention of a differentiated membership in the local church (elders) is this verse important.[137] One of the problems the Church as communion most illuminates is the relationship between office or office-holder in the Church and the community at large. It is, therefore, most valuable to note that the great apostle of freedom, St. Paul, is himself not adverse to appointing elders (Acts 14:23) and dealing with them (Acts 20:17–38). This is, of course, of greatest value in confronting those who are tempted to maintain that a communion ecclesiology excludes or eliminates legitimate authoritative, official differentiation within the Church. These and similar texts indicate that differentiation and office do not fracture the communion. Rather, they make it practically possible. The office-holder is there not in opposition to, but in support of the community. Insofar as Church office matured into the episcopacy, the ancient Church regarded the bishop as the focus and point of Church unity: communion with the bishop is communion with the whole Church. This is most succinctly expressed in verse 28 where we again meet the twofold missionary Jesus sent out (missioned) into the world to further his word and work: the Holy Spirit and the members of the Church:

> Be on your guard for yourselves and for all the flock of which the
> Holy Spirit has made you the overseers, to feed the Church of God
> which he bought with his own blood.

This verse is also important because it identifies the local community Church with the "Church of God" and of Jesus ("bought with his own blood"). The perichoresis or circumincession of the local and universal Church is clearly present in this verse. It is God's Church which is encountered (present, visible, graspable) at Ephesus. This makes it quite clear that the relationship between the local church (churches) and the universal Church (as well as the other local and/or particular churches) is not rivalry, hostility, competition, envy. Rather the local church is where the Church *simpliciter* happens. Church cannot be restricted to domestic, local, particular or universal.[138]

In the remaining chapters (21–28) of Acts the word *ekklesia* does not appear. The Church is designated as the "whole body" (21:22), the "way" (22:4; 24:22), the "saints" (26:10) or "brothers" (28:14,15). By outsiders the Church is referred to as a "sect" (24:14; 28:22). The value of this absence is that it indicates no single word, however important it might have been and may still be, is to be made into a fetish. Also noteworthy is that communion is also clearly evident in the other words used in the last eight chapters of Acts.

A similar perichoresis of the local and universal Church is discernible in the writings of St. Paul. In his earliest epistles Paul speaks of "the church in Thessalonika" (1 Thes 1:1; 2 Thes 1:1) as well as of "the church of God at Corinth" (1 Cor 1:1; 2 Cor 1:1). In the last chapter of his epistle to the Romans (16:16). he says, "All the churches of Christ send their greetings." This would doubtlessly refer to the local churches of Achaia. In the same chapter he also speaks of "Phoebe, a deaconess of the church at Cenchreae" (16:1,19). Paul speaks of the "churches in Galatia" and "all the churches of Asia." Statements like these at least hint of a "church" that is neither only local nor yet universal. It could be a regional church, although "particular" would perhaps be a better designation. "Regional" could signify merely a geographical fact or a kind of governmental administrative district. "Particular," although it can have separatist overtone, tends more to assert a proper or peculiar nature. This church would have something special about it, but this specialness would not be divisive or anti-universal Church. It would be, rather, a distinctive way of being Church in a given spatial and temporal situation, in an identifiable culture.

A further way (in addition to "local") of being a particular church is the *ecclesia domestica:* St. Paul extends his "greetings to the church that meets at their (Prisca and Aquila) house" (Rom 16:5; 1 Cor 16:19). There is also explicit reference to "the church that meets in your house" in the Epistle to Philemon (v. 2).

All these texts contain strong emphasis on the local church as a definite, identifiable community with further emphasis on this community as assembled, with even further emphasis on this community assembled for the celebration of the Eucharist. Such emphasis could easily lead to a sort of "Eucharistic ecclesiological actualism," as has been the case among certain Eastern Orthodox theologians.[139] That kind of ecclesiology is, of course, not required by the above texts. However, it is only in the later Pauline literature that the non-local, non-assembly Church receives much emphasis.[140] A possible exception to this could be urged on the basis of the Latin text of 1 Corinthians 11:16, which has the plural *ecclesiae,* although a significant variant does have the singular *ecclesia.* However, the Greek text has the plural, with no variants. In the Epistle to the Ephesians the word Church is used nine times, all of which are consistent with the first occurrence, in 1:22, "the head of the Church, which is his body, the fullness of him who fills the whole creation." There is the one Church, everyplace, which is the body of Christ. The same universal ecclesiology is also dominant in the Epistle to the Colossians, where Paul speaks "of his body, the Church. I became the servant of the Church . . ." (1:24,25). However, this epistle also contains a verse which reinforces the perichoresis of universal and particular (local and domestic) Church (4:15,16):

> Please give my greetings to the brothers at Laodicea and to Nympha and the church which meets in her house. After this letter has been read among you, send it on to be read in the church of the Laodiceans; and get the letter from Laodicea for you to read yourselves.

The New Testament texts themselves do not attempt to reconcile theologically these various ways of being Church. Indeed, later theology itself generally concerns itself with this problem only occasionally, the occasion usually being a dispute, if not a crisis about some particular problem in the life and practice of the Church. It is important to recall that originally the domestic, the local, the particular (regional) and the universal Church all simply coincided—in the church of Jerusalem, however briefly. The Church would have enjoyed a perfect perichoresis among its various actualizations. It is not merely fanciful to suggest that this was the symbolic state of affairs that obtained on the first Pentecost (Acts 2:1–13), especially if Luke's text does indeed intend a parallel between the proclamation of the torah on Mount Sinai and of the new covenant of the Spirit on Pentecost, as the phenomenon of speaking in tongues hints.[141] The remaining later years of the Church would simply be the actual fulfillment or realization of this Pentecostal prophecy and event.

Only because of and during the persecution, as we have seen, did the problem of the one and many church(-es) really enter into ecclesiology. Had there been various smaller communities within the church at Jerusalem, they would still have been regarded as the church at/of Jerusalem. As the dispersal of Christians increased, not only because of persecution but even more so because of missionary activity and conversion, the original one Church of God in Christ was no longer so simply evident. However, it did become clear that wherever a church was, there was the Church, the chief condition being that any given church be in communion with the other churches and thus in communion with and in the Church.[142]

Two items support this thesis. First of all, as we have already seen, the Acts of the Apostles attests to the visitation of outlying local churches (local communions) by delegates from "the [central] Church" (Acts 8:14–17; 15:30–35; 18:24; 19:1–7). These texts also reveal Luke's concern to show how incipient local and perhaps imperfect, only partial Churches are brought into full communion with the Church, and thus into full ecclesial existence.

The other supporting item is the Pauline theology which so emphasizes the one Church, the one Spirit, however many and diverse may be the gifts and local communities (Eph 4:1–12; 1 Cor 12:4–11). As Acts 14:23 together with Philippians 1:1 at least hints, the "presiding elders and deacons" are there to provide definite focal points of unity, both within the local community, but perhaps especially among the local communities and therefore within *the* (universal, worldwide) Church as such. Thus, monarchical is not precisely the choice term to describe what eventually is known as episcopacy.

The purpose of these extensive New Testament considerations is not to fall prey to a fundamentalist biblicism, but to point out how the *de facto* experience of the Church's growth reflects a perichoresic ontology which calls for both a theory and practice of local and universal Church, which can best be understood as communion. In the following section I shall attempt to provide some clarification, both conceptual and terminological.

We have already noted above the inherent difficulty in providing an adequate definition of the Church, because of its very nature as a trans-physical entity. The question can be posed whether Church is a univocal, equivocal or analogical term. Without wishing to fall prey to accusations of ecclesiological lukewarmness (see Rev 4:16) I shall attempt to show that the term is analogical. In its various applications (local, domestic, particular, universal) the term always sustains its essential meaning, that of the historical and traditional memory of Jesus wherein the theandric communion of God and man is celebrated, both enjoyed and preached and witnessed. Although a variety of terms and designations might be useful and desirable in some sense, I think that the term Church has to be retained for all these various instances of the Christian communion precisely in order to preserve the perichoresic communion of the one and the many church(-es) in explicit memory. The difficulty in the terminology of Church is not in the word, but in the very reality of the Church-communio itself.

The entire ecclesiological enterprise is, of course, enormously exacerbated by the legitimate diversity as well as the illegitimate divisions within Christianity, as well as within the civilization or culture at large. All too briefly, but nonetheless, I shall at least try to provide some intimations of an ecumenical and "ethnic" ecclesiology based on a perichoresic communion model of the Church. In so doing, I shall also attempt to provide some conceptual and terminological clarification of the term Church. First of all, it is important to keep in mind that the basic terminological contrast is between local and universal. Some wish to restrict "local" to an episcopal local church. There are valid reasons for doing this. I think it is better to allow "local" to designate all non-universal actualizations of the Church. "Local" would itself be variously articulated into domestic, parish, diocesan, regional-particular, patriarchal. I think that such an approach is advisable because, as we have seen, the term "Church" is polyvalent. Its analogical nature makes my suggested usage legitimate. Its history makes my suggested usage advisable.

Terms to designate various instantiations of the Church are not only scriptural, they are not only theological, they are also canonical (juridical). They reflect changing cultural conditions throughout the Church's history.[143]

Like office in the Church and the sacrament of holy orders, Church has been theorized and practiced differently at different times. But both orders-office and the Church retain their nature and identity. Thus, for example, the office of priesthood has at some times been able to perform some functions, at other times not. Confirmation is a good example. We shall see more of this in Chapter 4. Episcopal local churches have varied tremendously in size and hence ecclesial responsibility over the centuries. Many, if not most, large urban parishes today would be larger than many if not most dioceses had been for much of the Church's history. In previous centuries the priest who is today a (simple) pastor would have been a bishop—not because of his personal qualification, but because of the magnitude of his ecclesial responsibility, to which, it was hoped, his personal qualifications would positively correspond. The clear teaching of Vatican II is that episcopal and priestly office are participations in the one pastoral responsibility for the orderly life of the Church. Not all pastors, which would include bishops, and Pope, have the identical responsibility, but all share in the same responsibility. The priest-pastor is not in the local parish (local church) because the bishop-pastor is absent. Rather, because of the sacramental communion ontology of Judeo-Christianity, the bishop-pastor is present precisely in and through the priest-pastor. Hence, the parish-local church is not identical with the diocese-local Church. But neither is it sufficiently different to warrant being deprived of the name "local church," for it also is the memory of Christ, the tradition of Christ, the people of God, the body of Christ, the temple of the Holy Spirit and the spouse of God/Christ, where the good news of salvation preached by Christ is preached, the Eucharistic memory of Christ is celebrated, and the footwashing ministry of Christ is continued. Theologically, then, although not univocally so and not canonically, "local church" can, may and does signify *the* Church except precisely as universal. After this preliminary caution, we can now proceed to a brief description of the various ways in which the one Church actualizes itself and presents itself publicly.

1. *Divine Universal Church*. Every ecclesiology must begin with the basic texts of 1 Timothy 2:4–6 and John 3:15–18. The Church "makes sense" only in the context of God's entire plan of salvation for the whole world, of which saving will the Church is, according to Vatican II, the sacrament or effective sign. The *de facto* apostolic and traditional Church, whether local or universal or both, exists only as a consequence and manifestation of the divine salvific will. If this divine universal Church escapes the attention of the theologians, ecclesiology inevitably deteriorates into inner-ecclesiastical introversion, that illegitimate ecclesiocentrism criticized earlier. The Church is also in grave danger of becoming merely one more power group among many, a sociological reality of greater or lesser value, but no longer truly the sacrament

of theandric communion and salvation. In passing it may and must be noted that this universality is to be understood not only spatially, but also temporally. No finer image of this exists than the graphic scene from Hermas the Shepherd, to which we have so frequently referred. The Church is not for the world, the world is for the sake of the Church, the body of Christ. The Church was first in the intention of God, although it appeared in history only at the appointed time, in the fullness of time (Eph 1:10; 3:1–13; Col 1:25–27; Gal 4:14), the last days (Heb 1:1–4).

2. *Local Church.* The transition from the Church created before all things to the local church is proper because God's saving will, respecting as it does the nature of the world divinely created, must consequently have a local nature, a local realization. As corporeal creatures, human beings cannot just be in general. They must be someplace. The local church is, in reality, nothing other than the divine universal Church having happened in a given time and place. We often say that something took place. The local church is precisely the divine universal Church which has taken *place*. That is, the local church is basically man's response to God's saving will. Since human being is by nature social, its act-ual response is also social. Although there is a very valuable theology of every soul being the Church,[144] the Church is fundamentally a spatial, temporal, historical communion, people who have together accepted Jesus Christ as the revelation and presence of God in this world. For this reason we have suggested that tradition of Christ and memory of Christ are significant attempts at providing descriptive definitions of the Church, although these definitions would not be restricted to the local church as such. The local church achieves its most intense realization and symbolization in the celebration of the Eucharist, for nowhere else is it more explicitly the memory of Christ (1 Cor 11:25). However, the local church is not only liturgical celebration of the Eucharist. It has a perduring sacramental presence in the people and the institutional structures.

3. *Papal Universal (Catholic) Church.*[145] This Church corresponds to the divine universal Church insofar as the latter is not limited to any given time and place—that is, insofar as a particular local church and all of them precisely as local churches do not adequately reflect and exhaust the divine salvific will. The universal papal Church and the local church, whether episcopal or other, are always to be kept in closest tandem. Alone, neither is capable of reflecting the real actualization of God's saving will in the world. The relationship of the most basic local church and the universal Church has been well described by Karl Rahner:

> All this means that the Church, in its innermost essence, is itself directed to a localized concretization; and this in no way harms or lessens its universal destiny and mission to all men.
>
> Not only does the Eucharist, as local event, take place in the Church, but only in the local celebration of the Eucharist does the

Church become fully event in the most intensive sense of the word. It is not only true to say that the Eucharist is because the Church is, but it is also true, correctly understood, to say that the Church is because the Eucharist is. Hence the local church is not only—in a certain sense secondarily—an authorized agency of the one universal Church which could just as easily dispense with such an appendage; rather, this local church is the event of this very universal Church itself. This starting point for a theology of the parish does not lie in a deduction of the parish from the monarchical summit of the Church through the episcopal territories to a narrowly boundaried local ecclesiastical organization. The parish church is not only the result of an atomizing division; it is, rather, the highest degree of actuality of the total Church.[146]

Although the term "papal" is not universally beloved, I have retained it for lack of a better. Historically and theologically this office in the Church has developed in the context of the relationship of the local to the universal Church. For all its abuses, the papacy remains a prime symbol of unity, the communion of the one Church in many churches throughout the world. With due precautions, one can say with St. Thomas Aquinas that within the apostolic college and the entire Church the papacy enjoys an office similar to that of the Holy Spirit:

> The error of those who claim that the Vicar of Christ, the Pontiff of the Roman Church, does not enjoy a primacy of the universal Church is similar to the error of those who claim that the Holy Spirit does not proceed from the Son. For Christ himself, the Son of God, consecrates his Church and seals it for himself by the Holy Spirit as if by a character or seal. So, likewise does the Vicar of Christ, as a faithful minister, by his primacy and providence preserve the universal Church subject to Christ.[147]

Elsewhere St. Thomas continues the same line of thought, emphasizing again that the office of papacy is for the sake of the unity of the entire Church. The office of the papacy can be regarded as a sacramental presence (in the general or expanded understanding of sacrament) of the divine shepherding.[148] In the universal Church on earth, the papacy is to be a visible manifestation and effective means of representing the truth, theological and pastoral, "God is not a god of disorder but of peace" (1 Cor 14:33). But this is also clear: People are set apart according to differing dioceses and states. Yet, as the Church is one, so must the Christian people also be one. Therefore, as in the specific congregation of one church, one bishop is required, who is the head of that entire population, so for the entire Christian people there must be one who is head of the entire Church.

Therefore, the unity of the Church demands that there be one who presides as the head of the entire Church. . . . In its necessities Christ has not failed the Church. Therefore, one must not doubt that by Christ's ordering there is one who is at the head of the entire Church. It is not sufficient to say that the one head and one shepherd is Christ, who is the one spouse of the one Church; for, clearly, Christ Himself perfects all the sacraments of the Church. By the same reasoning, then, when He was going to withdraw His bodily presence from the Church, He had to commit it to someone who would, in His place, have the care of the universal Church. Hence it is that he said to Peter before His ascension: "Feed My sheep"; before His passion: "And once you have recovered you must strengthen your brothers" (Lk 22:32); to him alone did He promise: "I will give you the keys of the kingdom of heaven" (Mt 16:19), in order to show that the power of the keys was to flow through him to others to preserve the unity of the Church.[149]

Furthermore, the reaction of many Protestant theologians and churchmen to "good Pope John" indicates at least the possibility that the papacy as such (at least in certain possible configurations) is not simply unacceptable to Christians who are not Roman Catholic. In fact, Luther himself, and precisely in the Leipzig disputation where he formally rejected, for the first time, the fundamental nature and constitution of the ancient Church, could exclaim, "There is no doubt whatsoever that the entire world would welcome such a man with open arms and profuse tears."[150] Luther was referring to a possible Pope who would have been a truly pastoral "primate." Unfortunately, the style in which the papacy is lived and practiced has not infrequently obscured the essentially pastoral ministry which it embodies. This is not to say that an abuse-less papacy would have been and would be acceptable to all Christians. Furthermore, one ought not to forget the principle which maintains that abuse does not *ipso facto* take away or invalidate use. On the other hand, abuse certainly does obscure legitimacy and desirability. Although primacy is also not a universally beloved term, it is not without (perhaps irreplaceable) value in ecclesiology. In any case, simply not using a term hardly makes the reality represented by the term go away.

The Petrine office has a primacy in this sense, that it is a single, unsurpassable focal point of unity reflecting and emphasizing the universal salvific will of God and its realization in Christ. As we shall see, the pyramidal monarchical model of the Church is illegitimate, and was in fact never an ecclesial reality, but only a theological theory. The papacy is not to be thought from the top down and out, as if the Church were a triangle or pyramid. Rather, the papacy is to be thought of as a center which sacramentally helps to keep vitally present in the Church the faith that "there is one body, one Spirit . . . one Lord . . . and one God who is Father of all" (Eph 4:4–6), whose Son is the "only one mediator between God and mankind" so that "everyone (might) be saved and reach full knowledge of the truth" (1 Tim 2:4–6). Within this context the papal office, the Petrine ministry/primacy, has a legitimate and significant role to play in understanding the Church as the communion of God with all humankind. Neither the office nor the term need be sacrificed. For this reason I have chosen to retain the terminology of "papal universal Church." Unaware, perhaps like Caiaphas in John (11:51), Harry Truman may well have uttered a valuable theological insight in his famous "The buck stops here." In any society or community, there is always an ultimate, a final instance. This final instance may be structured in many ways. It need be neither monarchical nor dictatorial nor totalitarian. It can be "good shepherdly." Such is the ideal of the papal position in the universal Church: the Pope is to be a good shepherd in imitation and representation of the "good" (Jn 10:14) "chief Shepherd" (1 Pet 5:4).

4. *Particular (Regional) Local Church.* This church is an intermediate stage between the "purely" local church as this or that definite, locate-able individual community and the universal Church which is not easily and readily graspable. This fourth way of being Church also reflects the real historical and cultural nature of the human being. The human being surpasses his immediately local condition, but does not thereby dissolve into pure and mere "humanity." This dimension of human being is sometimes called regional or ethnic or sub-cultural. In any case the reality of particular ways of being human together is culturally undeniable. To this human nature corresponds the grace of the regional church. Here we must immediately recall what was said of the local church, namely, that it is not merely an administrative unit or quantitative deduction from a sort of neutral universal Church. There is a priority to the local and regional/particular church, for grace does not destroy, but builds upon nature, expanding, elevating and intensifying it ontologically. It is perhaps this way of being Church which has suffered the greatest attrition from the increased emphasis on the universal and papal Church and the corresponding theology. However, it is also precisely this area which allows for the greatest possibilities in both religious denominational and ethnic cultural ecumenism. The particular diversity of the Church must be allowed to flourish again so that its universal unity will enjoy its due profundity. Due care must be exercised, of course, so that separatism, divisionalism, factionalism are avoided. But equal care must also be exercised that all legitimate diversity and difference, whether ethnic, national, racial, artistic, or whatever, may flourish in the historical and traditional Church, the communion of God with human beings and of human beings with one another. It is here that rite, in its full meaning and import, and its decisive difference from sect, must again be allowed to flourish.[151] Like the Church itself, rite is not easy to define. Basically it is a particular group of people who have a particular way of being the church (in a particular place), but always in unity with the whole Church.[152] This "particular way" is complex, including liturgy, law, devotions, theology,

spirituality, music, art. "Particular place" is in parentheses because geographical location is no longer nearly as important as it used to be. Long ago a rite really did tend to be located in a particular place. But travel and migrations have scattered members of these rites all over the world. Greek, Ruthenian, Byzantine, Russian, Serbian, Maronite, Ukrainian rites were originally located in the Near East, Eastern Europe, Russia and India as their names indicate. But now they are also found in North and South America, without ceasing to be rites. Of course, these rites experience special problems because of the conflict between the modern urban American culture and the old country culture in which their liturgy is still celebrated—and where their spirituality was developed.

About eighteen rites are officially recognized in the Church. Other Western rites which once existed were simply overwhelmed by the Roman rite, the one that is predominant in the United States. It is possible to transfer from one rite to another, although some legal technicalities are required. The traditional rites have been a source of communion in the Church. They have provided considerable diversity within the unity of the one Church.

As these traditional rites struggle to survive in a new cultural situation, it is possible that other rites are struggling to be born. Although the forces of centralism are still strong, there is also strong movement toward greater recognition of local groups and their own particular cultures. Worldwide, but especially in Latin America, there is the phenomenon known as *communidades de base*. This term does not translate well. The usual translation is base or basic communities. What the term means is well expressed by this definition: "homogeneous groups of eight to forty Christians who share common interests, values, and objectives and who live an ecclesial experience in which primary interpersonal, on-going relationships predominate and who view themselves as an ecclesial unit."[153] Any single such community would not be considered a rite. It is not unthinkable, though, that a larger group of these would want to join together for certain common interests. This would not, of course, require nor should it result in the dissolution of the small units themselves. That would be to fall prey to the same malaise the base communities were supposed to heal. The great advantage of these communities is that they take seriously the *local* nature and dimension of the Church. They are not necessarily separatist. They could be, of course. But, then, so can anything. These base communities may be a bright spot on the current Church scene precisely because they understand and practice that the Church of Christ is truly present here and now—not only in Rome, not only everywhere in general, but right here and now. They may be a contemporary means of assuring that diversity without which there can be no communion.[154] Concerned to guard the legitimate diversity of the Church against excessive Roman centralization and concentration, Joseph Ratzinger has suggested that new patriarchates be created.[155] This would ameliorate the uniformist tendencies which flow partly from the confusion caused by the concentration of three offices in one person, the Pope: bishop of Rome, patriarch of the West, Pope of the universal Church.[156] New patriarchates, in the East, but especially in the West, would also have beneficial effects for the ecumenical dialogue.

Increased patriarchates would certainly highlight the Church as a communion in which diversity in unity and unity in diversity is not only a beautiful theoretical principle, but also a practical way of life. Increased patriarchates would also provide a means of reinforcing the identity of the local churches and of protecting them from a leveling amalgamation and fusion into some kind of giant corporation.

As we have seen, an ecclesiology which is truly perichoresic, truly sacramental communion, means that the local and particular church is not merely a minor ecclesiastical jurisdictional administrative unit, completely beholden to Rome for everything. Rather, in the local church everything is present that is present in *the* Church as such, only that being excepted which can be in the Church only as and insofar as it is universal. Thus present in the local church are the saving will of the Father, the headship of Christ, the Spirit Paraclete, grace, revelation, sacraments, charisms, Scriptures, official sacramental and jurisdictional ministry. This is not to assert that the local church as such is the sole source or guarantor of these gifts, merely that they are truly present in the local church.

As such, the local church cannot sustain only a few ecclesial realities, for example, worldwideness, the papacy as the focus of unity of the worldwide Church, the college of the heads of all the regional local particular churches, especially insofar as these assemble in ecumenical council, indefectibility in faith-being as well as infallibility in faith-thinking against the kingdom of death (see Mt 16:18 with Rom 5:12 and 1 Cor 15:22). Such indefectibility in being and truth would not properly belong to a local church, for local instances of human nature are not apt for such attributes. No single human being lasts as long as human being all told. Indefectibility is not an attribute of the Church as local, but as universal. The local church is "indefectible" only insofar as it is the event of Church as such, which is the worldwide sacrament of the worldwide communion between God and humanity.

As we remarked above, the local, particular church and the universal Church are equally necessary. The exclusion of the one leads to monochromatic totalitarianism, of the other to chaotic anarchism.

Ecclesially and ecclesiologically, the precise advantage of the universal Church is its anti-sectarian and anti-elitist emphasis. The advantage of the local church is its concreteness and definiteness. Of course, in neither is there a magical formula for success in responding to God's saving will in Christ and practicing ecclesial perichoresis and communion. Both must reckon with failure and sin. The Church will be not only theandric communion of God with humanity and historical, traditional, sacramental communion of human beings with another. It will also be the holy and sinful Church of sinful saints and holy sinners, the Church of Jesus, the friend of sinners (Mt 11:19; Lk 7:34), and of the Holy Spirit who is their forgiveness (Lk 24:47–49 with Acts 1:8 and 2:4, 38). Thus will the Father's saving will be accomplished (1 Tim 2:4–6; Jn 3:16). But, even sinfully, it remains the sacrament, sign and cause of theandric communion in the world. As the Church of Jesus, the friend of sinners, could it do otherwise? In fact, this Church does not merely tolerate sinners at the periphery of its communion; this "Church embraces sinners in its very bosom" (*The Church* 8).

Even sin cannot destroy God's communion with the world. Even the fallen world is where God's communion with the non-Godly takes place. I think it unwise to say that the motive for the incarnation was the redemption of humanity from sin. That gives sin too much status, too much importance. The motive for the incarnation is most properly the fullest possible self-communication of God into and in the non-Godly. Does this mean that the Holy Saturday liturgy is wrong to speak of Adam's sin as "O felix culpa"— O happy (or blessed) fault, which merited such a great redeemer? No, but we should understand that sin highlights the greatness of God's saving love in the Incarnate Son. It does not cause, evoke or even occasion the incarnation or the Savior or salvation. Properly understood, salvation is not only from the non-being which sin tries to cause. Salvation is properly and primarily from not being at all. Hence, God's first saving act is creation. All others are articulations of this original saving act. Salvation is not primarily "from." It is essentially "for." It is, first of all, the relationship of God *for* the non-Godly. Subsequently, it is divinely enabled response by humanity. That is, salvation is essentially communion of the non-Godly with the Godly. In this salvation, sin plays a real but entirely secondary and subordinate role. The entirely primary and principal role is God's effective will to be in communion with the non-Godly, so that the non-Godly may be at all and thus be in communion with God-Father-Son-Holy Spirit.

Thus we return to that sacramental communion ontology which makes the conceptualization of the Church as communion so apt and desirable. Being is communion both within the very divine being itself and in the relationship of the divine being with the non-divine. Creation and redemption establish the salvation of man, from ontic nothingness in creation and from hamartiological nothingness in redemption.

Creation establishes humankind as the image and likeness of God and redemption establishes humankind as the new creation, hence not only the image and likeness of God, but the very body of Jesus Christ. This "new" creation, theandric communio, both historical and traditional, is known as the Church. This Church is both one and many, a unity in diversity and diversity in unity. The local and universal Church share in the perichoresic ontology and communio of the Trinity and the Incarnation. Just as the three persons of the one God can be understood as dancing together and the human and divine natures of the one Christ can be understood as dancing together, so must the local and universal Church be understood as dancing together in joyful communion.

We may sum up by noting once more that ecclesiology makes sense only within the horizon of an entire ontology or comprehensive theory of being. In the Judeo-Christian ontology, being is understood primarily as communion. Unity and diversity, the one and the many, are, as such, not hostile, antagonistic, mutually exclusive. Rather they are a dancing together in joy, harmony and, indeed, communion. There is a threefold perichoresis: Trinity (*Deus in se;* God in himself); Incarnation (*Deus in alio;* God in the other, singular); Church (*Deus in aliis;* God in the others, plural.)

Thus the Church is most properly thought of as the divine will of God the Father, to save all people through both his Incarnate Son Jesus, who is in hypostatic union with humanity, and the Holy Spirit, the other paraclete and power of God in a fallen world, who is the bond of union within God as well as between God and humanity and within Christ-ed humankind. The Church is the special event and sign of this new creation which God has more wonderfully reformed and restored. The Church is, indeed, "nothing less than the house of God" (Gen 28:17), "a sacrament of intimate union with God, and of the unity of all mankind" (*The Church* 1). The Church is indeed a communion.

Precisely because the Church is a communion, it allows for diversity within unity. We have seen this in regard to the Church as domestic, local, regional-particular, universal. It also allows for diversity within unity on the part of the individual members' perception of and participation in the Church. Not all the members need practice their ecclesial faith in exactly the same way. To facilitate appreciation and practice of this diversity, Avery Dulles' book *Models of the Church* can be highly recommended.[157]

"Model" describes a "basic ecclesiological type." Each type has certain "major affirmations." Each model brings into a "synthesis a large number of biblical and traditional data." Models "illumine certain phenomena but not others."[158] Models are valuable for our purpose because they help us understand various particular ways in which the Church as way has existed in the past and exists in the present. They also intimate how new models can be created for the future. No model is absolutely sufficient, and no person lives exclusively within only one model. Creative rearrangement of the Church's "major affirmations" is fundamentally enabled by already actual models as well as future, potential ones.

Dulles lists five models: institution, mystical communion, sacrament, herald and servant. What we have done in this chapter provides some understanding of each of these models. The great advantage of Dulles' book, apart from his legendary orderliness and clarity, is the detailed listing of the individual components of each model, along with its advantages and disadvantages and an indication of the population best served by each model. Such models, theoretical and practical, are possible only because the Church is a communion. Communion provides for the accommodation of all, however diverse. Models not only accommodate the diversity of all members. They also provide patterns of being Church, so that different people can find ways of participating in the Church according to their natural talents and supernatural gifts. Models are, then, a means of making the diversity-in-unity communion of the Church practiceable and practical.

Church as communion is also important ecumenically, since communion immediately allows for diversity within unity. A communion spirit rather than a spirit of excommunication is a prime requisite, if currently divided Churches are to discover and create sufficient communion among themselves, so that they can be diverse and different, but not divided and divisive.[159] Obviously, good will and a communion spirit are not sufficient to achieve the communion of the Churches, but without them . . . The Catholic Church took a major step in promoting ecumenical communion in what Thomas Stransky calls "perhaps the most important one-word change in Vatican II."[160] This change was the substitution of the verb "subsists in" for "is" in article 8 of *The Church:* "This Church [of Christ], constituted in the world as a society, subsists in the Catholic Church, which is governed by the successor of Peter and by the bishops in union with that successor, although many elements of sanctification and of truth can be found outside of its visible structure. These elements, however, as gifts, properly belonging to the Church of Christ, possess an inner dynamism toward Catholic unity."

In this statement, and others, the Roman Catholic Church acknowledged that it and the Church founded by Christ and existing by his Holy Spirit are not purely and simply identical, co-terminous.[161] This allows for other bodies of Christians to enjoy the status of being Church, although the Catholic Church would still claim a certain preference in regard to being a fuller instance and realization of the Church of Christ. On this count it would claim a greater resemblance to the Church founded by Christ than other ecclesial communities can. The advantage of Vatican II's approach is that it puts the emphasis on the similarity of Churches, not their dissimilarity, without sliding into doctrinal and ecclesial indifference. It emphasizes what the Churches have in common, not what each lacks in comparison to the others. It starts with what unites the Churches, not what divides them. One could well argue that theoretically such a statement is only possible in a communion ecclesiology and that historically it was made at Vatican II only because ecclesiology had rediscovered its communion dimension. A long journey still remains, of course, until all churches enjoy explicit and full communion with one another. However, the one-word change at Vatican II has established a principle which enables an ecumenical communion of diversity in unity, and which makes full communion at least not impossible, if, nevertheless, still improbable for the time being.

Other insights at Vatican II and within the contemporary Church also indicate that we taking ever more seriously Pope Pius XI's statement: "Men were not made for the Church, but the Church was made for men: for us, men, on account of our salvation."[162] This means that the Church must take us more seriously precisely where it finds us. Salvation happens not in a universal vacuum, but in this real world. Karl Rahner has suggested that the Church did take a giant step in this direction at Vatican II. He contends that this Council marks "the transition of the Western Church to a world Church . . . a break such as has occurred only once before, that is, the transition from Jewish to Gentile Christianity."[163] In this "third epoch" of the Church's history, the full glory of God's universal saving will in creation and Church can be brought into sacramental visibility and fulfillment throughout the whole world, with all its personal and cultural diversity.

Rahner is speaking of the Roman Catholic Church, but his remarks, as he notes, are not restricted solely to that Church. Were the Catholic Church to achieve such worldwide diversity in unity, it would be even more strikingly the sacrament of the universal salvation God wills for and is effecting in the world. More than the First Vatican Council could have realized, it would truly be a banner raised high among all the nations, signaling the saving faith of God's gracious revelation (DS 3014). Of course, world-wideness has not become a concern of the Church only recently.

Catholicity, which means universal or worldwide, is a word that belongs to the essence of the Judeo-Christian revelation and tradition. Both Judaism and Christianity have been sorely tempted to become elitist and separatist. Although they have not always succeeded in resisting these temptations, rigorist exclusivism has never succeeded purely and simply. "Catholic" has been claimed as one of the notes or characteristics of the Church of Christ from early on. This is due, at least partly, to the Church's firm monotheism. If there is only one God, then this God must be the God of everyone, however unappealing some might appear. If this one God is a saving God, then salvation must be for everyone, at least in principle.

It is possible to argue that the Catholic Church has succeeded better than Protestant Churches in promoting this Catholicity. Yves Congar and others have described Catholicism as the search for plenitude and fullness, Protestantism as the passion for purity.[164] Cardinal Newman, who knew both sides of the fence at least to some extent, once said that "they [Protestants] are ever hunting for a fabulous primitive simplicity; we repose in Catholic fullness."[165] Protestantism has tended to emphasize "either-or" and "alone." Thus, its predilection for the three great "sola's"—"faith alone," "grace alone," "Scripture alone." It delights in disjunctions like "faith or works" and "Scripture or tradition" and "belief or reason." On the other hand, Catholicism delights in "both-and."

Hans Urs von Balthasar and Karl Rahner have both spoken of the "Catholic and." Balthasar has noted that Protestants are uneasy and suspicious of this "and," which, he says, belongs to "the very heart and core of Catholicism." According to him, ecclesial Catholicity is rooted in "the Catholicity of God . . . because by his very nature, God is Catholic and because in Jesus Christ and finally in the Holy Spirit this Catholicity of God has opened itself to the world."[166] In support of our approach, which emphasizes creation as the beginning of the Church as the sacrament of universal salvation, the Catholic communion of God with worldwide humanity, we can invoke Herman Volk: "This 'and' is already unavoidably present as soon as one begins to talk about God and the creature. The foundation of this 'and' is not the identification and identity of the creature with God. Rather, God's freely willing and creating the creature makes that very creature to be real. This same principle applies to creation, but also and equally to the hypostatic union of Jesus and grace"[167]— and, we could say, to the Church as the society of grace, a favorite theme of St. Thomas Aquinas.[168] One does not do well to start talking about the Church of God as remedy for and salvation from sin. That is much too late. Even Jesus and Abraham, even Adam, are much too late. Rather, as Hermas the Shepherd saw so well, the only proper place to begin talking of the Church is not a place at all. Before there even was the world—that is the right "time" to start speaking of the Church. For there are space and time only so that there might be the Church. For all that is not purely and simply God is purely and simply for the sake of God's Church. For Church is but the preferred name in history for the communion of the triune God, Father-Son-Holy Spirit with the non-Godly.

From chthonic creation in the beginning to celestial consummation in the end, all is for the sake of the communion of God with humankind. Of this sacramental communion ontology, of this theandric communion, the Church, as communion, is the sacrament.

NOTES

1. *The Shepherd* of Hermas, Second Vision, IV, the "Copying of the Book," tr. Joseph Marique, The Apostolic Fathers, ed. Francis Glimm (New York: Cima, 1947) 239.

2. *De Oratione Dominica*, 23 (PL 4, 553).

3. St. Cyprian, *The Unity of the Catholic Church*, 6 (Ancient Christian Writers, 28, tr. Maurice Bevenot. Westminster: Newman, 1957) 49.

4. Tertullian, *On Purity*, 21 (Ancient Christian Writers, 28, *Treatises on Penance*, tr. William P. Le Saint. Westminster: Newman, 1959) 121.

5. Heribert Muhlen, *Una Mystica Persona* (Paderborn: Schoning, 1968) passim (see "Wir" in the index). Yves Congar, "Die Wesenseigenshaften der Kirche," MS 4/1, 393.

6. Robert Kress, *Whither Womankind* (St. Meinrad: Abbey, 1975; now Westminster, Md: Christian Classics) 265–290. Attempts like Donald Gelpi's to name the Holy Spirit "Mother" strike me as strained, and basically sterile. In the preceding chapter, I noted the unsuccess of Jenson's attempt to justify the preference of Father as the name for God. As an expression of the desire to counter and rectify the customary sexist or exclusivist language Gelpi's attempt is commendable. In this case, however, one may wonder whether the cure is not worse than the disease. If a feminine name is to be used in regard to God and one of the divine persons, it should be the first person, as the unoriginated orgin/originator. From what is currently available to me, I would think that, rather than de-sexistizing God and theological-religious language, Gelpi's

approach reinforces sexist language. See Mary Ann Donovan and Donald Gelpi, "Naming the Spirit," CTSAP 37 (1982) 159–161. In this respect, I have generally used what is called inclusive language. In a few instances I have foregone this, noting here that dictionaries certify that "man" is a collective noun denoting humanity, not masculinity.

7. Karl Rahner, ST, V, 125, 203–205.

8. Yves Congar, *Jesus Christ* (New York: Herder and Herder, 1966) 28–31.

9. Already St. Thomas Aquinas noted this: ST, I, q. 37, a. 1. See also Walter Kasper, *Der Gott Jesu Christi* (Mainz: Grunewald, 1982) 274.

10. Werner Kummel, "Heilsgeschichte im Neuen Testament?" *Neues Testament und Kirche,* ed. Joachim Gnilka (Freiburg: Herder, 1974) 434–457.

11. Yves Congar, *De la communion des Eglises a une ecclesiologie de l'Eglise universelle* (Paris: Cerf: 1962) 227–260.

12. Jerome Hamer, *The Church Is a Communion* (New York: Sheed and Ward, 1964) 13–96.

13. Raymond Brown, "The Unity and Diversity in New Testament Ecclesiology" *new Testament Essays* (Milwaukee: Bruce, 1965) 36–50. Yves Congar, "Kirche," MS, I, 790–812; "Laien," MS, II, 7–25. For detailed expositions of the New Testament ecclesiologies, Rudolf Schnackenburg, *The Church in the New Testament* (New York: Herder and Herder, 1965) and Heinrich Schlier, "Ekklesiologie des Neuen Testaments," MS, IV/1, 101–221.

14. *Crises Facing the Church* (New York: Paulist, 1975) 45–62.

15. Garden City: Doubleday, 1978.

16. "Imaging the Church for the 1980's," *Thought* 56 (1981) 121–138.

17. *Images of the Church in the New Testament* (Philadelphia: Westminster, 1960), 26.

18. MS, IV/2, 404–405.

19. "New Testament Background for the Concept, the Local Church." CTSAP, 36 (1981) 4.

20. *The Church Is a Communion,* 174–176.

21. Ludwig von Hertling, *Communio. Chiesa e papato nell' antchita Christiana* (Rome: P.U.G., 1961) 7–9.

22. On the ecumenical dimensions and possibilities of this text, see Franz Mussner, "Eph. 2 als oekumenisches Modell," *Neues Testament und Kirche,* Gnilka, (Freiburg: Herder, 1974) 325–336.

23. Even Vatican II is very circumspect in this regard, saying that "Christ inaugurated the kingdom of heaven on earth. . . . the Church, or, in other words, the kingdom of Christ now present in mystery. . ." (*The Church* 3).For all the caution of scholars today, it is quite noteworthy that even in 1970 C.H. Dodd still felt able to entitle his book about Jesus *The Founder of Christianity* (New York: Macmillan, 1970).

24. We need not recall only Hermas. Notker Fuglister has been able to write almost one hundred pages on "Strukturen der alttestamentlichen ekklesiologie," MS IV/1, 23–100. One of Yves Congar's best known articles is entitled "Ecclesia ab Abel," *Abhandlungen uber Theologie und Kirche,* ed. Marcel Reding (Dusseldorf: Patmos, 1952) 79–108.

25. *Sociology of Religion* (Chicago: University of Chicago Press, Phoenix, 1962) 341.

26. *Religion in Essence and Manifestation II* (New York: Harper and Row, 1963) 651 (no. 101).

27. *Die Kirche* (Freiburg: Herder, 1967) 90–96.

28. *Christsein* (Munich: Piper, 1974) 275.

29. For a comparison of Karl Rahner and Hans Küng on this, see Francis Fiorenza, "Rahner's Ecclesiology: Jesus and the Foundation of the Church—An Analysis of the Hermeneutical Issues," CTSAP 33 (1978) 229–254.

30. Michael Nicolau and Joachim Salaverri, *Sacrae Theologiae Summa* I (Madrid: BAC, 1955) 511–590. Timothy Zapelena, *De Ecclesia Christi* (Rome: P.U.G., 1955). 120–515. Even more recent ecclesiologies, trying to be "updated," can easily remain captivated—and captured—by this approach and its terminology. For example, Albert Lang, *Fundamentaltheologie, II: Der Auftrag der Kirche* (Munich: Huber, 1968) entitles the pertinent sections of his book "Die Errichtung des Apostelamtes durch Jesus," "Die Einsetzung des Primats durch Jesus," 57–68, 68–95.

31. This distinction is especially developed in *Jalons pour une Theologie du Laicat* (Paris: Cerf, 1954), but it appears refrain-like throughout all his writings.

32. "The Foundation of the Church: Biblical Criticism for Ecumenical Discussion," *Theological Studies 34* (1973) 15, 3.

33. F.M. Braun, *Neues Licht auf die Kirche* (Einsiedeln: Benziger, 1946) was able to show this even for liberal Protestant theology already in 1942 when the original French version appeared.

34. "Der historische Jesus und die Kirche," *Wort und Wahrheit* 24 (1971) 306.

35. Edward Schillebeeckx has warned about "the triumphalism of counter-triumphalism" in *Vatican II, The Real Achievement* (London: Sheed and Ward, 1967) 89. There is a similar sentiment about "ecumenical triumphalism" by Oscar Cullmann, "Sind unsere Erwartungen erfullt?," with Karl Rahner and Heinrich Fries, *Sind die Erwartungen erfullt?* (Munich: Huber, 1966) 60. Older texts, indeed, but no less necessary now than then. Perhaps even more so now.

36. "Hat Jesus eine Kirche gestiftet?," *Theologische Quartalschift* 16 1/2 (1981) 81–96, here 82.

37. I have resorted to the phrase reign/kingdom of God to translate the original Greek and Aramaic term, which is not adequately conveyed by either reign or kingdom alone. Rudolf Schnackenburg, *God's Rule and Kingdom* (New York: Herder and Herder, 1963), is still the best introduction to this topic.

38. Rosemary Radford Ruether, *The Church Against Itself* (New York: Herder and Herder, 1967) 57. In this opinion, Ruether admits her basic dependence on Martin Werner, *The Formation of Christian Dogma* (New York: Harper and Row, 1957). This is probably unfortunate. As Walter Kasper has noted, although Werner's theory of the deeschatologizing and Hellenizing of Christianity does contain a kernel of truth (229, 308; on page 308, fn. 71, *Eschatologisierung* must be a typo for *Enteschatologisierung,* as on p. 229), it is an "an sonsten monomane These"—an otherwise monomanic thesis (308, fn. 71).

39. *Religion,* 651.

40. Edward Schillebeeckx, *Christ* (New York: Seabury, 1980) 907, uses "Tanach," when he refers to the canonical bodies of Jewish Sacred Scripture within Jewish history and context, "Old Testament," when he refers to the same books in the New Testament Christian context.

41. Lohfink, 92–93. It has been suggested that the early Christians may have chosen precisely the word which has come to be translated Church (*ekklesia*) precisely to distinguish themselves from the Jewish synagogue as a community/communion. This would hold for the Church both as a local and a universal social unity. See L. Rost, *Die Vorstufen von Kirche und Synagoge.* BWANT IV/24 (Stuttgart: Kohlhammer, 1938).

42. *Super Epistolas ad Romanos Lectura,* ed. Raphael Cai (Turin: Marietti, 1953) I, 171 (no. 913).

43. In the next few pages I summarize the material which I have developed at length in *Christian Roots* (Westminster, Md.: Christian Classics, 1978) 23–40, 65–122, 207–218. See also Karl Thieme, "Das Mysterium der Kirche in der christlichen Sicht des Alten Bundesvolkes," *Mysterium-Kirche,* ed. Ferdinand Holbock and Thomas Sartory (Salzburg: Muller, 1962) 37–88.

44. W.F. Albright and C.S. Mann, *Matthew* (Garden City: Doubleday, 1971) 71–72; also 232.

45. I trace this theme through both Old and New Testaments in *Christian Roots.*

46. Albright and Mann (CLXXXV) properly decry the eighteenth century notion, especially fostered by German Romanticism, that Jesus was something of a simpleton or country bumpkin, with hardly minimal talents and intelligence, much less the superior ability which would have been necessary for him to accomplish what he did, however embellished the Gospel accounts may be. One also wonders how influential this romantic portrait of the "simple Jesus" might still be, however subliminally, among exegetes and theologians today. Why else such great reluctance to accord Jesus any of the abilities which one would otherwise unhesitatingly accord a normal human being?

47. On the tensions between the early Christian wandering charismatic preachers and the more sedentary urban fixed communities, see Gerd Theissen, *Sociology of Early Christianity* (Philadelphia: Fortress, 1978).

48. We shall return to this theme in detail in Chapter 4.

49. See Robin Scroggs, "The Earliest Christian Communities as Sectarian Movement," *Christianity, Judaism and Other Greco-Roman Cults,* ed. Jacob Neusner (Leiden: Brill, 1975) II, 1–23. John Gager, *Kingdom and Community: The Social World of Early Christianity* (Englewood Cliffs: Prentice-Hall, 1975. Brian Wilson, *Sect and Society* and *Magic and the Millennium* (London: Heinemann, 1961, 1973).

50. For a more positive view of the Pharisees, see Joachim Jeremias, *Jerusalem in the Time of Jesus* (Philadelphia: Fortress, 1969) 246–269. Also John Pawlikowski, "On Reviewing the Revolution of the Pharisees," *Cross Currents,* 20 (1970) 414–434.

51. *Matthew* cvi-cxxiii; 278–283.

52. Joachim Jeremias, *The Parables of Jesus* (New York: Scribner's, 1963; rev. ed.) 223.

53. Ibid. 231.

54. *The Manual of Discipline,* i; ix: in Theodore Gaster, *The Dead Sea Scriptures* (Garden City: Doubleday Anchor, 1956) 39, 59–60.

55. The Bible of Jerusalem note on this verse.

56. Nicholaus Kehl, *Die Kirche in Neuen Testament* (Innsbruck: Theologische Fakultat, 1970; mimeo) 85.

57. Oscar Cullmann, *Jesus and the Revolutionaries* (New York: Harper and

Row, 1970). Martin Hengel, *Was Jesus a Revolutionist?* (Philadelphia; Fortress, 1971).

58. "Violence and the Kingdom," *Source,* 10 (1982) 5. "Jesus no more intended to change the social system than he did the political order. He never assumed a definite attitude on economic and social problems. Jesus did not in any way attack the system of property. He made no attempt to share out the goods of this world more fairly"—Rudolph Schnackenburg, *The Moral Teaching of the New Testament* (New York: Herder and Herder, 1965) 122–123. A striking example of the "passion for social justice" ideological interpretation of the Gospel without the requisite social scientific and "real world" practical competence, and the consequent harm to faith and faithful, is in the book of Robert McAfee Brown, *Gustavo Gutierrez* (Atlanta: John Knox, 1980) passim, especially 43–49, 68–76. Jesus may well have had books like this in mind when he decided on reticence in regard to social advocacy.

59. Andrew Greeley, "Politics and Political Theologians," *Theology Today 30* (January 1974) 341.

60. Robert Daly, "Seminar on Patristics: Military Force and the Christian Conscience in the Early Church: A Methodological Inquiry,"*CTSAP 37* (1982) 178–181.

61. For example, Raymond Brown is able to speak of the ecclesiology in Johannine theology in *The Gospel According to John,* I-XII (Garden City: Doubleday, 1966) CV-CXI. Furthermore, the relationship between Peter and the Beloved Disciple is not without considerable significance for the orderliness of Church structure and life. Brown, XCVI-XCVIII; *John XIII-XXI,* 984–986, 1004–1007.

62. Jean Giblet, "The Twelve, History and Theology," *The Birth of the Church* (Staten Island: Alba, 1968) 65–82. Karl Herman Schelkle, *Theology of the New Testament* IV (Collegeville: Liturgical Press, 1978) 61–85.

63. On the transformation of the Twelve's role after Pentecost and their gradual disappearance from the ecclesial scene in the New Testament writings, Paul Gaechter, "Die Sieben," *Petrus and seine Zeit* (Innsbruck: Tyrolia, 1958) 136–154.

64. Franz Mussner, *Der Galaterbrief* (Freiburg: Herder 1974) 423; "Das Wesen des Christentums ist sunesthienai," *Mysterium der Gnade,* ed. Heribert Rossmann and Joseph Ratzinger (Regensburg: Pustet, 1975) 92–102.

65. Schelkle, *Theology* IV, 145–162.

66. This is not because Jesus was originally or later on became a sectarian. "From the very beginning Jesus directed his efforts to the whole of Israel, and he persevered in this to the very last." Patrick Dias, *Kirche in der Schrift und im 2. Jahrhundert* (Freiburg: Herder, 1974) 29.

67. It is at least clear that "for the first Christians the song of the suffering servant of Yahweh was of decided significance from the beginning on." Karl Lehmann, *Auferweckt am dritten Tag nach der Schrift* (Freiburg: Herder, 1968) 247.

68. The New Testament accounts of the Last Supper institution are basically reliable accounts going back to the event itself. Rudolf Pesch, *Wie Jesus das Abendmahl hielt. Der Grund der Eucharistie* (Freiburg: Herder, 1978).

69. On the importance of this text for St. Thomas Aquinas, see Josef Pieper "Kreaturlichkeit, Bemerkungen uber die Elemente eines Grundbegriffs," *Thomas von Aquin 1274–1974,* ed. Ludger Oeing-Hanhoff. (Munich: Kosel, 1974) 47–72.

70. R. Brown, *The Gospel of St. John* XIII-XXI, 1135–1144. Rudolf Schnackenburg, *Das Johannesevangelium* III (Freiburg: Herder, 1975) 156–173.

71. *Jesus Christ* 31.

72. LTK, IV, 336–364.

73. *Pfingsten—Erfahrung des Geistes* (Stuttgart: KBW, 1974) 61.

74. *In Joannem* cxx, 2; PL 35, 1953.

75. It is usually pointed out that Jesus began his public preaching and mission by "proclaiming the good news from God. The time has come . . . and the Kingdom of God is close at hand. Repent, and believe the good news" (Mk 1:14–15). It should also be noted that kingdom remains a constant throughout the mission of Jesus. He speaks of it sixty-one times in the synoptic Gospels. Raymund Schwager, *Jesus-Nachfolge* (Freiburg: Herder, 1973) 67.

76. Even as cautious a scholar as Joachim Jeremias says: "Honesty and the duty to honesty require the answer, 'Yes, Jesus had expected the end to come soon' " (*Neutestamentliche Theologie,* I, 139). However, whether therefore error should be attributed to Jesus is a quite different matter, as pointed out by Karl Rahner and Wilhelm Thusing, *Christologie—systematisch und exegetisch* (Freiburg: Herder, 1972), 28–33. As Oscar Cullmann has well said, "The crucial question is whether Jesus himself believed in a fulfillment already in the present without thereby excluding the expectation of a consummation to take place in the near future, but yet only after his death. The words of Jesus cited above show that this question is to be answered affirmatively. In this connection see especially W. Kummel, *Promise and Fulfillment. The Christology of the New Testament* (Philadelphia: Westminster, 1963; rev. ed). Furthermore, on the relativity of "soon" or "a little while," see the comments of Raymond Brown on John 13:33 in *The Gospel According to John* XIII-XXI 607. St. Thomas Aquinas lived in an age hardly less feverishly apocalyptically expectant than either Jesus' or our own, for that matter. His words, as usual, are models of the equilibrium and confidence Christ has enabled. "Since the last days are not long . . . some have concluded that since the days of the Apostles . . . so much time has elapsed that the time of the Antichrist must be near . . . However, (according to the tradition of even the primitive church), no definite span of time whatsoever, whether long or short, can be reckoned according to which the end of the world in which Christ and Antichrist would be expected would occur." *Contra Impugnantes Dei Cultum et Religionem, Opuscula Theologica,* II, ed. R. Spiazzi (Turin: Marietti, 1954) 104 (nn 529, 531).

77. *Jesus* (Reinbek bei Hamburg, 1968) 87.

78. *Einfuhrung in den Glauben* (Mainz: Grunewald, 1972) 54.

79. Ernst Fuchs, *Zur Frage nach dem historischen Jesus* (Tubingen: Mohr, 1960) 155.

80. Karl Rahner (with Wilhelm Thusing), *Christologie—systematisch und exegetisch* (Freiburg: Herder, 1972) 67–69.

81. Whether for the many, for us, for sinners, for forgiveness of sins or sinners, this insight belongs to the earliest understanding of Christ, his life, his sacrifice at the Last Supper and on the cross. Karl Lehmann, *Auferweckt* 87–157; 247–257. On the importance of "for" in the Judeo-Christian tradition, Joseph Ratzinger, "Stellvertretung," HtG II, 566–575.

82. Karl Rahner locates the precise distinctiveness of Jesus in that his grace is not only for him but also precisely for us, ST. V, 212.

83. This verse has given rise to the Petrine ministry and office also known as the Petrine primacy and the papacy. An excellent summary of the discussions about Matthew 16:16–19 as well as the papacy can be found in Otto Karrer, *Peter and the Church* (New York: Herder and Herder, 1963). Later developments are expertly examined in

the Roman Catholic-Lutheran bilateral dialogues: *Eucharist and Ministry* (1970); *Papal Primacy and the Universal Church* (1974); *Teaching Authority and Infallibility in the Church* (1978, 1980; all are available from the Augsburg Publishing House in Minneapolis). Also worth consulting is *The Final Report* of the Anglican-Roman Catholic International Commission (Washington, D.C.: U.S.C.C. Office of Publishing Services, 1982). Although its focus is precisely the problem of infallibility, the symposium edited by Terry Tekippe offers an excellent history of the theology of the papacy. *Papal Infallibility* (Washington, D.C.: University Press of America, 1983).

84. Yves Congar, *L'Eglise de saint Augustin a l'epoque moderne* (Paris: Cerf, 1970) 271–281.

85. How Jesus the preacher became Jesus the preached is well presented by R. Schwager, *Jesus-Nachfolge* 83–86.

86. An airy survey of the sinful Church, including the papacy, as the "Chaste Harlot," has been done by Hans Urs von Balthasar, "Casts Meretrix," *Sponsa Verbi* (Einsiedeln: Johannes, 1961) 203–305.

87. Dermot Lane has noted the influence of "the Lutheran principle of justification by faith alone (*sola fide*)," baneful for the most part, on the "question of the Jesus of history and the Christ of faith." *The Reality of Jesus* (New York: Paulist, 1975) 160. Everything in Lane's argument applies equally to our question, namely the Petrine office. When all is said and done, as we shall see in Chapter 4, office and and organization in the Church are primarily a matter not of divine revelation, but of human nature and human being. In any group of human beings there is structure and organization. There is usually a final and ultimate instance of authority and authoritative decision. Harry Truman's famous principle of government also has ecclesiological dimensions and validity: "The buck stops here!" There is nothing about Christ, supernatural revelation and grace that exempts ecclesial reality from these general societal (political) principles.

88. After Henry Rikhof has discussed the semantic, lingustic and grammatical problems involved in conceptualizing and defining the Church, he suggests as the quintessential definition-description: "The Church is the communion of the faithful." Of course, he immediately concedes that this only "indicates a network which determines the coherence of a possible ecclesiological discourse." *The Concept of the Church* (London: Sheed and Ward, 1980) 232, 234. Although I also think that communion is the best and preferable term to describe the Church. I would also think that quintessential is not a fitting term for any image or definition-description of the Church. Because of its theandric nature, the Church is probably not patient of any quintessential terminology. Josef Ratzinger has emphasized the role that the political misuse of excommunication by Popes and bishops in the Middle Ages played in "discrediting and devaluing the Church as communio." The primitive Church's self-concept as communion was emptied of meaning, and the word Church came to signify only the institutional, the structural. "Opfer, Sakrament und Priestertum," *Catholica* 26 (1972) 116–117.

89. "Wort und Sakrament," *Glaube und Geschichte* (Mainz: Grunewald, 1970) 309.

90. Otto Semmelroth, *Die Kirche als Ursakrament* (Frankfurt: Knecht, 1953) 14–25.

92. "Um die Einheit des Kirchenbegriffes," *Fragen der Theologie heute,* ed. Johannes Feiner et al. (Einsiedeln: Benziger, 1957) 326.

93. *De Paenitentia* (Innsbruck: Theologische Fakultat, 1955, mimeo.) 299–303.

94. *Meditation sur l'Eglise* (Paris: Aubier, 1953, rev. ed.) 175.

95. Epist. 187; PL 38: 845.

96. "The People of God," Miller 200; also 205, 241.

97. ST, X, 403, note 24. It is interesting to note how strong habitual ways of speaking are. Herlinde Pissark-Hudelist, who also notes this suggestion of Rahner and agrees with it, immediately reverts to calling the Church *Ursakrament*. "Zur Diskussion um des priestertum der Frau," *Wagnis Theologie,* ed. Herbert Vorgrimler (Freiburg: Herder, 1979) 423.

98. *Grundkurs des Glaubens* (Freiburg: Herder, 1976) 396.

99. Brian McNeill, "The Spirit and the Church in Syriac Theology," *The Irish Theological Quarterly* 49/2 (1982) 91.

100. Heribert Muhlen, "Das Verhaltnis zwischen Inkarnation und Kirche in den Aussagen des Vaticanum II," *Theologie und Glaube* (1965) 190.

101. See Robert Kress, *A Rahner Handbook* (Atlanta: John Knox, 1982) 56–61, 79–85.

102. *Sermo* 96, 7; PL 38: 588. Thus Juan Alfaro does well to emphasize that the Church is the sacrament of the glorious, glorified, risen Christ. "Christus, Sacramentum Dei Patris: Ecclesia, Sacramentum Christi Gloriosi," *Acta Congressus Internationalis De Theologia Concilii Vaticani II* (Rome: Typis Polyglottis Vaticanis, 1968) 4–9.

103. Max Keller, *Volk Gottes als Kirchenbegriff* (Einsiedeln: Benziger, 1970) 13–15.

104. M.D. Koster, *Ekklesiologie im Werden* (Paderborn: Schoning, 1940).

105. Nicolaus Timpe, *Das kanonistische Kirchenbild vom Codex Juris Canonici bis zum Beginn des Vaticanum Secundum* (Leipzig: St. Benno, 1978) 72–119.

106. Yves Congar, "The People of God," Miller 204, says: "Karl Rahner thinks that this is sufficient to justify extending the expression people of God to all humanity. Scriptural usage as well as liturgical and patristic tradition does not justify this way of speaking, but the Council neither adopted nor rejected it." However, on page 199, Congar had said, "We shall see that this people of God is *de jure* co-extensive with humanity."

107. Henri de Lubac, *Corpus Mysticum* (Paris: Aubier, 1948, rev. ed.) esp. 279–295.

108. *Ekklesiologie* (Münster: Theologische Fakultat, 1965, mimeo.) 65. See also the article in note 88 above. Also, "Leib Christi," LTK 6, 176.

109. *Des Volk Gottes* (Oslo: 1941) 278.

110. "Leib Christi," LTK 6, 908.

111. Yves Congar, *Le Mystere du Temple* (Paris: Cerf, 1957) 7: "The entire enterprise of God is, in effect, to make of humanity, created in his image a living, spiritual temple, where he not only dwells, but where he also communicates himself and where he receives the worship of an entirely filial obedience."

112. Heinrich Schlier, *Der Brief an die Epheser* (Dusseldorf: Patmos, 1965) 91–99.

113. Heribert Muhlen, "Sakralitat und Amt zu Beginn einer neuen Epoche," *Catholica* 26 (1972) 71, 81.

114. *The Gospel According to John* I-XII, 180.

115. Cited by Henri de Lubac, "Lumen Gentium and the Fathers," Miller, 171.

116. "Das Verhaltnis," 186, 190. See also his *Una Mystica Persona* (Paderborn: Schoning, 1964) IX, passim.

117. This is the leitmotif of Muhlen's works cited in note 116. See also Yves Congar, *Eglise Catholique et France Moderne* (Paris: Hachette, 1978) 111.

118. This image of the Church is frequently accompanied by another, the Church as Mother. As Hippolytus states, "The Church never ceases to bring forth the Logos, man and God, from its heart." Cited along with other texts by de Lubac, "Lumen Gentium," Miller, 159–160. Not only the universal and hierarchical Church is Mother. As every soul or Christian is Church, so does every Christian beget the Logos and contribute to the Logos being begotten in those around it. Hugo Rahner, "Die Lehre der Kirchenvater von der Geburt Christi aus dem Herzen der Kirche und der Glaubigen," *Symbole der Kirche* (Salzburg: Muller, 1964) 13–90. Yves Congar, "Preface," Karl Delahaye, *Ecclesia Mater chez les Peres des trois premieres siecles* (Paris: Cerf, 1964). Henri de Lubac, *Les Eglises particulieres dans l'Eglise universelle* (Paris: Aubier-Montaigne, 1971) 154–165, 167–174.

119. Robert Kress, *Christian Roots.* Also, "Imminent Apocalyptic or Patient God? Toward an Eschatological Ecclesiology," *Communio 5* (1978) 392–397.

120. The Eucharistic accounts of the New Testament are traceable back to Jesus himself. Raymund Schwager, "Geht die Eucharistie auf Jesus zuruck?" *Orientierung,* 39 (1975), 220–223. Also, Rudolf Pesch, *Wie Jesus das Abendmahl hielt. Der Grund der Eucharistie* (Freiburg: Herder, 1978).

121. Karl Rahner and Angelus Haussling, *The Celebration of the Eucharist* (New York: Herder and Herder, 1968) 33.

122. Karl Rahner ST, II, 140–141.

123. *Faith in History and Society* (New York: Seabury, 1980) 88–115, 184–204. Also, "The Future in the Memory of Suffering," *Concilium,* 76 (1972) 9–25.

124. *The Emergent Church* (New York: Crossroad, 1981) 34–47.

125. Robert Kress, "Theological Method: Praxis and Liberation, "*Communio 6* (1979) 118–120.

126. John Headley, *Luther's View of Church History* (New Haven: Yale University Press, 1963) 106, 118–124, 179–187.

127. Joseph Ratzinger (with Karl Rahner), *Revelation and Tradition* (New York: Herder and Herder, 1965) 29; also 27, 60–63.

128. Jean Puyo, *Congar* (Paris: Centurion, 1975) 34.

129. Krister Stendahl, "The Question Concerning the Gospel as Center and the Gospel as Totality of the New Testament Witness" *Evangelium-Welt-Kirche,* ed. Harding Meyer (Frankfurt: Knecht, 1975) 103.

130. Yves Congar speaks of "The Holy Spirit and the Apostolic Body, Continuators of the Work of Christ," *The Mystery of the Church* (Baltimore: Helicon, 1960) 147–186.

131. Notker Fuglister, "Strukturen der alttestamentlichen Ekklesiologie," MS 4/1, 39.

132. Ludwig Rost, *Die Vorstufen von Kirche und Synagoge* (Stuttgart: Kohlhammer, 1938).

133. Olof Linton, "Ekklesia," *Reallexikon fur Christentum und Antike* (Stuttgart: Hiersemann 1959) IV, 905–921.

134. See Burkhart Schneider, "Bemerkungen zur Kritik an der Kirche," *Gott in*

Welt, ed. Heribert Vorgrimler (Freiburg: Herder, 1964) II, 246–266.

135. Robert Kress, *The Difference That Jesus Makes* (Chicago: Franciscan Herald Press, 1982).

136. For the ecclesiological dimensions of this "is–ought," see Rudolf Schnackenburg, *The Moral Teaching off the New Testament* (New York: Herder and Herder, 1965) 268–186, 342. Also his *Die Johannesbriefe* (Freiburg: Herder, 1963) 184–204.

137. See Myles M. Bourke, "Reflections on Church Order in the New Testament," *Catholic Biblical Quarterly,* 30 (1968) 493–511. Also Raymond Brown, *Priest and Bishop* (New York: Paulist, 1970).

138. On all of the above see Burkhard Neunheuser, "Eglise universelle et eglise locale," *L'Eglise de Vatican II,* ed. Guilherme Barauna (Paris: Cerf, 1966) II, 607–638.

139. On the dangers and avoidability of an actualistic eucharistic ecclesiology, see Yves Congar, "Die Wesenseigenschaften der Kirche," MS 4/1, 400–408. Also Joseph Jungmann, "Liturgy in the Parish," *The Parish* ed. Hugo Rahner (Westminister: Newman, 1958) 64–71.

140. However, see Raymond Brown, "New Testament Background for the Concept of the Local Church," *CTSAP* 36 (1981) 4–12.

141. As we saw earlier, although the account of Pentecost in the Acts of the Apostles may not contain a reference to the Genesis account of the tower of Babel, it nevertheless contains, on the basis of its parallelism to the rabbinic theology of the universal intelligibility of the proclamation of the Torah, an undeniable impetus toward the universalization of the Christian tradition and communio. Jacob Kremer, *Pfingsten— Erfahrung des Geistes* (Stuttgart: KBW Verlag, 1974), especially 58–70.

142. Thus there is legitimated once again the usage of perichoresis to describe the nature, constitution and being of the Church. See also Raphael Schulte, "Kirche and Kult," *Mysterium Kirche,* Ferdinand Holbock and Thomas Sartory (Salzburg: Muller, 1962) II, 770–772.

143. Henri de Lubac, *Les Eglises Particulieres* 29–56. Oskar Saier, *Communio in der Lehre des Zweiten Vatikanischen Konzils* (Munich: Hueber, 1973) 141–181.

144. Henri de Lubac, *Catholicism* (New York: Longmans, 1950) 17–34, 161–205.

145. Rome and the papacy have long been points of contention, not only among Roman Catholic, Orthodox and Anglican Churches, but also within the Roman Catholic Church itself. As there has been an exaggerated papalism, so has there also been an illegitimate anti-Romanism. Hans Urs von Balthasar, *Der antiromische Affekt* (Freiburg: Herder 1974) 15, 58, 152, 284, 291. Congar is cited to the same effect on page 16, note 4. Karl Rahner, ST, XIV, 368–381, *Toleranz in der Kirche* (Freiburg: Herder 1977) 105–125.

146. Karl Rahner, "Theology of the Parish," *The Parish,* ed. Hugo Rahner (Westminister: Newman, 1958) 28–30.

147. *Contra Errores Graecorum,* II, 32; *Opuscula Theologia,* I, ed. Raymond Verardo (Rome: Marietti, 1954) 340.

148. One must be careful of inflating the various institutional dimensions of the Church. Nevertheless, Yves Congar has thought it possible to speak of "Rome as center, ikon and servant of unity." *Eglise Catholique* 89–102.

149. *Summa Contra Gentiles, IV,* 76 (Turin:Marietti, n.d.) 541.

150. See Joseph Ratzinger, "Widerspruch im Buch von Hans Küng," *Zum Prob-*

lem Unfehlbarkeit, ed. Karl Rahner (Freiburg: Herder, 1971) 102–105. We shall consider the papacy in greater detail in Chapter 4.

151. The advantages for the relationship of the Eastern and Western Church(es) are too obvious. The point need not be belabored, but perhaps one should often recall the sad history narrated by Yves Congar, *After Nine Hundred Years* (New York: Fordham University Press, 1959).

152. Polycarp Sherwood, "The Sense of Rite," *Eastern Churches Quarterly,* 12 (1957–58) 112–125.

153. Tomas G. Bissonnette, "Communidades de Base: Some Contemporary Attempts to Build Koinonia," *The Jurist,* 36 (1976) 24.

154. Leonardo Boff has suggested that these communities may rediscover, refound, reinvent the Church. *Eclesiogenesis, Las communidades de base reinventan la Iglesia* (Santander: Sal Terrae, 1980; tr. from the original Portugese, *Eclesiogenese)* 37–50.

155. *Das neue Volk Gottes* (Dusseldorf: Patmos, 1970) 142.

156. Charles Moeller, "History of Lumen Gentium's Structure and Ideas," Miller, 151, note 114: "It is important not to confuse diverse aspects of the papacy: the Pope is bishop of Rome and patriarch of the West. Since the West was never but one patriarchal church, there was a risk of 'telescoping' this dignity into that of the universal pastor."

157. (Garden City: Doubleday Image, 1978). In "Imaging the Church for the 1980's, *Thought* 56 (1981) 121–138, he retraces the original five models and adds a sixth, discipleship.

158. Dulles, *Models* 13, 28, 29, 32.

159. Robert Kress, "Leise Treten: An Irenic Ecumenical Hermeneutic," *Theological Studies* 44 (1983) 407–437.

160. Thomas Stransky, "Discussion," Miller, 179.

161. James McGovern, *The Church in the Churches* (Washington: Corpus, 1968).

162. Cited by Henri de Lubac, *Catholicism* 26.

163. "A Basic Interpretation of Vatican II," *Theological Studies 40* (1979) 723.

164. "M.J. Guitton has thought it possible to characterize the Protestant attitude as a quest for purity, the Catholic attitude as the quest for fullness or plenitude. That seems quite right to us. . . ." Yves Congar, *Vraie et fausse reforme dans l'Eglise,* 2nd ed. (Paris: Cerf, 1968) 278. See also Yves Congar, *Sainte Eglise* (Paris: Cerf, 1963) 150–161.

165. "Milman's View of Christianity," in *Essays Critical and Historical,* reprinted in C.F. Harrold, ed. Essays and Sketches II, New York: Longmans, Green and Co., 1948) 258.

166. K. Rahner, *Herausforderung des Christen* (Freiburg: Herder, 1975) 84; Hans Urs von Balthasar, *Katholisch* (Einsiedeln: Johannes, 1975) 18, 22, 167. *Gott Alles in Allem* (Mainz: Grunewald, 1958) 149–151.

168. Yves Congar, "Traditio Thomistica in materia ecclesiologica," *Angelicum,* XLIII (1966) 421–424; "The Idea of the Church in St. Thomas Aquinas," *The Mystery of the Church* 97–117. This is helpful, for it shows that the ecclesiological use of the term "society" is not exhausted by the model of the Church as "perfect society."

3

THE CHURCH AS SACRAMENT

From the consideration of God-Father-Son-Holy Spirit as the source and paradigm of created being and of the Church as the sacrament of the salvation of created being, we now move to a more detailed consideration of the word and reality "sacrament." In the preceding chapters we have used "sacrament" in a general way, assuming the fuller development that is contained in this chapter. In a way, this is in keeping with the actual history of both Church and theology. The reality which has come to be designated by the term "sacrament" existed long before it received this name. As we have seen, sacrament is a wide-ranging term. In recent centuries it had been applied almost exclusively to seven special sacred ritual actions, the chief of which are baptism and Eucharist. However, it describes not only these actions, but also the very way or mode of the Church's and Christ's being. Indeed, it can even be applied to God insofar as the second person of the Trinity is the word, the sign, symbol, sacrament of the Father. In the Christian tradition sacrament has emphasized the visible form achieved by invisible grace. Sacrament is the *Gestalt* in two ways—in the very being of the history or economy of salvation in general and in the various actions in which salvation becomes history in particular. For this reason the chapter on the Church as sacrament provides a most fitting transition from the Church as communion to the Church as communication.

Before we can proceed to the more detailed explanation of sacrament in the Judeo-Christian Catholic tradition, a few philosophical insights must be mentioned.

In philosophy one distinguishes between first act and second act. As in all such distinctions, caution is advisable. But the distinction is helpful in spite of possible dangers and misuses. First act describes the very being of a thing or person. Thus, for example, we speak of man precisely as human being. The term "being" can be used in two ways. Minimally, it can simply designate that the thing or person in question is not not. That is, it means that the object in question is not nothing, that it exists. One technical meaning of exist is that something stands out from nothing. This minimalist use is truly helpful, but it is also so general that it can be misleading. Included under its umbrella are God, angels, humans, animals, vegetables, minerals, ideas, artifacts—indeed anything, as long as it is not nothing and exists at all. The minimalist use of

"being" tends to blur distinctions among various beings and to make everything the same, ignoring the precise identity and dignity of different beings.

The maximalist use describes being as subject, that is, being that is free,
intelligent (knowing) and volitional (choosing). Or, put another way, being is
understood primarily as the ability to know, love and be free. Any being that
can't know and love freely is not nothing, but it does "be" less than other
beings. Higher beings, like humans, are "more" being than lower beings, like
rocks. There are levels, grades, degrees of being. When we think of beings, we
can start from the highest being or the lowest. We can think truly both ways—
one is not right and the other wrong. But there is a difference.[1]

And this difference can make a big difference in our subsequent thinking.
Here is where the distinction between first and second act can be misleading.
For example, do we define the human being primarily as not nothing? Or do
we say with St. Thomas Aquinas that "the human being has its being more
truly where it loves than where it [merely] is?"[2] In the first case, acts of knowing and loving would be "accidental." That is, they would be something that
"happens" to the human being, already otherwise fully constituted. They
would tend to be subsequent and subordinate, secondary in and for human
being. In Aquinas' understanding, on the other hand, the very being of the human being, truly human being, would be constituted precisely in and through
the love and the knowing of the human being. This does not mean that the human being ceases to be at all when not actively knowing and loving in individual actions. Here we must recall what we said above about being as act,
actuality. Being is not primarily a static absence of non-being, a merely not
not existing. Rather, this not "not being" is a secondary and negative consequence with accompanies the primary and positive meaning/nature of being
which is knowing, loving, being free. Insofar as a being does not and cannot
know and love freely, it is not simply nothing. But it is definitely less being (It
"bes" less!) than human and Godly being.

All this is a consequence of the world being (created in) the image and
likeness of the triune God, who is pure act (actuality) and the fullness of being,
for whom to be is to know and to love. It is also why Church as sacrament is
such good transition from Church as communion to Church as communication. Because of its *de facto* development in the history of the Church and its
theology, the term "sacrament" designates both the being and the act-actions
of the Church. It well describes the first and second act of the Church. It reminds us emphatically of the philosophical axiom, *agere sequitur esse*. To act
(acting) follows upon (is in accord with) to be (being). Too often the intimate
inner connection between first and second act is disregarded. Applied to our
consideration, this means that the Church is always sacrament—the very being
of the Church is sacrament-al. This sacramental being (first act of the Church)
actuates itself further in distinct different actions in different times and places
(the second act-s of the Church) throughout history. These sacramental actuations are many and diverse. A set of seven has achieved a privileged place in

the life of the Church. These are called the seven sacraments—baptism, confirmation, Eucharist, penance, anointing of the sick, marriage and holy orders. They are special, and their specialness must be respected. But they must be respected in such a way that their privileged status does not destroy or obscure the sacramentality of all the being and all the acts, actions and actuations of the Church, which is itself the sacrament of Christ who is the sacrament of the Word-Son, who is the sacrament of God-Father.

The above is intended to emphasize the sacramental nature of the Church. Sacrament does not describe merely a few actions which the Church does now and then. Rather, the Church is thoroughly sacramental. Its being and its actions are sacramental, its first act as well as its second act(-ions). It could not be otherwise, of course, since the Church is the sacrament of God's salvation and since this God is triune communion and communication and since salvation is participation in the very nature of this triune God (2 Pet 1:4). In the preceding chapter we summed all this up in the phrase "sacramental communion ontology."

We shall now proceed to examine the etymology of the word sacrament and how this word came to be applied to the Church and its acts. We shall see that sacrament came to be the preferred term to designate the "saving mystery," which is ultimately God's very own self and which happened decisively and irrevocably in the world's history in Christ. Sacrament came to describe concrete saving realities, words and rites, precisely because and insofar as they are effective signs and signful causes, mediating Godly, Christly salvation to human beings throughout time and space. In the factual historical development of the Church, seven such signful mediations achieved special prominence.

ETYMOLOGY

Although "sacrament" was not an original biblical word, its basic religious dimension made it an apt (at least not an inapt) term to designate the ritual, signful mediation of God's saving grace to human beings. The word originated in the Latin root *sacr-*. It designated a relationship to the numinous, the divine, the Godly. Two verbs, *sacrare* and the more common *consecrare,* described the action whereby a thing was transferred from the secular or profane to the sphere of the divine or holy—from *jus humanum* to *jus divinum.* This transfer required an official public act. It was not a merely private, personal religious action. The noun *sacrum* (*sacra*) was the preferred term to describe all human relations, especially sacrifice, to the deity. In sum, the Latin *sacramentum* had a triple etymological meaning: (1) actively, the means (object) whereby something was consecrated to the deity; (2) passively, that which was consecrated; (3) the consecrating action.

Sacramentum was used especially in regard to military and judicial procedures. Militarily, it meant the special official oath a soldier took before a public official. By this oath the soldier reinforced his promise and petitioned the gods to bless him if he spoke truthfully and kept his oath, to punish him otherwise. Again, this was an official public act which transferred and elevated the object, in this case the soldier, to the divine sphere. Consequently, the soldiers who had made this oath were known as *sacrati milites* (consecrated soldiers) and *solemnis et sacrata militia* (solemn and consecrated or sacred military service/army).[3]

In a judicial procedure, *sacramentum,* designated the sum of money which each litigant deposited in a sacred place or with the high priest. The winner received his back, the losers forfeited his to the public treasury, to be used for religious purposes. It is quite possible that this "sacramental process" was so named because the litigants took an oath (consecrated themselves) before the gods that they were telling the truth. The importance of the oath and its subsequent obligation for the meaning of *sacramentum* is indicated by a letter of Pliny the Younger to the Emperor Trajan in 96 or 97. Of the Christians he says: "It is their custom to gather together before dawn, both to sing a hymn to Christ as God and simultaneously also to bind themselves by oath (*sacramento*) not to commit any evil [or sinful] act."[4] Clearly, then, the original pagan Latin word *sacramentum* was a religious term. As Christian writers and theologians looked for Latin words to translate their Hebrew, Aramaic and Greek Christian language and literature, sacrament would have been readily available.

SACRAMENT AND MYSTERY

Sacrament was the preferred Latin translation for the Greek *musterion* (mystery). *Musterion* itself is a somewhat mysterious term, neither its etymology nor its original meaning being entirely clear. It probably came from *muein,* meaning to close, to lock—for example, to close one's mouth or lips; to shut (up); to be silent. A mystery was a secret or hidden thing, about which one had to be silent. Mystery did not imply that something was unintelligible, only that its meaning was hidden from most, known only to a few. It was not a precisely religious term although it originated precisely in the religious realm. From there it moved over into general profane and secular usage. In the Hellenistic culture, *musterion* played roles in the mystery religions or cults, in philosophy and Gnosticism.

In the mystery cults *musterion* appeared almost exclusively in the plural, probably because of the multitude of diverse cultic actions which it designated. Since, as the very name indicates, the mystery cults were secret (mysterious), not too much is known about them.

They did flourish from the seventh century B.C. to the fourth century A.D. They are generally regarded to have been terminated with the destruction of the temple of Serapis in Alexandria in 389. However, some mystery cults may well have survived into the sixth century, in spite of official imperial condemnation and persecution. According to Odo Casel, the mystery cult was "a sacred cultic action in which a saving act or deed became present in the rite; in that the cultic community performed this rite, it participated in the saving action and thereby acquired salvation for itself."[5] Through their ritual actions, the mystery cults made the fate of the deity present for a select group of the initiated, so that these adepts might share in the fate of the deity. An initiation rite was required, by which the select few adepts were separated from the mass of people. Through the celebration of the sacred rites, the initiated achieved salvation, which, since the gods were chthonic, was a continued and increased share in the life of the cosmos.

The philosophical mystery has this in common with the mystery cults—both promise salvation as well as reveal the way to this salvation, which consists of the vision of the divine (deity). They differ in that for philosophy the mysteries are no longer ritual actions, but secret and hidden doctrines or truths. One *ascends* to this salvation through various steps or stages, in which one is purged of earthly, bodily obscurations and advances serially to a final stage of perfection in which one is able to see the truth of being itself.[6] Because of its philosophical transformation, mystery no longer meant cultic, ritual encounter with the deity, but the divine ontological foundation or source of the world itself.

In one sense, Gnosticism[7] combined elements of both the mystery cults and mystical philosophy. Through the disclosure or relevation of the hidden mysteries, redemption occurred. Everyone who received (heard) the hidden mystery in silence became a pneumatic (a spiritual person; for the Gnostics matter was at best imperfection—really, evil; salvation meant deliverance from matter). For the Gnostics, mystery referred to everything connected with the hidden heavenly sphere beyond this earthly cosmos. In this heavenly sphere were to be found both the origin and the redemption of humanity. The revelation of these transcendent mysteries granted knowledge (*gnosis*). This knowledge was not only information, but transformation—the deification of the human being. Since this knowledge was divine, a mysterious saving power, it required strict secrecy.

The pagan religious background of the Greek word "mystery" makes the biblical writer's reluctance to use it readily understandable. It is noteworthy that the Greek Septuagint translation of the Old Testament never once uses mystery to translate the Hebrew equivalent, *sod*. In fact, in the entire Septuagint the word mystery occurs only twenty times, all in the later books of the Hellenistic period. In the Wisdom literature, mystery usually means nothing more than something private or hidden, which is not to be made public or revealed. Mystery is used in a more religious sense to designate the saving plan of divine wisdom which, although hidden, is not meant to be restricted to a select few (Wis 2:22–23; 6:22). It is worth noting that in the Old Testament myster never refers to sacrifice or other cultic ritual action. The most important Old Testament texts are in Daniel (2:18–19, 27–30, 44–47; 4:9). Mystery signifies the divine knowledge and will to save as well as the events which symbolize and effect this salvation in the future. Late Jewish apocalyptic literature continues and develops the understanding of mystery as the divine eschatological will to save and its gradual, obscure revelation and actualization. Although there is some similarity between the biblical-apocalyptic and the Greek cultic, philosophical, Gnostic understandings of *musterion,* the differences are greater by far. These differences are located in the understanding of God and humanity as well as the point of departure, means and term of salvation.

MYSTERY IN THE NEW TESTAMENT

Against this whole background, we can now briefly turn to the New Testament usage of mystery. Even in the New Testament we do not find a direct, immediate, and explicit application of the words mystery and sacrament to that which later came to be described by the technical term "sacrament." On the other hand, Paul does use mystery to describe the salvation achieved by Christ and mediated through the Church in the sacraments. Mystery appears only once in the Synoptic Gospels, not at all in the Gospel of John. The Book of Revelation uses it in the late Jewish apocalyptic sense. Mystery is, then, basically a Pauline term.

The Synoptic usage (Mk 4:11–12; Mt 13:11–15; Lk 8:10–11) states that the mystery(-ies) of the kingdom of God (of heaven) is made known to the disciples of Jesus, while it remains hidden from others in parables. This verse contains no allusion to sacrament as a cultic, ritual action. On the other hand, it does speak of the kingdom of God as a mystery, and kingdom of God is the Synoptics' standard designation for salvation, whose sacramental mediation belongs to the essence of the Church.

The key texts in the Pauline writings are Romans 16:25–26; 1 Corinthians 2:7–10; Ephesians 1:8–10, 3:3–12; Colossians 1:26–27; 2:3; 4:3; 1 Timothy 3:16. For Paul the mystery is clearly and emphatically the "Christ-event, from its eternal hiddenness in God to its realization in Christ and its proclamation through the apostles."[8] This Christ-event is, of course, the divine saving will, which has existed from all eternity, which embraces all human beings in principle, which is incarnate in Jesus Christ, and which is made effectively and symbolically present throughout human history in and by the Church. According to the Epistles to the Ephesians and Colossians, God wills to effect human salvation not alone, not all by himself as it were, but in and through the Church. The Church, which is human and visible, has a proper role to play in the mystery of God.[9] It is not blasphemous to say that the time between the ascension and parousia of Jesus is the "time of the Church."[10] Herein lies the precise scriptural foundation for the category of the sacramental, although, as we have already often noted, the term itself would be developed only later. This is worth emphasizing, since nowhere does even Paul apply the term mystery (or sacrament) to a sacred ritual action like baptism or Eucharist. Even the oft invoked 1 Corinthians 4:1 ("People must think of us as Christ's servants, stewards entrusted with the mysteries of God") does not refer directly to the sacred rituals and signs we know today as the sacraments. Of course, neither does it deny that there are sacraments and official ministers of sacraments. Furthermore, it is legitimate to use such a text in the later clarification of the Church's sacramental being and activity, as long as one remains aware that a theological deduction, not a revelational proclamation is what is at play here.

Two final remarks will complete these considerations. The contention that Christianity was but one more version of the Hellenistic mystery religions is no longer made. Likewise, the contention that Paul transformed the simple religion of the simple Jesus into an elaborate mystery and Gnostic religion is no longer a seriously urged theory.[11] On the other hand, there are parallels in the understanding of mystery in the Epistle to the Ephesians and the Qumran literature.[12] I emphasize parallels or similarities, since no direct causal relationship has been established. Such similarities are hardly unexpected, since certain ideas become common currency in a given period, and even the Qumran adepts were not completely isolated. Hence, it is quite possible for the Epistle to the Ephesians and the Qumran documents to speak of God and God's saving plan in terms of eschatological mysteries, originally hidden in God but now revealed in the end times.

Since the New Testament does not directly and explicitly designate any rituals or actions as sacraments, some think that their total absence in the Gospel of John decisively proves that sacraments are not biblical, but, rather, intrusions from the Greek mystery religions. They interpret John's Gospel as not only un-sacramental, but also as anti-sacramental. Thus Rudolf Bultmann can assert: "It is therefore permissible to say that though in John there is no direct polemic against the sacraments, his attitude toward them is nevertheless critical or at least reserved."[14] For them, Jesus is the living bread as well as the true light and life. Access to this Jesus is available solely through faith itself. Faith alone is sufficient. Nothing else is needful, certainly not ritual actions which would supposedly mediate saving grace and salvation. Indeed, such rites must be excluded, because they easily tend toward magic and superstition, and came, after all, from the pagan mystery cults.

On the other hand, both Catholic and Protestant exegetes find hints and intimations of sacraments not only throughout the New Testament, but especially in John's Gospel. For example, Oscar Cullmann is emphatic: "We mean to go further, however, and show how the Gospel of John regards it as one of its chief concerns to set forth the connection between the contemporary Christian worship and the historical life of Jesus.[15]

Obviously also against Bultmann is Franz Mussner's statement: "Precisely the opposite is true. The Johannine presentation of Christ is permeated with cultic traits. One can speak of a cultic background in regard to the Johannine Christology.''[16] Rudolf Schnackenburg treads a middle way.[17] He emphasizes that John's Gospel is primarily an interpretation of Jesus' earthly ministry. Hence, the Christological interpretation must not be displaced or obscured by a sacramental interpretation. On the other hand, Schnackenburg also finds definite sacramental traits in the Gospel. Indeed, ecclesiological and sacramental considerations went into the very composition of the Gospel. And Raymond Brown asserts:

> In addition to the more explicit references to the sacraments, some of which may come from the final redactor, there is in the very substance of the Gospel a broad sacramental interest; and in this respect John is quite in harmony with the Church at large. . . . This Johannine sacramentalism is neither merely anti-docetic nor peripheral, but shows the essential connection between the sacramental way of receiving life within the Church at the end of the first century and the way in which life was offered to those who heard Jesus in Palestine.[18]

An insightful remark of Barnabas Lindars may serve to conclude this discussion: ''John has no wish to belittle the importance of either baptism or the Eucharist. They are practices with which his readers are expected to be familiar, so that he can simply take their existence for granted.''[19]

The Synoptic Gospels and the epistles and even the Johannine writings[20] contain clear and distinct references to ritual actions which can legitimately be included in the ''overarching category''[21] of sacrament in its later technical sense. In general, Jesus not only preached a message about the divine dignity and human response thereto. He also proclaimed the reign/kingdom of God to be present in his very own corporeal person. His personal existence-being and actions were manifestional mediations of the divine saving will and grace to his world and contemporaries. These manifestational actions are not to be restricted exclusively to the miracles. They include just as well those signs which were customary in religion in general and in Judaism in particular, and which Jesus himself used in his saving mission.

Among these signs, the imposition of hands and anointing with oil played a prominent role. Especially against the background of the Jewish Old Testament and contemporary Jewish practice does Jesus' institution of the Last Supper intimate a sacramental understanding. Paul's interpretation of the primitive Church's baptism and Eucharist (Rom 6:2–11; 1 Cor 6:11; 10:14–22; 11:26–29), his understanding that eternal salvation can be mediated through the combination of matter and word (Eph 5:26), and John's understanding that salvation is available through corporeal gifts given by the Lord (6:53–58) also indicate a sacramental understanding. As this ''sacramental'' mentality became more intensive and extensive, other ecclesial acts could also be interpreted in a sacramental manner. It was, indeed, such reflection on the practice and lived reality of the Church that eventually led to and culminated in the doctrine of sacrament in general and the seven sacraments in particular. A decisive step in this reflective development was taken by Tertullian.

TERTULLIAN

Of all the early theologians of the Church, Tertullian (160–220) was most influential in the development of sacramental doctrine. Although he was not the originator of the new Christian interpretation of the word *sacramentum,* he was certainly the one who solidified this interpretation in the Christian theological tradition.[22] Tertullian was familiar with *sacramentum* in pre-Christian literature as well as the translation for *musterion* in the African versions of the Bible. Most important, though, was his use of *sacramentum* to designate both baptism and the Eucharist.

Tertullian used sacrament in the classical sense of oath, and he compared the baptismal rite with the soldiers' oath-taking. The similarity is strengthened when one keeps in mind that in antiquity religions were thought of as God's militia. It is possible that the soldiers' oath was accompanied by an external sign during Tertullian's lifetime. To this would have corresponded the baptismal ablution, further strengthening the parallel. Tertullian also used *sacramentum* to translate *musterion* (only later did the neologism *mysterium* appear), probably because the mystery cults were also understood to constitute their members as God's militia and because the mystery cults influenced and modified the religious understandings of the soldiers. He also used *sacramentum* in a salvation history sense. He delighted in discovering allegorical and symbolic relationships between Old Testament figures and Christ. They were called sacraments because these persons or objects were signs of a mysterious reality which was made known through a revelation. *Sacramentum* was also applied to institutions and events in Israel's history insofar as they pointed to the divine saving will, finally fully revealed in Christ. Tertullian also applied *sacramentum* to the contents (articles) and confessions or creeds of the faith. The Christian religion itself is a *sacramentum fidei* (sacrament of the faith).[23] *Sacramentum* signified not only cult, but also doctrine, orthodoxy and preaching. It was a synonym for truth, saving discipline, the rule or canon of truth.

Most importantly, though, Tertullian also used *sacramentum* in a more restricted sense, more like the modern use of sacrament with which we are familiar. He was led to do this by his desire to show that what was sought in the pagan religious mystery cults was fulfilled in the Christian mysteries or sacraments. He even went so far as to describe the pagan rituals as a diabolical aping of the Christian sacraments. This was especially true for baptism. The crucial steps in Tertullian's theology of the sacraments was provided by the parallel between the soldier's oath *sacramentum* as initiation or entrance rite into the military order and baptism as the Christian initiation rite into the Church. Both were thought of as the *militia dei*. This pagan *sacramentum* is really and truly fulfilled and perfected in Christianity, where, and only where, it enjoys its full meaning. Through baptism the catechumen becomes a *miles Christi* (soldier of Christ) and assumes an obligation in regard to the faith similar to the obligation to the state assumed by the soldier in his *sacramentum*. Baptism is *sacramentum* in the truest and most proper sense. This understanding of sacrament also emphasizes the obligation as well as the consecration of the baptized person. Tertullian has a highly developed symbolism of water, tracing its saving and spiritual (pneumatic) dimensions all the way back to the creation account in Genesis:

> All waters, therefore, in virtue of the pristine privilege of their origin, do, after invocation of God, attain the sacramental power of sanctification; for the Spirit immediately supervenes from the heavens, and rests over the waters, sanctifying them from himself; and being thus sanctified, they imbibe at the same time the power of sanctifying.

It is consequent, then, that Tertullian should find the sacrament of baptism prefigured in the Old Testament, especially in the exodus and passage through the Red Sea. He called baptism the "happy sacrament" *(felix sacramentum)*,[24] for it frees us from all the failures of our past and frees us for eternal life. Not only, then, the parallel between baptism and the military oath, but also the fact that *sacramentum* translated *musterion* and baptism is the true mystery-consecration, enabled, even compelled, Tertullian to emphasize baptism as the true *sacramentum*.[25]

Tertullian also spoke of the Eucharist as sacrament. In this instance, the category of symbol, image, pictorial representation played a significant role. The Eucharistic discourse in which Jesus described himself as bread was very important in Tertullian's sacramental theology. It enabled him to understand that a reality had to be present, of which the bread is the symbol or figure. The bread cannot be merely a cipher or reminder if it is truly a symbolic image or picture. It must point to something which is present, albeit invisible, and which gains visibility in the picture or symbol. This is very similar to modern sacramental, symbolic theology, which, in German, speaks of an *In-Erscheinung-Treten*. This means that a hidden or invisible reality "comes-into-appearance." It achieves visibility, becomes sensibly perceptible. Thus, Jesus is truly present "behind" or "underneath" what looks like bread. He achieves a true, real visible presence among believers by means of the breadly appearance.

Tertullian's sacramental theology was not nearly as sophisticated and complicated as that of some later theologians. Nevertheless, he was able to lay a firm foundation for further development. In his theology the crucial elements of sacramental theology are already present: the sanctifying God and the theandric Savior Jesus as well as grace in a *Gestalt* which includes both effective causality and symbolic signification. The consecration caused by this grace both evokes and enables the consecrated person to respond morally, to assume the duties of that state in life which is membership in the Church, which is "our Mother,"[26] the "true Mother of the living."[27] On this foundation subsequent theologians built their own theories and elaborations of the sacraments as signifying causes and causing signs of the grace of salvation.

Although Tertullian fell prey to the rigorist heresy of Montanism, his sacramental doctrine remained the lasting basis for all further sacramental theologizing. After him, Cyprian continued to emphasize the sign-full-ness or signification-al dimension of the sacraments. Sacrament also continued to enjoy a wide range of meanings. With Cyprian and his contemporaries, however, words such as sign, figure,type, image, similitude and likeness became almost synonymous with sacrament. Cyprian's overarching concern for the unity of the Church, threatened by heretical movements, led him to emphasize the Church as "this holy mystery of oneness [*hoc unitatis sacramentum*] . . . portrayed in the Gospel by our Lord Jesus Christ's coat, which was not divided or cut at all. . . . By the sacred symbolism [*sacramento et signo*] of his garment was proclaimed the oneness of the Church."[28] In support of our contention in the preceding chapter that a choice definition of Church is tradition, we may invoke Cyprian's description of the Church as the *sacramentum traditum*,[29] the *sacramentum divinae traditionis*.[30] Insofar as the Church is the complex of the entire teaching of Christ, the revelation of God, which is accepted in faith, it is synonymous with the *traditio Christi*. It is also fitting, therefore, that Christ be described as sacrament, since, in the final analysis, he is the end-all and be-all of all salvation-history, the mysterious, sign-full revelation of the mystery of the saving God. Although Cyprian increasingly emphasized the Eucharist as sacrament, baptism remained the chief sacrament. Likewise, at this time the term sacrament still covered a multitude of realities—various and many rites, the faith itself and the doctrines of the faith. Nevertheless, there was a discernible tendency to focus attention on certain ritual celebrations of the Church's faith as sacraments.

By the time of Ambrose, sacrament had definitely begun to signify definite ritual celebration, although many more than the later classical seven were deemed sacramental. Indeed, sacrament still applied to type and symbol, as well as saving facts, acts and truths. Especially the incarnation and passion of Christ were regarded as sacramental. On the other hand, the "specialization" of the term sacrament to designate certain ritual actions definitely intensified during this period. Ambrose emphasized the initiatory rites of baptism and confirmation as well as the Eucharistic sacrifice. He also laid the foundations for the "anthropological" explanation of the sacraments. In regard to baptism, he noted: "Since man is constituted by two natures, that is, by a soul and body, the visible part is consecrated by a visible element, the invisible part by an invisible element. For the body is washed by water, the sins of the soul cleansed by the Spirit."[31] Ambrose also emphasized that a sacrament is composed of two elements: one is external and visible, the other is internal and invisible. In the visible element there occurs a divine activity or, as later terminology would say, causality.

In the entire patristic development, which culminated in Augustine, there was one constant: sacrament, especially as the translation of mystery, became the preferred term to designate the "objective reality" of the sensibly perceptible presence of the divine saving will and plan in the cosmos, already created and ruled by God, and in the history of this cosmos. Concretely, this objective reality/sacrament was first of all the objective incarnate divine Word-Son, Christ, and his objective Church, in which the saving plan is effectively mediated throughout history to the end of the earth. Christology and ecclesiology are parallel reflections on the "objective reality" of various stages of the divine saving will at work in the world, reconciling it with God and within humanity (2 Cor 5:18–21). Both reflections, on the lived reality of Christ and of the Church, had (and have) to combat similar heresies, which would make the "objective reality" unreal—unworldly, acosmic, "spiritualistic."[32] Both had to affirm concrete particular realities and objectivities, in both Christ and the Church, so that the saving plan of God might be truly and really present in the world.

It is not only a divine desire in heaven, not merely a pious human aspiration on earth, not a vague and hazy ghost-like emanation floating about the cosmos, safely removed from the harsh, and sweet realities of everyday human life. No, the saving will of God has became flesh; it is part of the cosmos (Jn 1:14; Gal 4:4). To affirm this general saving objective reality, theology has invoked other more limited, particular objective realities.

Of these particular objective realities, a key if not the key one has been sacrament.[33] This reality and its theology have been invoked repeatedly to protect the incarnation of God's saving will/plan in Christ and the Church. Sacraments "make" the divine saving will present in history, in the concrete realities of everyday life. As we have seen, the word itself has shared in the vicissitudes of everyday life. No single reason compelled the choice of *sacramentum* to translate the "objective reality" as described in the Bible as *musterion*.[34] Neither was there a single compelling reason for its selection as the term designating that particular "objective reality" which came to be known as sacrament (and the seven sacraments) in the Christian tradition, a development which was, in a way, "canon-ized" by the Council of Trent. That the term was chosen to avoid (other) pagan terms such as *mysteria, arcana, sacra, initia* in Roman usage is important, but not sufficient of itself to explain the dominant position assumed by *sacramentum*.[35] Neither do the positive reasons recounted above. For these reasons we are justified in describing the choice of *sacramentum,* its emergence and predominance, as arbitrary. Arbitrary, that is, not capricious, for there were good and serious reasons for this development, although they were not mathematically pure and absolutely compelling. Capricious would describe a choice or development without (weighty) reasons at all. This is quite in keeping with the finite and historical nature of human beings, creatures that they are, who must often make serious decisions on adequate and reasonable, but not absolute and exclusive grounds. Thus, the reality of God's mysterious saving will, effectively and signfully present in human being and history, came to be called sacrament. Although the term itself may not be scriptural, the reality and theology are.

We have briefly considered the development of sacramental theology in the Church's earliest history. Since our purpose is not a detailed history of the sacraments, we shall briefly highlight only a few later theologians and ideas insofar as they played decisive roles in the development of the theology of the sacraments.

AUGUSTINE

As elsewhere in theology, so was Augustine also most influential in regard to sacramental theology, especially in the West. That he continued the earlier theology is indicated by the combined appearance of mystery and sacrament 2,279 times in his writings.[36] Although these two terms are often paired and used synonymously, there is a growing tendency for mystery to designate the doctrinal and sacrament the ritual dimensions or aspects of the one mystery—God's saving will in Christ and the Church. Sacrament itself is used in a broader and in a narrower sense. Broadly, it designates any reality that points beyond its own immediately perceptible earthly reality to a supernatural, supersensible reality which is beyond the perception of the "fleshly" or unholy person. Israel already enjoyed sacraments, but these only promised salvation, whereas the sacraments of the New Testament give salvation. In the Sacred Scriptures there are many sacraments, that is, profound and mysterious insights which must be believed by all and whose meaning must be investigated by those capable. Similarly, all the ceremonies of the new law can also be regarded as sacraments. In this broader use of the term, the fundamental application is to the "sacrament of the incarnation . . . the sacrament of the divinity and unity of Christ manifest in his flesh."[37] Thus, "Christ is the life of all [the other] sacraments,"[38] especially of the sacrament of the Church with which he is always united,[39] for "the full mystery of all the Scriptures is Christ and the Church, the *Totus Christus.*"[40]

As important as this general sense of sacrament is in Augustine's theology, the more restricted sense is even more important. Indeed, it is predominant and refers most frequently to baptism and Eucharist. Augustine reinforced earlier theology's emphasis on the sign-full-ness of the sacraments. He was aided in this by the philosophy of Plato which emphasized that invisible (incorporeal, immaterial) being is real and true being, that visible being is only (but truly) a reflection and image, a picture of this invisible reality. Invisible *being* is represented in and by visible *beings*. Within this philosophical perspective, sacraments were classified as signs. "A sign is a thing which, by its very nature, is apt to cause something beyond the image it impresses on the senses to come to be known."[41] Thus, [they] "are called sacraments because in them one thing is seen, another is understood."[42] A distinction is made between natural signs (*naturalia*), which are in the very nature of things, apart from any rational or human intervention, and given (*data*) or conventional signs which result from human intersubjectivity and agreement. Of course, in these conventional signs every effort is made to find the most fitting, most inherently "natural" expression for the reality to be sign-ified. The purpose of these conventional signs is to enable that which one person has within to be shared with another. Of all such human signs, the word is the most important, the most wide ranging, the most versatile.

Thus, God, who is the origin of the sacraments, arranged for there to be the greatest possible "natural" affinity between the sacramental signs and the reality they signify: "If the sacraments would not have some similarity with those things of which they are the sacraments, they would not be sacraments at all."[43] Sacraments differ from ordinary signs in that sacraments are "signs which pertain to divine things,"[44] they are "sacred signs."[45] The sacramental sign is complex, consisting of a corporeal or material thing like water (*elementum*) and a word (*verbum*). In regard to baptism, Augustine stated that "the word comes [*accedit*] to the element and a sacrament happens [*fit;* is constituted or made], itself then a visible word"[46] (*verbum visible*). Elsewhere, corporeal sacraments are also called *verba visibilia.*[47] Of course, this word is not just any word, not just a human word. It is the word of faith. In the "sacramental word" the faith of the Church becomes sensibly perceptible, both audible and visible. The sacramental sign is the manifestation of the faith of the Church, which is precisely the Church of the Incarnate Word. This "wordly" origin of the Church along with Augustine's predilection for the word-sign can readily account for the expression "visible word." However, there is also a more precisely sacramental theology element at work here. For Augustine, the reality to which the sacrament-signs point, the reality which they signify, is not immediately and directly the grace which they mediate, but they mystery of Christ[48] (himself *the* "Visible Word"), who, as we have seen, is the source of all grace and sacraments. The sacraments are not merely rememberings or memories by which Christians might recall or think about Christ. Rather, they are in a certain sense (*quodammodo*) that which they contain and that to which they point, that which they signify.[49] The sacraments are a representation (*representatio*) of the saving events of Christ's life, especially his passion and death.[50] Therefore they are truly powerful (*virtus, vis*), for in their visibility the invisible Spirit of God is at work. Certainly, the recipient of the sacrament must be properly disposed and willing to appropriate the grace offered by the sacraments. But the sacraments themselves are power-full because they are filled with the grace of God: "*Gratia, quae sacramentorum virtus est.*"[51] Therefore, the sacraments are not subject to the moral probity of their human ecclesial ministers. The power of the sacraments comes from the triune God Father-Son-Holy Spirit, not from the desire or holiness of the creatures for whom they are intended as the *means* of salvation. They signify, contain and cause salvation, but they are not to be purely and simply equated with salvation. For Augustine, finally, a "sacrament consists in some kind of celebration, in which the commemoration of the deed done happens in such a way that what is to be received piously is also understood to be signified."[52]

The centuries after Augustine were dominated by his theology, much of which was more or less commentary on his writing. It should be noted that not all these commentators agreed unanimously. By and large, though, sacramental theology remained within Augustinian perimeters. Isidore of Seville did give the Augustinian doctrine a certain direction, one which emphasized commemoration and signification less, hiddenness and mystery more.[53] In these centuries was developed the classic formula "a sacrament is the visible form of invisible grace" (*invisibilis gratiae visibilis forma*).

Widely attributed to Augustine, it cannot be found in his own, authentic writings and seems to have been used first by Berengarius.[54] Similar formulas spoke of sacrament as "the visible sign of an invisible grace" and as "the sign of a sacred reality." Berengarius' theory about the real presence of the body and blood of Christ in the Eucharist forced the theologians to greater precision, not only in regard to the Eucharist but also in regard to sacramental theology and terminology in general.[55] Because of his philosophical presuppositions, Berengarius had difficulty understanding the real presence of Christ in the Eucharist. In particular, he was unable to accept the theological explanation of the conversion of the bread and wine into the body and blood of Christ. Transubstantiation was not an acceptable term or explanation for him. As a consequence, he "saw in the Eucharist merely a figure (*figura, similitudo*) of the body and blood of Christ transfigured in Heaven. The words of Christ, 'This is my body,' are . . . To be taken in a metaphorical sense, just as is the phrase: 'Christ is the cornerstone.' "[56] For him, then, the elements of the Eucharist remain what they were before the consecration. In the Mass the consecration effects a conversion "not of the Eucharistic elements themselves [the bread and wine], but of the sentiment of the believer with respect to them. . . . They become the body and blood of Christ in the contemplation of the recipient. . . . The Eucharistic activity begins and ends within the consciousness of the believer himself."[57] The good result of the controversy incited by Berengarius was the clarification of the sacrament as *veritas* (truth) and *figura* (figure, sign). In the sacrament of the Eucharist, and in the others too, there is both symbol and reality. The reality can be understood as Christ, grace, a share in the divine life. The symbol is polyvalent, designating, in the context of the natural elements and the ritual activity, Christ, especially his passion and resurrection, the whole Christ (Church), the nourishment of the life of grace and holiness, the forgiveness of sins, the bond of love which unites all who eat the Eucharist, etc.

In this dispute, then, emphasis was placed on the content or thing (*res*) of the sacraments, to balance the previous emphasis on the sign of the sacraments. Sacraments are truly symbol and grace. The beginnings of later theology's emphasis on the sacraments as *causes* of grace are visible in these discussions. From our point of view, this development is important because it reflects the concern of the Church for the sacraments as signs and means of the real communion of the divine with the human. Thus, the sacraments are not merely artificial signs which give information about God's relationship to the world. Like the incarnation itself, they make that which they signify, God's communion with man, to be present in the world and history. It is in this context that the use of the word substance in regard to the Eucharist must be understood.[58] It is intended to guard against the reduction of the sacraments to the status of *figura* or mere signs, signs which would be without the content (*res sacra*) which they signify. Substance, used primarily in regard to the true and real presence of Christ in the Eucharist, a presence mediated through the *species* of bread and wine, is properly contrasted with appearance or accident. It is a particular philosophical language and conceptualization whose value should be neither exaggerated nor condemned. Its secondary significance is for the other sacraments, which, as we have noted, are protected from being more artificial, informational signs. Although transubstantiation is not used properly of the other sacraments, its use in regard to the Eucharist "guarantees" that the other sacraments contain and/or confer the grace which they signify.

This "realistic" understanding of sacrament is continued in the definitions developed by the Scholastic theologians. Hugh of St. Victor's definition was to become classic: the sacrament is "the sign of a sacred thing . . . because through it something visible is perceived externally, something else invisible is signified internally." However, the sacrament is not merely a sign like other signs. "The sign signifies solely from its institution; the sacrament also represents by virtue of its similitude. Likewise, the sign can [only] signify a thing, but cannot confer it. On the other hand, in the sacrament there is not only signification, but also effectiveness or efficacy (*efficacia*)."[59] In another work Hugh gives a more detailed definition: "Sacrament is a corporeal or material element externally proposed to the senses and representing by similitude, signifying by institution and, by sanctification, containing some invisible and spiritual grace."[60] This definition, which Hugh considers "perfect and proper," can be misleading. The phrase, "containing grace" (*continens*), can, at least out of context, place too much emphasis on the material element, albeit consecrated, of the entire sacramental complex, which embraces action as well as thing. Indeed, subsequent theologians substituted *gra-*

tiam conferens for *gratiam continens*. They were thus able to emphasize the action-al and the causal character of the sacrament, as well as its significational dimension.

The same trend is illustrated by the definition in the collection of authorities (*auctoritates*) known as the *Summa Sententiarum*. A *summa* was an attempt to provide a more orderly and systematic procedure for theological study. It consisted of quotations from previous authorities, that is, significant theological and magisterial sources, as well as summaries of doctrinal positions. The scholastic *summa,* which had predecessors in earlier collections of patristic texts known as *florilegia* or *flores patrum,* flourished in the twelfth century and served as the basis for the flowering of systematic theology in the thirteenth. According to the foundational *Summa Sententiarum* "sacrament is the visible form of the invisible grace granted in it, which, to wit, the sacrament itself confers. For it is not only the sign of a sacred thing, but also its efficacy (*efficacia*)."[61] This definition, widely accepted, was quickly surpassed by that of Peter Lombard, whose *Book of Sentences* quickly became the standard theology textbook on which anyone who wanted to be taken seriously as a theologian had to write a commentary. According to Lombard, "Properly speaking, a sacrament is that which is the sign of God's grace and the form of this invisible grace in such a way that it effects the image and exists as cause."[62] Here the nature of sacrament as not merely sign, but also cause of grace is clearly and emphatically present. This definition also moderates the previous emphasis on the material element and speaks simply of sign, within which an action might also be included. In this spirit, the most widespread sacramental axiom becomes "*Id efficit quod figurat.*" That is, a sacrament effects (causes) that which it symbolizes.

Again, I note that these definitions of sacrament further emphasize the real presence of God in the world and the world's realities. It is not, of course, that the world compels God to be present. It is, rather, that God's desire to be in communion with creation is so intense and so effective that even the things of this world can be mediators and "containers" of this divine presence and communion. In a prayer to the "God of Knowledge," Karl Rahner has admirably summed up this sacramental ontology: "For You (God) are the first and last experience of my life. Yes, truly You Yourself, not Your concept, not Your name, which we have given You. . . . You have become [in baptism] . . . the destiny of my heart. *You have seized me, I have not comprehended You.* You have transformed my very being" (my emphasis).[63] Sacraments as visible signs of invisible grace do not, then, mean that we have taken hold of and overcome God. It is just the opposite. Sacraments mean that God has seized the beings he originally created and made them even greater means and signs of the divine communion with the human. Of this entire sacramental doctrine, ontology and salvation there is hardly a better shorthand summary than St. Thomas Aquinas' definition: "*Signum rei sacrae inquantum est sanctificans homines*"[64] (A sacrament is the sign of a sacred thing insofar as it sanctifies human beings). According to William van Roo, the "it" refers not immediately and precisely to sign, but to sacred thing (*res sacra*).[65] Thus, sacrament is an incarnation of the "grace which makes human beings holy."

The Councils of Florence and Trent gave the sacramental theology of St. Thomas Aquinas a sort of official status in the Church. Proper appreciation of this fact requires awareness that neither St. Thomas nor these councils had solved all the problems of sacramental theology. Neither had they provided complete, fully articulated systematic treatments. Many questions were left untreated, many inconsistencies were left unreconciled. Strangely enough, even these councils did not offer an official, strictly dogmatic definition of sacrament.[66] And, according to van Roo, no such universally binding definition has been provided by the consensus of the theologians.[67]

Has, then, nothing or, at best, very little been accomplished by centuries of theological reflection on the religious tradition which began with Abraham and which was given a decisive articulation by Jesus and which has been handed on by and since the apostles? Do we still wander about in a wasteland of ignorance or wallow about in a swamp of equivocity? Does sacrament mean everything and, therefore, nothing at the same time? Is it at best a nonsense, at worst a pagan seduction from the (biblical) revelation and truth? We can and may easily and peacefully answer in the negative. We have already seen that an unexpected advantage of the word "sacrament" is that its very etymological and semasiological history indicates the ability of God and salvation to be present even in the vicissitudes of finite, contingent human being and history. That is, even a word with a diffuse and checkered history like *sacramentum* can serve the revelation of God, the salvation of humanity. It can be transformed into a choice, preferred theological term to designate the reality of theandric communion of God with his human creation and creatures. Of course, the term is not univocal, but then how many of our really important human words are? If sacrament is not Cartesianly clear and distinct, neither is it equivocal. In regard to *juramentum* or oath, St. Thomas points out that sacrament is used analogically. Although sacrament is used diversely and although it is indeed applied to different things, it designates these different objects insofar as they all have a diverse reference to (or various relationships with) *one single object or thing which is a holy thing (analogice, scilicet secundum diversam habitudinem ad aliquid unum, quod est res sacra).*[68] The diversity of the term and reality, sacrament, and the unicity of the reality to which sacrament refers, namely *res sacra,* has an added unexpected benefit: it focuses attention on the most important thing, namely the source, cause and goal of all holiness, the holy thing, God and God's grace.

The many-meaninged sacrament is clearly exposed as (merely) means toward an end. And this end, this *res sacra,* is God, who is essentially holy and whose holiness calls for and enables all other beings to be holy (Lev 19:2),each in its own way. One of these ways is known as sacrament. Finally, sacrament's analogical nature as a many-meaninged term and reality also makes it apt to reflect the universality and unity of salvation history in its entirety. This salvation history itself is discrete both spatially and temporarily, geographically and chronologically. In this context, Thomas Aquinas notes that, "as Augustine says . . . different sacraments are fitting (*congruunt*) for different ages, as, indeed, different ages are signified by different words, namely present, past and future."[69] The greater specification which may have been achieved in the signification and sign-full-ness of sacraments throughout history does not mean that the earlier sacraments were not at all significative of the grace of Christ. Or, put positively as Thomas does, later Christian sacraments enjoy and offer a "more explicit/expressive signification of the grace of Christ, through which the human race is sanctified" (*expressiorem significationem gratiae Christi, per quam humanum genus sanctificatur*).[70] Likewise, their causality of grace is also more tightly bound up with Christ as the source of all sacramental grace and life. However, in addition to these more expressly Christian sacraments, there are also other sacraments which are different, but still truly sacramental. Sacrament is, then, truly apt to designate the whole of salvation history as well as its particular, specific objects and contents as the objective incarnations and signful embodiments of grace, of God's saving will for creation. Against this general background of the history and meaning of the term sacrament, which describes the incarnation of God's powerful will and mysterious plan to save humanity through Jesus Christ, his Church, and its specific, objective realities, we can now proceed to consider the seven special sacraments and their double use and function, namely "divine worship and human sanctification."[71]

WORSHIP

The entire history of salvation is a history of the relationship between God the Creator and man the creature. Another word used to describe this history is religion. I recall our definition of religion as the organization of one's life, individually and socially, on the basis of values and insights perceived to be ultimate. We also noted that religion has a theoretical dimension (our thinking and understanding) and a practical dimension (our acting and behaving). Worship is considered to be the primary and principal act of religion. As such, it implies the theoretical dimension of religion, for it implies or presupposes an understanding of God as the ultimate truth and good. To understand why Thomas Aquinas speaks of the sacraments as both divine worship and human sanctification, we must recall a few general truths about religion as such and the Judeo-Christian religion's understanding of the God to be worshipped and God's relationship to the world to be sanctified.

We can begin by summarizing Thomas Aquinas' treatment of religion in the *Summa*.[72] Whatever may be the etymological origin of the term "religion," and whatever its precise definition, it is concerned with the order or relationship of creatures to God the Creator (a. 1). In religion we acknowledge, honor and reverence God because of the divine excellence (a. 2, 4). We do this either by presenting something to God or by accepting something from God (a. 3). An offering to God is called, in general, cult (adoration, worship; a 5). Strictly speaking, religion is concerned not immediately and directly with God himself, but with the things which pertain to and relate to God. Hence, worship, which is the experienced and expressed relationship of human beings to God, is the proper act and expression of religion (a. 6). Now we come to the crucial part of these considerations for our particular purpose.

Thomas asks whether divine worship has some sort of exterior or external act (a. 7). He begins his answer by quoting Psalm 84:2, "My heart and my flesh sing for joy to the living God."[73] He understands this verse to mean that "as interior acts belong to the heart, so do exterior acts pertain to the members" (basically synonymous with body, flesh, although each has its own peculiar overtones). He then emphasizes that "we show reverence and honor to God not for his own sake, for he is already replete with glory, to which nothing can be added by creatures, but for our own sake, because, namely, when and insofar as we reverence and honor God, our mind (we) is properly ordered (*subiicitur*) to him, and in this consists our perfection." In Thomas' understanding, it is clear that the worship of the divine God and the holiness of the human worshiper coincide. There is, we could say, recalling Trinitarian and Christological terminology, a perichoresis of divine worship and human sanctification. This worship and sanctification are properly done only when the nature of God, man and their relationship is respected. Thus, "in order for the human mind to be in communion with God, it needs the guidance and assistance (*manuductione*) of sensible things." In a sense, we are taken by the hand by the things of this world and led to the proper worship of God, the result of which is our own sanctification. Among these sensible things are to be found what Christians call sacraments. Although the interior acts of religion are primary and principal, the secondary and subordinate external acts are nonetheless appropriate and necessary, for these "external acts and works are presented to God as signs of interior and spiritual works, which God finds *per se* acceptable." The principle of incarnation operates in two directions. From God giving, the invisible divine grace takes visible form in many ways throughout salvation history. From man receiving, the invisible grace received is celebrated in many different visible forms and rituals. Here the intimate affinity of the incarnational and sacramental principles is clearly visible.

In these few lines, Thomas sums up much of the sign-full, sacramental theology we have related thus far. The key is always God, God's relationship with us and ours with God. In this relationship, our very being is religious, and this religious being is exercised (performed, put into practice) by our actions, which, since we are bodily and spiritual, are also visible and invisible, exterior and interior. Our "spiritual" actions are also "sensible." Most importantly, our religious being and actions are not alienating and oppressing. They are our very fulfillment and perfection. Religion is not the demotion, but the promotion of human being. Why? Because the relationship between the God-Creator and the man-creature is one communion, effective and symbolic. Therefore our acknowledgement of the excellence of God is simultaneously and inevitably the acknowledgement of our own excellence. And that is also why our acknowledgement of God's superior excellence is also necessarily the sanctification of our own excellence, however less than God's it may be.

Here we need only recall that in the Judeo-Christian tradition God is not the annihilator but the Creator, not the destroyer but the Enabler (Wis 1:11–13). As we have seen, God is the great philanthropist[74] (Tit 2:11, 3:4), in Jesus even the friend of sinners (Ez 18:23; Mt 11:19), in the Holy Spirit their powerful forgiver (and forgiveness: Lk 24:47–49 with Acts 1:8; 2:38). Indeed, precisely because of our creation by God, there is *no* "infinite gap between God and man . . . yawning abyss."[75] Quite the contrary. Because of creation there is communion between the divine and the human, so that the latter is truly the image and likeness of the former. God and man are meant for each other. They are friends who walk together in the cool of the evening breezes. Even human sin has not been able to rupture this theandric covenant and friendship. In spite of all this evidence to the contrary, some theologians persist, perversely it seems to me, to insist that God is *totaliter aliter*—totally other, entirely other. This contention of theirs may have some value as hyperbolic rhetoric to guard against flippancy in regard to the divinely created and graced theandric familiarity to which the entire Judeo-Christian tradition testifies. In truth, though, God is not entirely other than we, who, after all, are created in his image and likeness. We are not like the Jains of Hinduism who worship the Tirthankaras who are so distant from each earthly creature that they neither know nor care that they are being worshiped.[76] Given the truth of God's creation, how could God be entirely other than we, with whom he is in communion? God is indeed entirely and totally other, but only than nothing and evil or sin. James Ross is correct when he suggests that God is "significantly other:"[77]

> Furthermore, he [St. Thomas] also argues that if God is to have such properties as self-existence and omnipotence, He must be a significantly different kind of thing from anything in our experience. . . .
> I have said here "significantly different" because Aquinas is not commited to the absurd notion that God is entirely different from creatures. In fact, the analogy theory is designed to permit expression in language of the similarity between God and creatures while protecting our discourse from a claim that God is directly similar to creature.

This is also what the Fourth Lateran Council (1215) meant when it said that a "similarity (likeness) cannot be asserted between the Creator and the creature unless greater dissimilarity (difference) is also asserted."[78] Were we totally different from God, or totally the same, we could not worship God. In the second case we would not need to. In the first we could not, for we would not even know that there was a God to worship. It is, rather, our communion with God which makes us able to know, enjoy and worship God. Thus, worship is clearly not a sign of our worth-less-ness, but of our worthness. Our worship of God is a sign not only of God's worth-ship, but also of our own worth-ship as well.

Yes, I said "worth-ship." This word is no longer familiar. But it is the origin of our word "worship." It described the worth or value which someone or something enjoyed. There are traces of this meaning in the language by which royalty, civil or ecclesiastical, is addressed: Your eminence, Your Highness, Your Lordship. From English plays we can recall people being greeted as "Your Worship." It was customary for such a greeting to be accompanied by a gesture like genuflection or kissing the hand. In these actions and words we have an excellent illustration of ritual and symbol. These actions and words were not merely external tags or labels. They were the sensible embodiment of the inner being of the person performing them. In the course of history the language describing this entire activity changed. The emphasis was no longer on the worth of the person being honored but on the activity of the person doing the honoring. Worth-ship became worship. And this latter word gradually came to designate the action acknowledging somebody's worth rather than the worth-ness of the person itself. Henceforth the word refers to the inner attitude and external expression whereby we respond to the dignity (the worth-ship) we perceive in another. Adoration, another word for worship, comes from the Latin, and means literally to speak to. When we worship and adore, we speak to or toward the adored one. What do we say? That we acknowledge his or her goodness, value, worth.

Some philosophers have deemed worship humanly demeaning and destructive because they have conceived God as a tyrant.

For example, Friedrich Nietzsche thought that "only when there is no God will man become free."[79] In the same vein, Jean-Paul Sartre thought that human beings could never be free as long as they believed that there was a god or gods.[80] On the other hand, the Judeo-Christian tradition thinks that we can be at all only because there is God—of course, not just any God, but God Father-Son-Holy Spirit. This God does not enslave us to himself, but frees us from ontological nothingness in creation and harmartiological nothingness in redemption. This God is primarily Creator, for this God both gives and forgives created being.[81] It is precisely this God and this giving-forgiving relationship which we celebrate in our worship in general and in our sacraments in particular.

In our religion this understanding of God, God's nature and God's relationship to the world is the theory. It is the faith which we believe and profess. Our profession of this faith is the practice of our religion. This practice has two dimensions. One is ethics—the way we acknowledge God's superior excellence in our daily lives and in our behavior in general. The other is ritual—the way we acknowledge God's superior excellence in certain special, sign-ful celebrations. Together, these two professions constitute our worship. We must always be careful, lest worship be restricted to formal prayer and ritual worship, as is sometimes—often?—done. Since there is but one God for all of creation, adequate and proper worship must include both our everyday ethical behavior and our special ritual behavior as well. Since the God we worship is precisely our Creator, and since we exist at all only insofar as we exist in, better, as relationship with this God, our acknowledgement of God's excellence is the acknowledgement of our own excellence. To recognize and honor God's worth-ship is to recognize our own. For this reason Karl Rahner was right on target when he contantly warned in his lectures at Innsbruck that one does not make God greater by making man lesser. And St. Thomas was also right on target when he said that the sacraments are for divine worship and human sanctification, precisely because the worship of God is the sanctification of man.

To describe this positive, benign and enabling relationship from the point of view of God, the Christian tradition has decided to call God "Father." Unfortunately, our patriarchal past is such that the word "Father" is not well received by all. However, the term "God the Father" need not, as such, have any patriarchal overtones or connotations. Since God is not bodily or biological, the term God the Father cannot, as we have already emphasized, be invoked in favor of male sexism and chauvinism. Rather, as we have also seen, God is called or named Father precisely because God enables being, which had not been before and which cannot be on its own, to be.[82] And having enabled it to be in the first place, God continues to nourish and promote this being. The designation of God the Creator as Father also protects creation, especially human, from being sourced in, beholden to, and the image and likeness of chaos, blind fate, capricious chance, divine mistake, unbending necessity and inexorable retribution.[83] For the Judeo-Christian tradition God the Creator and Redeemer is Father precisely because of the divine power, wisdom and love which enable the triune God to be the *lieto fattore,* the joyful, joyous maker of the world, precisely as material, corporeal, sensual and sensuous.[84]

Therefore we have ritual worship and sacraments which are the visible forms of invisible grace. It is important to emphasize the theological as well as anthropological origin of ritual and sacrament. Our sensible worship with material things is possible, proper and necessary precisely because we believe in this "happily creating God." People who accept the anthropological agreement for visible, ritual worship because human beings express their inner feelings in external actions might nevertheless object that theologically such worship is at best superfluous, perhaps even blasphemous. How could material being ever be fitting for worship of the spiritual God? Platonic and neo-

Platonic philosophers and theologians might think thus, since matter exists so far down on the scale of being. Indeed, the material human body (*soma*) could be regarded as the tomb (*sema*) or prison of the immaterial soul.[85] For the Gnostics the whole material would was essentially flawed, a mistake which proved that Yahweh, its Creator, could not be the true God.[86] In fact, matter was basically the "condensation of the original failing . . . the crystallization of fault and guilt in the visible realm."[87] In this perspective holiness can be achieved only by abstention from this world, salvation by flight from it. Religions rooted in this mentality could only illogically have ritual worship and sacraments as visible forms of invisible grace.

In contrast to Gnosticism's "cosmic fault" and "cosmic pessimism,"[88] Christianity has spoken of the "cosmic liturgy."[89] One can speak of a "cosmic liturgy" because of "the cosmic history of grace."[90] This universal cosmic liturgy does not eliminate or trivialize our local here-and-now liturgies. Rather, these particular liturgical celebrations enable the cosmic liturgy to be celebrated with greater concentration and intensity on certain occasions, as befits our human nature. In the "cosmic liturgy" the theological and anthropological justifications of ritual worship and sacrament come together. Because the cosmos is God's to begin with, cosmic beings can certainly be used in the human recognition and honor of this God. Since human beings are the cosmic image and likeness of this God, they can and must use cosmic things in their worship. Otherwise, they would be disrespectful of God, of the cosmos God created, and of themselves. Acosmic worship is both vain and sinful, for it would exclude from human nature's second act behavior what God had put in human nature's first act being.[91] These considerations emphasize once more the sacramental communion ontology which we have emphasized throughout this book. Visible signful celebrations are not impositions on God, but God's expressions of himself and his saving will and plan for the human creation originally made in the image and likeness of God. In this creation, material and sensible being plays its own proper role as mediator and manifestation of God's communion with the non-Godly. Hence there are sacraments and sensible, ritual worship not only because of human nature (a composite of invisible soul-spirit and visible body), but also because of the divine nature (the friendly Creator of the material cosmos, which is the visible image and likeness of the invisible God). So, once again we are brought to the perfectly theandric being, to the hypostatic union of the human and the divine, Jesus Christ.

Before we proceed to Jesus as the "founder" or "author" of the sacraments of the Christian Church, we must briefly consider Jesus himself as sacramental and ritual person. We know that Jesus was familiar with ritual worship. He himself went to the temple to pray. He also gave a classic admonition about the relationship of external and internal worship: "So then, if you are bringing your offering to the altar and there remember that your brother has something against you, leave your offering there before the altar, go and be reconciled with your brother first, and then come back and present your offering'' (Mt 5:23). Jesus also upbraided hypocrites, who honor God ''only with lip-service, while their hearts are far from [God]. The worship they offer . . . is worthless'' (Mt 15:7–9, quoting Is 29:13). Finally, we must also keep in mind Jesus' many admonitions about the relationship between ritual worship and ethical worship, both of which are necessary, both of which must coincide, in order for the excellence of God to be properly acknowledged and honored (for example, Mt 15:1–9:23).

Of course, Jesus not only lectured about this, he also practiced it, manifesting it in his life in general and in certain actions in particular. Until now we have not spoken of sacrifice, which is a crucial concept and reality in religion in general and in Christianity in particular. How often and spontaneously we speak of Christ's sacrifice on the cross and the sacrifice of the cross. However, as important as this crossly sacrifice of Jesus was, it can be unduly emphasized. Furthermore, certain aspects of this crossly sacrifice can also be mis-emphasized. For example, in spite of all the preaching rhetoric to the contrary, the pain of the crucifixion is not of supreme significance. In fact, it is strictly secondary and subordinate. Likewise, the degree of difficulty involved in Jesus' sacrifice on the cross is not the precisely important element. Difficult things or actions are not necessarily meaningful, important or even good, for that matter. Of course, sometimes good actions are both painful and difficult, and then it is virtuous to endure and persevere. But the key element, the fundamental element, is always the intrinsic value, goodness and worth of the action itself. Even death, even the deathly sacrifice of Christ on the cross, precisely as deathly, is not the primary and principal characteristic of Christ's vocation and mission. It was not precisely Christ's dying by which he acknowledged God's excellence and offered himself to the Father as a pleasing sacrifice. It was, rather, by doing his Father's will which, of course, could not be done in this case unless Jesus was willing to die. The significance of Jesus' sacrifice on the cross is that it was the way in which Jesus acknowledged God's excellence, and the way that he manifested this unconditional acknowledgement in the concrete circumstances of history.

Sacrifice is not primarily slaughter or destruction. It is rather *the* chief act, really and symbolically, of religion and religious worship. Sacrifice is the recognition of the worth of another and the affirmation of this worth through the dedication of oneself to the worthy one. This dedication is usually symbolized in some kind of action. A preferred symbolic action has been the destruction of something, especially something living. This destruction symbolizes that the life of the worshiper, the sacrificer, is completely dedicated to the worthy one.

However, it is clear that this total dedication could also be present without the symbolic destruction of an animal. Sacrifice as recognition and total dedication can take place in one's daily life without any ritual. Indeed, it must. The sacrifice of daily living will naturally seek some kind of symbolic ritual expression. Nevertheless, the ritual is not the sacrifice. The Epistle to the Hebrews (10:5–7) emphasizes this when it says, and this is what Jesus said, on coming into the world:

> You who wanted no sacrifice or obligation prepared a body for me.
> You took no pleasure in holocausts or sacrifices for sin; then I said,
> just as I was commanded in the scroll of the book, "God, here I am!
> I am coming to obey your will."

According to Jesus, then, human beings are sacrificial and priestly by and in their very lives—as long as they live for and not against God. Jesus was not priest and sacrifice only on the cross. His entire life was priestly and sacrificial, for it was completely given over to the recognition of God's worth-ship and the expression of this recognition in his daily life. That is what "to obey your (God's) will" means.

Sin made Jesus's sacrifice difficult at times and finally even bloody and destructive. But that is because sin is destructive and deadly—not because sacrifice is! Since we live in a sinful world, our worship will also have to deal with sin. But once again, sacrifice is not because of sin.

Sacrifice is because we are in communion with the perfect worth-ship of God, not because we are sinfully out of communion. Our worship and sacrifice must never become preoccupied with our guilt and sin. They must always be preoccupied with God's gift and grace, our creaturely communion with God. This is always the primary element, not our sinful fall and flight.

To emphasize once more, sacrifice is in no wise dependent on sin. This is because worship does not depend on sin. Worship is the acknowledgement and celebration of our relationship with God. Our relationship to God is not based on sin. It is based on the gift-giving nature of God and his communion with his creation. As Karl Rahner insists, "Our guilt and sin alone are not the horizon or context within which our lives and salvation happen. By itself the experience of being lost or fallen is not sufficient to call forth the expectation of redemption and it is certainly not able to explain how such redemption is to be understood."[92]

If this is so, neither worship nor sacrifice can be the attempt to placate an angry God. In any case, it is clear that we cannot make, cause or compel anyone to forgive us. The word itself tells us that *forgiveness* is a gift. It is not earned, but given. If this is the case among humans, how much more so between man and God. So, sacrifice is not something we do to make God forgive us and like us. Not even the crossly sacrifice of Christ could do this.

To quote Rahner once again, "Because the saving will of God exists, the cross and resurrection of Jesus exist—this is true. Because the cross exists, God's saving will for us exists—this is *not* true. God is not transformed from a wrathful, vengeful justice to a forgiving love by the cross. Rather, the originally and unfathomably forgiving God, who communicates himself to the world in spite of its guilt, thereby overcoming this guilt, evokes the event of the cross into existence.'' Further on the same context he says that ''the cross enjoys a primordial originary causality (*ursakramental Ursachlichkeit*) for the salvation of all men insofar as it mediates this salvation through the saving grace which is effectively present throughout the world. The cross is the sign of this saving grace and its insuperable victory in the world. The efficacy of the cross lies therein, that it is the *ursakramental* sign of grace.''[93]

Why is Christ the perfect priest and perfect sacrifice? Not because he died on the cross, but because he is the perfect dedication of human being to the divine being. Of course, had Jesus refused the cross, his dedication would not have been perfect. But this perfect union with God enabled him to undergo the cross, not vice versa. Even apart from sin and the cross, Christ would still have been the perfect priest and victim, hence the perfect sacrifice, hence perfect worship. But on the cross Christ's perfect sacrifice achieved visibility in history—in his own personal history, in the history of his people, Israel, and in the history of the world. The above considerations clarify the relationship between the interior and exterior dimensions of religion and worship, sacrifice and sacrament. Because of the Judeo-Christian ontology, it is not a question of the visible material forcing the invisible spiritual to do or become something. Rather, the visible material is the expression of the invisible spiritual and its communication of itself to the other.[94] This is consistently the case, from the beginning all through salvation history. The creation of the visible and material world by the invisible spiritual God clearly indicates that the material does not compel the spiritual, but is its expression, form, *Gestalt*—in our language, its sign, its sacrament. This continues through the incarnation, the Church and the individual sacraments of this Church. Of course, these sacramental incarnations of the grace of God's saving will are not univocally identical. But they are similar, analogical.

Creatures do not compel God, they do not cause God to become gracious, as if he were not already so. This applies to the cosmos, to the human nature of Jesus and the visible forms of the sacraments. Neither our rituals in general nor our sacraments in particular compel God. They do not even compel us, although, as we have seen, they lead and guide *(manuductione)* us in our relationship to God, in our religion and worship. What ritual does do is bring invisible divine grace and invisible human response (faith) into social, public sensibility and graspability (*Greifbarkeit*). Sacraments are the social and public intersubjectivizing of the personal grace and faith which are divine gift and human response.[95] We can say that all religions do this, in their own ways. One of the most striking manifestations of this is the ritual of atheistic Marxist, communistic nations. Their ''spirit'' expresses itself in material objects and, thus expressing itself, reinforces its presence among the ''true believers''— the members of the party and the citizens of the state.[96]

In a similar way, Jesus' faith (Heb 12:2) expressed itself in various ways throughout his life—his visits to the temple, his prayers, his healings, his sermons, his gathering and instructing disciples, his meals with disciples and even sinners, especially his last supper, yes, even his crucifixion and death on the cross. But we may not stop here; we must also include his resurrection, for even this was no merely invisible, interior, spiritual event. It too was sacramental, for the victorious saving will of God in Jesus ''showed itself by many demonstrations: for forty days he continued to appear to them'' (Acts 1:3) in ordinary (Jn 20:14–15, 20) and emphatic (Jn 20:27) ways. Even his ascension did not purely and simply ''invisibilize'' this incarnate saving will of God, this sacramental Jesus (Jn 14:9; 12:45), for he left memorial life-giving signs—sacraments—of himself as the bread of life and life of the world (Lk 22:19–20; Jn 6).

Therefore, M.-D. Chenu correctly emphasizes that ''Christianity is not constituted soley by the moralizing of human life, but chiefly by the sacramentalizing of certain essential acts by which it is constituted as the mystical body of Christ.''[97] He also correctly emphasizes that ''the Church is not only a society of cult and worship. It is also a communion of faith, hope and charity.'' And now we have come full circle, back to our explanation of religion as the organization of one's *whole* life—ethics (or morals) and ritual, which together, and only together, constitute the *proper* and adequate recognition and honor of God's excellence: worship. Or, in Christian terminology, our faith, hope and charity, which together constitute the fundamental act or performance (*Vollzug*) of our Christian being/life,[98] exercises and expresses itself one way in events of our daily, everyday life, another way in special ritual, liturgical, ceremonial celebration.

Although rite or ritual usually designates one part of human life, it can also describe the entirety of human life. This is because human life always expresses itself in external, visible, sensibly perceptible actions. These actions are both impromptu and spontaneous on the one hand, planned and patterned on the other. Spontaneous expressions readily repeat themselves and thus establish themselves in patterns. Peter Berger has gone so far as to maintain that people can survive the intensity of the demands of daily living only because they ritualize it.[99] There is a further general sense of rite or ritual which is important for our considerations. It leads right into the Christian sacraments as such.

St. Thomas says that ''entire rite of the Christian religion is derived from the priesthood of Christ.''[100] In the next chapter we shall treat priesthood in greater detail. Here it suffices to note that, like worship, priesthood has a wider (daily life) and narrower (ritual) meaning. We have customarily associated priesthood with ritual worship, but are learning that it is equally, yet differently applicable to the daily worship of God. Both ''priests'' offer worship and sacrifice. Through various sacraments we are given various participations in the worship—sacrifice and priesthood—of Jesus. We are thus enabled to share in both the daily and the ritual worship that Christ offered his heavenly Father and that he has shared with us in and through the Church. This is our faith, which we live in faith, hope and charity and celebrate in the sacraments. Chenu's statement means more than that we human Christians invent our own signs to signify our faith. Its fullest import is that we, precisely as Christians, constitute the Church which is the sacrament of Christ. Not only in the seven special sacraments or in all the individual ritual, sacramental actions of the Church are we sacramental. Rather, our very being as the Church makes us *to be* sacramental. Our Christian religion not only has sacraments and rites. It is sacramental and ritual. And these sacraments, this entire religion/Church "rite is derived from the priesthood of Christ." That is, it is the sacrament of Christ's priestly being and behavior throughout time and space. This is the faith which we invisibly believe in our minds and practice in our actions, both ethical and ritual (sacramental).

These considerations are also valuable because they encourage us to keep the faith and sacraments in constant tandem. St. Thomas emphasizes the mutuality and complementarity of faith and sacraments throughout his theology. These two words (and realities, of course) describe our relationship with Christ, our connection to his saving work, and communion with his saved (resurrected) and saving person. Thomas insists that "the power of Christ's passion is shared (*copulatur nobis*) with us through the faith and the sacraments of faith."[101] A contemporary theologian, Edward Schillebeeckx, points out that St. Thomas was not a solitary exception: "In continuity with the preceeding tradition St. Thomas never hypostasized the Church's sacramental principle and system. Therefore he always speaks in one breath of 'faith and sacrament' and of the 'sacrament of faith.'[102] Likewise, according to St. Thomas, the sacraments are the "insignia of the Church."[103] They sign-ify the Church, revealing its nature through its actions. Recall the philosophical axiom that the actions (the "to act") of a thing follows its nature (its "to be"). We have seen this in John's Gospel in regard to Christ whose actions represent his "beloved sonship" with God (Jn 10:25–38). As the person Jesus is the sacrament of God, so are his actions/works the sacraments of his person. As the Church is the sacrament of Christ, so are its actions likewise sacraments—of the Church and through the Church, of Christ. As ritual, a sacrament is "a certain profession of faith through exterior signs."[104] Again, "All ceremonies are certain professions (*protestationes*) of the faith which constitutes the interior cult of worship of God. Thus, a human being can profess his faith in deeds or actions as well as words."[105] St. Bonaventure also insists that "in their (the sacraments) reception there is a profession of faith not only in word but also in deed (action)."[106]

The faith, then, is incarnated, incorporated, given visible form in the ritual celebrations known as sacraments. This is true for us and the Church now. It was also true of Christ then. We need to recall that faith, religion, worship all, each in its own way, describe the relation of someone to God. This relationship, which is in our personal interior (Thomas speaks of the *mens* or mind), expresses itself externally in words and other signs. Human intersubjectivity, as Augustine already clearly recognized, requires communication in signs and words. Jesus as truly divine and also truly human was not exempt from this human existential factor. If he wanted to share his experience of God with others, he had to use words and other signs, whether these other signs were ordinary everyday actions or special symbolic acts. In this context we may and must understand Jesus as the "institutor" of the sacraments. The question of Jesus' role in the institution of the sacraments is parallel to the question of his founding of the Church. In both cases the Church has insisted that Jesus is the origin, source, founder, author, *conditor* of the sacraments (DS 1601, 3439). However, official Church documents so insisting decline to provide explanations how these terms are to be understood or how Jesus actually performed this function. This is helpful, for it indicates that a strict, historical chronicle of explicitly instituting actions by Jesus and described in equally explicit proof texts in the New Testament is not to be expected and is not what the council has in mind. Even the Council of Trent did not stipulate the details of Christ's institution of the sacraments, allowing theologians to speak of mediate and immediate institution. In the first case Jesus would have empowered others to determine, in the second he would have himself determined the significance, efficacy and rites of the grace to be given in the sacraments.

More recent sacramental theology has been concerned less with this kind of historical institution by Christ and has concentrated on a more sacramental-ontological explanation.[107] It has emphasized Jesus himself as the originary and primordial sacrament, the Church as the fundamental sacrament and the individual (seven) sacraments as logical and consequent, from both theological/Christological and historical points of view, articulations of this Church-sacramentality. Here we need to recall what we said earlier about Jesus as founder of the Church: Wach's emphasis that no "founder" of a religion really wanted to found a religion. He wanted, rather, to share his religious experience with others; Leeuw's emphasis that a religion has many founders, and that a single person can play many "founding" roles.[108]

How, then, did Jesus found or institute or author the sacraments? Let us first note how misleading the term "author" is here. Every author, of course, wants to be read, wants an audience. Why else write (although some do apparently write only for themselves; such rare exceptions, however, only strengthen the point I want to make)? Although the author must have an audience in mind, the audience itself does not participate directly and immediately in the writing of the book. The audience must wait until the book has been completed and is already finished before it can read the book. In a true sense, the book can exist on its own, without readers. It can be written without being read. It certainly does not require the readers' participation in order to come into existence. Such is not, however, the case with the sacraments. It is, therefore, not good to speak of Christ as the author of the sacraments. Christ alone, by himself, is not the founder of the sacraments. There is an equally

necessary (not equally important) co-founder, for Jesus cannot found or institute the sacraments without the participation and cooperation of those others
known as disciples.

How, then, did the sacraments come into experience? First of all, Jesus
has an experience of God. He had to decide whether to keep this experience to
himself, all for himself, or to share it with others. We know that, in keeping
with his nature (Phil 2:6–11), Jesus decided to share his experience of God
with others. In order to do this, he had to objectify his experience, that is, put
it into concepts, words and other signs.[109] We know that Jesus did this because
he talked with his followers, preached to crowds, helped people in need, acted
ritually and symbolically (at least on some occasions). Some people who heard
him preach and act became his disciples. They received these objectifications
of Jesus' experience of God, preserved them, adapted them to their situation
and handed them on. In doing this, they kept the memory and tradition of
Christ alive in the world and thus became the Church. The objectifications
which they received and handed on entered into the very constitution of this
Church, into its life and being. In the Church, the spoken words objectifying
Jesus' religious experiences passed over into and became the Sacred Scriptures (the Bible); the ordinary daily actions of Jesus, his daily life, passed over
into and became the faith, hope and charity (religion as ethics-worship) of the
Church and its members; the symbolic actions of Jesus passed over into and
became the sacraments (religion as ritual worship). This is all intended as
commentary on and conclusion from such famous statements in sacramental
theology as: Augustine's "There is no other sacrament of God than Christ";[110]
Leo the Great's "What was visible (*conspicuum*) in Christ passed over into the
sacraments of the Church";[111] Ambrose's "You have shown yourself to me
face to face, O Christ; in your sacraments I have found you."[112] It is intended
to account for Jesus' statements about his real and true post-ascension presence among us, in many ways, until the ends and the end of the world. It assumes, most of all, the truth of the hypostatic union, so that Jesus' being and
actions have a greater ontological depth and intensity than those of others who
are indeed in communion with God, but not hypostatically so. Thus, we
should most properly say not that Jesus *has* an experience of God, although
this is true. We should say that Jesus *is* an experience of God by the non-
Godly. Indeed, Jesus is *the* experience of God by the non-Godly. Hence his
general objectification of his experience of God is also qualitatively (ontologically) different than and superior to ordinary people's objectifications of their
experience of God, as are his individual objectifications. This difference carries over into the intersubjective sharing and reception of these objectifications
by his disciples, so that they are not mere mental memories recalling an absent
Jesus. Rather, they are the visible sacramental signs making and signifying the
Christly experience of God present in the history of the world in and through
the Church, which is itself the sacramental memory and tradition of Jesus and
his (objectified) experience of God. In its being and activity the Church legit-

imately gives special status to some of these preserved and handed on objectifications because of their greater proximity/affinity/intimacy with Christ and
because of their greater relevance to the concrete conditions of social and individual human life. One of these special objectifications is called the Bible as
the inspired Sacred Scriptures; another is the seven sacraments as effective *ex
opere operato*. This Latin phrase means that the sacraments have a special efficacy because and insofar as they are the actions of the risen Christ operating
in and through the Church as itself the official sacrament of Christ. The term
has nothing to do with magic or superstition. It is, rather, the term that developed in history to describe the Church's faith that Jesus Christ is not only truly
the hypostatic union of the human and the divine, but also that this union per-
dures effectively throughout time and space in the Church and in a special
manner in some actions of the Church. It is a way of explicitly stating the faith
that the sacraments of the faith are divinely given and effective ways of preserving and promoting the communion of God with man. Sacraments as *ex opere operato* do not compel God to do what he didn't want to do in the first
place, nor do they excuse us from doing what we are supposed to do—rather,
they enable us to do it. To speak of Jesus as the founder of the sacraments as
we have done reflects the fundamental conviction of our entire book, namely,
that the relation between the divine and the human is of one of divinely initiated and effected sacramental communion. To emphasize that the disciples are
co-founders is to remain true to the Judeo-Christian and biblical insight that,
although human being comes entirely from and is entirely dependent upon
God, it is not merely passive in regard to God. This would be a negative evaluation of God's own creative power. As Thomas Aquinas argued, "The perfection of the effect manifests the perfection of the cause. To denigrate the
perfection of creatures is, therefore, to denigrate the perfection of the divine
power."[113] Passivity is not the proper term to describe the human relationship
with God. Receptivity is, for the human being cooperates receptively with
God precisely on the basis of the creation.[114] Hence, we may describe Jesus as
the initiating founder, the disciples as the receptive founder of the sacraments.
The initiative is always God's, but the effect of the divine initiative is human
capacity, receptivity.

God always respects the contingent creation which has come forth from
the divine power and wisdom. Thus, we can move from the theo-Christo-an-
thropological origin of the sacraments to their cultural and historical origins.
The New Testament makes considerable effort to emphasize that Jesus was not
a strange creature from outer space, neither God nor man. It emphasizes the
precisely historical and cultural conditionedness of Jesus (e.g., Lk 1:5; 3:1; Mt
2:23; Gal 4:3–6). In their own way these concrete cultural and historical factors are as important as the theological and Christological factors we have already examined. Since religion exists only in human beings, religion, like
them, always reflects as well as inspires the given culture of any age and place.

Paul Tillich was fond of saying: "Religion is the substance of culture and culture is the form of religion.''[115] Insofar as creation established congeniality between invisible Creator and visible creature, no material creatures as such would be excluded from use in ritual worship. Hence, the sacraments which originated in Jesus could use any material things and sensible rituals which the human mind could create.[116] On the other hand, since Jesus did not exist just in general, not just anywhere or anytime, but in a given place at a given time, we may expect the sacraments which he and his disciples co-founded to reflect (incarnate, embody) the culture, religious and secular, of that time and place. We have already briefly considered this culture in the section on Jesus as Founder of the Church.

Into the constitution of the sacraments originating in Christ will go not only his own (and his disciples') religious experience, but also that of humanity in general and Israel in particular. Theologians have been accustomed to speak of the sacraments of nature, of the old law and of the new law.[117] The sacraments of nature and the Old Testament are not only good in themselves, they are also "sacramenta futuri,"[118] sacraments of the future, for they point to the full revelation and presence of God's communion with creation in Christ. *Natura propter gratiam* has been a classic Christian theological axiom: nature exists for the sake of grace.[119] St. Thomas was bold enough to assert: "It must be believed that from a divine instinct, as if from some kind of private law, men would be led to a definite form of worshiping God, which would be suitable not only [to express] interior worship, but which would also be suitable (*congrueret*) to signify the mysteries of Christ,''[120] He even went so far as to assert that the Jewish sacrament of "circumcision conferred grace insofar as it was a sign of faith in the future passion of Christ," although the grace of baptism is "more copious" because "the effect of something present is greater than the effect of a [future] something hoped for.''[121] According to Schillebeeckx, Israel not only had sacraments, "Israel [was the] sacrament of God.''[122] Listings of both natural and Jewish sacraments vary, as do the explanations of their efficacy in conferring grace. The sacraments of the new law are generally considered to be more effective and preferable (DS 780, 1310, 1602, 1698), but the explanations of the difference and preference are neither uniform nor universally enlightening.[123]

What is at hand here is less a precise theology of the sacraments and more a general theory of salvation. The more optimistic the expectation of salvation, the more operative the conviction of God's universal salvific will, the greater the grace-efficacy of the natural and Jewish sacraments is perceived to be. For our purposes, though, it is sufficient to note the general conviction of Christian theology that there have always been sacraments—because of both the divine and the human natures. Nowhere has God left human beings without the offer of saving grace, and everywhere this grace has taken visible form, so that it might be truly Christian grace, in the pattern of the "one mediator between God and man, the man Jesus" (1 Tim 2:4–6).

We can expect, then, both similarity and dissimilarity between Christian sacraments and natural and Jewish sacraments. The material element and ritual action may often be similar or even the same—water and washing, oil and anointing, bread/wine and eating/meal. The specific Christian symbolism will be effected by the "word which accedes to the element," as Augustine pointed out in regard to baptism. This Christian verbal specification is but the continuation of the natural specification which takes place in all human signs, which are constituted of material element/visible action and clarifying, specifying word. These sacramental words (the Scholastic theologians called them the "form," giving formal identity and being to the more general "matter") bring the entire sacramental action into Christ-like sacramentality, as the Incarnate Divine Word brings the entire cosmos into Christ-like sacramentality. Our seven sacraments are the little sacraments (material element plus word) of Christ the Big Sacrament (cosmos plus Word). Such an understanding of sacrament eliminates all suspicions of superstition and magic.[124] All sacraments, whether natural, Jewish or Christian, are participations in the manifestations of that one sacrament who is Christ: "The sacraments are the mysteries of the flesh [bodily human nature] of Christ. His flesh and the mysteries performed in it are the means, the instrumental cause and the sign, whereby God gives the life of grace to the soul" [the human being].[125]

This understanding should also eliminate the erroneous, however old and venerable, custom of describing Protestantism as the Church of the word and Catholicism as the Church of the sacrament. Of course, various churches can and may emphasize some "specific traditional contents" and some "sacred objectivities" more than others. That is quite in accord with the finite and historical nature of human being. On the other hand, neither Protestantism nor Catholicism has ever, in theory or practice, simply eliminated word or sacrament, although some non-sacramental (as they are called) Protestant churches have come close.[126] But they haven't because they can't. And they can't because even the word is a sign, and of all human signs, words are most pervasive and effective. For Christians sacraments are "the highest levels/ degrees in which [God's] exhibitive, manifestational word of grace happens in the Church."[127] This explanation does not threaten the "word" with the possibility of being reduced to a deficient or "degraded mode" of sacrament.[128] Rather, both wordly signs and action-al signs are visible (sensibly perceptible) means which the invisible saving will of God uses to communicate saving life effectively and significatively to the human race in different times and different places. The various words, rituals and specific sacraments of the Church are the concrete here and now articulations of the whole Church as the sacrament of salvation signified and effected by God in Christ. There is, then, neither hostility nor rivalry between word and sacrament, since both are visible forms of invisible grace.

As Heinrich Schlier points out, the entire practice of the Church is the building up of the Church. Churchly life or practice (*kirchliche praxis*) is the actualization of the apostolic activity—here we meet again the co-founding of the Church and sacraments by Christ and his disciples. The Church builds it-self up in the worship of God. The high point of the public, official, formal worship is the Eucharist, which itself is the preaching or proclamation of the Lord (1 Cor 11:23–29). In the Eucharistic assembly there is an orderly table community which proclaims the memory of Christ, implanted in the commu-nity. The Eucharist itself involves a verbal liturgy of prayer and song which is an unfolding of the word of Christ (Eph 5:12–21) as is the preaching of the word a prophetic proclamation (1 Cor 14:23–25). There is, then, a pericho-resis of word and sign in the sacrament.[129]

According to 2 Corinthians 4:2: "The Gospel enables and allows the truth to shine forth" (*phanerosis tes aletheias*). This word of God took form in the apostolic word, and through this apostolic word continues in the Church's preaching proclamation. This divine and apostolic word resides not only in the word of verbal language but also in the "wordless word of things" and even in silence. For this reason there is not only language, but "sacrament, mysti-cism, and, as we say, religious art." These are all ways in which the Word of God reveals himself in history.[130]

Rahner's description of the sacraments as the "highest levels or degrees" of God's symbolic saving activity in Christ can be properly understood. Sac-raments degrade neither verbal nor non-verbal signs. Rather, sacrament com-bines them into a new and higher degree of sign-full-ness, of word-ness, precisely in connection with the incarnate word-sign, Jesus Christ. Here we have another way of saying what we have continually emphasized, that the whole order of creation and redemption is sacramental. Therefore Walter Kas-per well says, "Most importantly, one must give up the fixation on the seven sacraments and begin again to emphasize more the sacramental signfulness of all Christian life. This would require a creative and relevant renewal of the sa-cramentals. Only if the whole of human and Christian life is sacramental do the precisely full and 'perfect' [seven] sacramental forms make sense."[131]

Before we suggest how the number seven is to be understood, we want to restate the question. We could ask, "If grace can be mediated and signified in all of God's good, sensible creation, why are there only seven such signs which are called sacraments?" In a sense, the question contains its own an-swer. Since God shares grace with us in so many different ways in his sensible creation, it is not necessary for any individual sharing or experience of grace to be one of the official sacraments for it to be an effective means of grace.

It was already clear to Peter Lombard in 1158 that "God has not bound his power to the sacraments."[132] Even such a cautious thinker as St. Thomas could say, "As faith alone sufficed for adults in the law [state] of nature, so it could also suffice now for someone who does not omit or neglect the sacra-ments out of contempt."[133] Schillebeeckx has neatly restated this in our own days. The seven sacraments "do not limit the possibilities of salvation as if they were a fence. They are not a handicap to God's grace but the incarnation and visibility of his love in the world."[134] We can also recall Rahner's explanation that Christian life and the sacraments are not identical or the same; they do not simply coincide.[135]

To conclude from these statements that sacraments are superfluous or at best trivial would be entirely wrong. As we have seen, sacrament as such has theological, Christological, anthropological, and sociological roots. Sacraments are signs, and signs are part of our very human nature, especially insofar as it is intersubjective. Signs are also indicated by our discrete, historical nature, for signs, verbal and other, are effective means of achieving solidarity and communion with the past and providing communion for the future. Again, it is the historical dimension of human nature that provides the starting place for the discussion of the precisely seven sacraments. As we have seen, God's saving will, present from the very beginning, has been progressively revealed in what theologians distinguish as nature, grace and glory.

Salvation is the history of grace, whose two dimensions we call creation and redemption. Privileged manifestations of this "cosmic history of grace" in Christianity are the seven sacraments.

ONLY SEVEN?

But why are there only seven sacraments as the Councils of Florence (DS 1310) and Trent (DS 1601) insisted? This is a perplexing question. A survey of the latest writings on the subject reveals no overwhelmingly convincing answer.[136] It is generally agreed that such a determination could not be made until an adequate definition of sacrament had been achieved. This did not happen until the twelfth century. As we have seen, until then many visible signs and symbolic rituals had been counted among the sacraments. Even the Council of Trent which stipulated the number seven did not achieve a formal definition of sacrament.[137] Furthermore, as Yves Congar shows, in general and specifically at Trent, the seven sacraments have been distinguished into major (baptism, Eucharist) and minor, a practice which has roots in Scholastic theology in the Middle Ages.[138] Sacraments are not merely seven different instances of the same thing. So even though the Council of Trent specified the number of the sacraments, it did not provide an equally specific definition of the sacraments.

In view of this and other historical data, theologians have had recourse to a symbolic interpretation, which emphasizes that the number seven denotes fullness or completeness.[139] This interpretation also concentrates on the psychological explanation of the seven, which we shall examine in detail later. Suffice it here to note that this approach relates the seven sacraments to seven "peak experiences" in human life.

This symbolic approach is not entirely cogent, but it points in the right direction. Emphasis should not be placed on the number seven, but on the sacramentality of Christianity and of the Church in general. This general sacramentality expressed itself in many ways in the ministry of Jesus, in the primitive Church, and in the following centuries. Of these sacramental expressions, some were more popular among the people, some more central to the life of the Church, some more closely connected with Jesus. Above all, there was no universal *a priori* principle by which the Church could discern, in its popular piety as well as in its official decisions, which of all these sacramental expressions would survive and thrive, which would wither and fade. This became clear only in and through the events of history. The importance of the concrete circumstances of culture and of history is reflected in the gradual evolution of the term sacrament as well as the various enumerations of those signful expressions which were counted as sacrament in the stricter or fuller sense. There is clearly a correlation between the precision of the definition of sacrament and the enumeration of the sacraments.

As in so many other sacramental matters, Hugh of St. Victor exercised a decisive influence in determining their number. He suggested a threefold division of the sacraments.

(1) Sacraments of salvation, in which salvation principally consists: baptism, Eucharist, confirmation, the Consecration of a church, the place where the sacraments are celebrated. These are the principal sacraments.

(2) Sacraments of practice or exercise (*Exercitatio* in this context is not easily translated): blessings, holy water, ashes, etc. These are not necessary for salvation, but they promote and further it. These are the minor sacraments.

(3) Sacraments of preparation: consecration and blessing of sacred vessels, vestments, ordination. They serve the preparation and administration of the other sacraments.[140] The canonists suggested a fourfold division: salutary (baptism, Eucharist, confirmation), ministerial (vessels, etc.), venerational (feasts of the liturgical year) and preparatory (consecrations and dedications). Some suggested a further threefold division: necessity (baptism, catechesis, exorcism); dignity only (consecrations and dedications); necessity and dignity (confirmation and Eucharist).[141] The value of this for us is its emphasis on the capacity of natural material beings to be the mediators of supernatural spiritual grace and on the historical relativity of the seven sacraments as a definite, exclusive classification of sacramental signs in the Church. For this reason we have suggested that the number seven is certainly not capricious, but is indeed arbitrary, for it is the result of human choices on the basis of reasons which are serious and weighty but not absolute.

The definitive stipulation of seven sacraments was achieved in the middle of the twelfth century. Peter Lombard's presentation of the sevenfold enumeration is laconic, without even the hint of a defense of this number against other possible candidates. "Now we proceed to the sacraments of the new law, which are baptism, confirmation, the blessing of bread, that is, the Eucharist, penance, last anointing (*extrema unctio*), orders, marriage. Of these, some provide remedy against sin and confer helping grace (for example, baptism), some are only a remedy (matrimony) others strengthen and support us with grace (Eucharist and orders)."[142] Other theologians suggested different classifications of the sacraments, but Lombard's seven had gained a firm foothold in theology. Later Scholastic theologians attempted to explain the fittingness or convenience or congruence of the seven sacraments. Some went so far as to speak of the necessity of seven, but this was an extreme, not the usual approach. Some of these attempts may strike us as fanciful, using as they do such combinations as the three divine persons and the four winds (directions) of the earth, the seven gifts of the Holy Spirit, the seven lampstands and seals of the apocalypse, even the seven last words of Jesus on the cross. Similar efforts can also be found in the Eastern churches, which, in this case, were rather strongly influenced by the West.[143] Again, I note explicitly that the value of these sacramental definitions and classifications is their (at least implicit) emphasis on the general gracedness of human being and history. They imply that all of life is a rite, that the Christian religion is the ritual expansion of the priesthood of Christ, offering perfect sacrifice to God and enabling the universal sanctification of the human race and its cosmos.

There are "only" seven sacraments because the whole created and graced universe is "already" sacramental.[144] We are again reminded that worship is not restricted to just a few moments or parts of our existence. Rather, worship, the act of religion, and religion itself are our whole life. The sacraments are not momentary invasions of our human secular, profane world by divine grace which comes from outside. Grace is not like a pointille painting of individual dots,[145] so many of them so close together that eventually they don't look like individual dots anymore, but a "solid" painting. Too often one thinks of grace as many individual, discrete drops of rain falling on our world from heaven. But, as we have seen, the world is itself graced. It is, we might say, in the state of grace, for it has been "Christ-ed." The sacraments are not something sacred which comes from outside into a supposedly profane world. Rather, the sacraments bubble up from within our already graced world. There are not seven sacraments because the world needs grace, but does not have it. There are seven sacraments because the world needs grace and does have it. The seven sacraments are the concrete, sensibly perceptible form (*Gestalt*) of this grace. Why seven? The theological category of correlation offers some enlightenment in this respect.

SACRAMENTS: CORRELATION OF GRACE WITH NATURE AND HISTORY

According to Hans B. Meyer, "the sacraments and their symbolism are the answers to the fundamental questions of human existence." In the sacraments God has responded—and responds—superlatively to "the vague intimations, struggles and longings of all the earth's religions."[146] According to Paul Tillich, sacraments are the correlation of divine grace with human nature and history, both individual and corporate.[147] They can be this because they are the objectifications of Jesus' human experience of God. As the perfect love of God for the world and the perfect love of the world of God, Jesus is fully divine and fully human. His experience essentially includes *all* of human experience and existence. His worship as perfect priest and perfect victim, the perfect sacrifice, has definitively consecrated the world to God in holiness.

A classical explanation of the *seven* sacraments, sometimes called the psychological explanation because it relates the seven sacraments to the seven peak individual and social experiences of human life, elaborates and explicates this cosmic consecration and sanctification. Often, unfortunately, these correlations have been excessively concerned with the sins of human beings instead of "just" their natural developmental states and needs. However, as we have seen, such preoccupation with sin is not necessary for the sacraments to be or to be understood. It is sufficient to relate the sacraments as signful celebrations of supernatural grace to the natural needs of human beings, as this example from the thirteenth century illustrates.

> Baptism for beginners, confirmation for combatants, the Eucharist
> for wayfarers, penance for prodigals, extreme unction for the departing, orders for the ministering, and marriage for those who toil.

The same basic correlation is found in St. Bonaventure, except that he uses military metaphors. Matrimony is for those "who prepare new soldiers." Holy orders is "for those who bring in new recruits." At that time the Church on earth was frequently called the "Church militant" or the fighting Church.[148]

St. Thomas has a similar arrangement:[149] baptism corresponds to birth; confirmation corresponds to maturity; Eucharist corresponds to preservation and strengthening of life; penance corresponds to healing sickness for the restoration of health; extreme unction, anointing of the sick, corresponds to restoration of original strength and preparation for the journey through death to the glory of heaven; holy orders corresponds to governing for the sake of the common good; matrimony corresponds to continuation of the human family.

Such correlations became very "traditional." They appeared in official documents as early as 1439 in the Council of Florence's decree for the Armenians, as late as 1943 in Pope Piux XII's encyclical on the mystical body.[150]

Such a correlation is critically important, for it shows how the whole of human life and history is caught up in the saving will of God, how God's communion with the human is not restricted to this or that moment. By itself, however, it could give a false impression, as if the prime factor in the sacraments were psychological. In fact, it is theological and salvation-historical. In the concrete "cosmic history of grace" there are other and more important correlations. Franz Dander hints at this when he correlates the sacraments not only to "the spiritual life of man," but also to "the building up of the Church, the body of Christ" and to the "apostolate of establishing the Kingdom of

Christ'' on earth.[151] However, his correlations do not really surpass the psychological scheme.[152]

SALVATION-HISTORY CORRELATION

One especially important correlation has been mentioned above. St. Paul intimates it when he says that by baptism we are initiated into the death and resurrection of Christ (Rom 6:1–11). Since the sacraments are the objectifications whereby we share in the religious experience of Jesus, we should be able to show similar correlations for all the sacraments. This correlation has not been developed in theology, so our own effort here must be tentative.

Baptism . . . . .Incorporation into the death and resurrection of Christ.

Confirmation . . . . .Pentecostal ''enspiriting'' and ''empowering'' of the disciples of Christ to be the universal, world-wide Church as missionary witnesses of the tradition and the memory of Christ.

Holy Eucharist . . . . .Participation in the meals of Jesus, the Friend of sinners, with sinners, especially in the Last Supper where Jesus' priestly life-sacrifice for not only humans, but sinful humans, begins its consummation. This is also the quest for Wisdom's banquet, where the food gives everlasting life. Thus, eating the bread and wine of the Eucharist does not have the usual effect of turning bread and wine into our bodies. Rather, our eating this ''bread and wine'' turns us into the body and blood of Christ, thus establishing, sustaining, and intensifying the *whole Christ*.

Penance . . . . .Sharing in the many, many acts of forgiveness which Christ is, and in the Holy Spirit who is the divine power for the forgiveness of sin/sinners.

Anointing of the Sick. . . . . .Not only sharing in the healings of Jesus, but also sharing in Jesus' experience of the weakness and fragility of human existence, unto death, but also experiencing in and with Jesus the still

greater saving strength of God as
Abba, Father, into whose hands we
can commend our failing selves.

Holy Orders .Sharing in a particular way the shepherding of Jesus in regard to the or-
derly life and mission of the Church.

Matrimony . . . . .Sharing in the pleasure of being, as this
pleasure originates in the triune com-
munion of God and the theandric communion of Jesus insofar as this
pleasure is both friendship and (pro-)
creation.

All of this altogether mightily reinforces the conviction that the saving communion of God with man happens right in the very things[153] and in the very events of this world and its history. God is not way out there someplace. God's saving grace does not float mistily over the universe. Rather, through the creation by God and the incarnation of the Word and the mission of the Holy Spirit and apostles to the ends of the earth and the end of time the world's history is a history of grace, the cosmos already a liturgy. Temple no longer designates a special space, separated from the rest of the profane secular world. Temple is, rather, the space of the world, sanctified by the saving will of God incarnate in it in various ways.

For this reason Karl Rahner is fond of speaking of the "mysticism of everyday life,"[154] for God can be and is experienced not only in isolated moments or extraordinary experiences, but in the everyday life of Everyman and Everywoman. This cosmic gracedness expresses itself in a special way in the Church, where "Christians have been incorporated into a new cultic organism."[155] Not only in special sanctuaries, but in their whole lives they are "a royal priesthood, a consecrated nation, a people set apart to sing the praises of God" (1 Pet 2:9).[156] However, they sing this praise not only in their daily lives which are their "spiritual sacrifice." They also sing in special symbolic and ritual actions, which have come to be called sacraments and sacramentals. Because the world has been created by God, "There is hardly any proper use of material things which cannot be thus directed toward the sanctification of men and the praise of God."[157] Certain usages of material things in this sanctification and praise have achieved special status in the Church. As the most intense signs of God's salvation in and of the human, material cosmos, these have come to enjoy the full status of sacrament.

As we saw in our very brief history of the development of the theology of sacrament, the special seven sacraments do not exist in a vacuum. They do not form some special kind of strange being, unlike anything and everything else in the world and in religion. In fact, they have so much in common with other religious realities that their specialness was discovered only slowly and with considerable difficulty.

SACRAMENTALS

In this context we mention those blessings, prayers and rituals known as sacramentals. Although the experts do not agree about the precise nature and identification of sacramentals, Vatican II offers an acceptable definition:[158]

Holy Mother church has, moreover, instituted sacramentals. These are sacred signs which bear a resemblance to the sacraments: they signify effects, particularly of a spiritual kind, which are obtained through the Church's intercession. By them men are disposed to receive the chief effect of the sacraments, and various occasions in life are rendered holy.

We would prefer not to say that "various occasions in life are rendered holy." We would prefer to say that in sacramentals, like sacraments, the graced, holy state of life is celebrated. Through these ritual celebrations the grace which God has already given to the world comes into a certain visible signfulness in society and history. This already present grace is also intensified through the sacramentals.

For similar reasons William J. O'Shea's explanation is also lacking: "Through the sacramentals the Church brings all created things into the orbit of God's blessing, in reality touches everything with the grace of the redemption, making so many material things and persons instruments of the grace of God."[159] We think, rather, that the world is already graced, that the Church is the sign of this graced-ness. As this sign, the Church is also the cause of the continuing and increasing graced-ness of the world. For this reason it is the sacrament of salvation. The same understanding applies to the seven sacraments and all the sacramentals. We should, therefore, avoid everything that might give the impression that the Church is a holy enclave in an otherwise profane world, that the sacraments and sacramentals are moments of grace which spasmodically intrude into a pagan and profane world.

Hence sacraments, sacramentals, public devotions (in some kind of official connection with Church authorities) and private devotions (for example, in the family or in informal gatherings) have this in common: they are the grace-inspired visible celebrations of the grace God has poured into the world, and they bring this grace into sensibly perceptible forms in this world. This general sacramental view is very important for at least two practical reasons. First, it can help us avoid "over-seven-sacramentalizing" the practice of our faith, hope, and charity. Our entire graced life is already the "rite of the Christian religion.'' Second, it also indicates great possibilities in adapting the ''ritual of the Christian religion'' to any given age or culture, for such sacraments and sacramentals are the cultural forms of religion.

As we have seen, sacramental theology is a history of adaptation—of concepts, terms, ceremonies. This has been the case from the very beginning of the Church when Jesus adapted traditional Jewish concepts, terms and ceremonies to express and share his experience of God with others.

A classic expression of this adaptability is the admonition of St. Gregory the Great to Augustine, missionary to ''the new Church of [England]'':[160]

> You know the liturgical customs of the Church in Rome in which you grew up. But I find it acceptable (pleasing) that you should carefully select whatever you can find, whether in the Roman or Gallican or any other Church, as long as it is pleasing to almighty God, and from these many Churches build up a new structure particularly fitted to the Church of the Angles which is still new in the faith. . . . Choose, then, from all the individual Churches whatever elements you judge to be pious, religious and proper; and having put them together in an organic unity, establish them among the Angles as their customary liturgy.

There is no reason why a twentieth century Nigerian should have to worship like a sixteenth century Italian. In fact, why should a twentieth century Italian have to worship like a sixteenth century one? The Second Vatican Council took note of this:[161]

> For the liturgy is made of unchangeable elements divinely instituted, and elements subject to change. The latter not only may but ought to be changed with the passing of time if features have by chance crept in which are less harmonious with the intimate nature of the liturgy, or if existing elements have grown less functional.

This is elaborated further on:

> Even in the liturgy, the Church has no wish to impose a rigid uniformity in matters which do not involve the faith or the good of the whole community. Rather it respects and fosters the spiritual adornments and gifts of the various races and peoples. Anything in their way of life that is not indissolubly bound up with superstition and error it studies with sympathy and if possible, preserves intact. Sometimes in fact it admits such things into the liturgy itself, as long as they harmonize with its true and authentic spirit.
>   Provided that the substantial unity of the Roman rite is maintained, the revision of liturgical books should allow for legitimate

variations and adaptations to different groups, regions, and peoples, especially in mission lands. Where opportune, the same rule applies to the structuring of rites and the devising of rubrics.

Notice the immediate predominance given to the "Roman rite." Further on, however, greater expansiveness seems to be provided for:

> In some places and circumstances, however, an even more radical adaptation of the liturgy is needed and entails greater difficulties. Therefore: (1) The competent territorial ecclesiastical authority mentioned in Article 22, par. 2, must, in this matter, carefully and prudently consider which elements from the traditions and genius of individual peoples might appropriately be admitted into divine worship.

I include these lengthy quotations because they illustrate, from a different point of view, the conviction of God's saving will for communion with material, visible, sensible human beings is thoroughgoing. Nothing human is excluded from the worship and sanctification which this communion enables. Although ritual is not optional, no ritual is purely and absolutely necessary. This is the impact of the Council of Trent's declaration that the Church has power over the sacraments except for their substance.[162] This statement also illustrates the truth of what we have called the co-founding of the Church and sacraments by Jesus and his disciples.[163] There is an element which comes from the initiating Jesus and which is, therefore, beyond the power of the receptive disciples. Nevertheless, the sacraments, as ritual celebrations of divine grace, are also within the power and competence of the disciples who constitute the Church, which is itself an adaptable and adapting sacrament.[164]

All this is precisely a reaffirmation of the relentless will of God to "save all men and have them come to the knowledge of God through the one mediator between God and man, Jesus" (1 Tim 2:4–6). Although the sacramental ritual is human and open to wide-ranging adaptation the sacraments themselves are not primarily the acts of human beings, but the gifts of the divine being.[165] It is also clear that the sacraments are not primarily remedies of sin, not even of human moral weakness and failure. In fact, they are not primarily remedies at all, at least not in the usual sense of that word. We can even say that the sacraments are not primarily redemption.

What are they then? Here we must borrow a term from the Churches of the East. They have traditionally spoken of *theiosis*, a Greek word meaning divinization. It means that God is making us "divine." St. John Chrysostom is famous for his concise formulation of this whole idea. "The Word became flesh (human) so that we humans might receive the Holy Spirit. . . . God made himself to be a bearer [carrier] of the flesh [human being] so that the human being can become the bearer [carrier] of the Spirit (of God)."[166] The

Eastern tradition has been even more emphatic, saying simply that "God became man that man might become God." According to one of their great contemporary theologians, "The human being becomes by grace what God is by nature."[167] In a word, God became man in order that man might become God. This becoming happens in the material things of this material world, which is, therefore, already sacramental. The sacramentality of the world becomes even more intense in the Church and its sacraments, which are themselves the sacraments of Christ, who is the sacrament of the saving God Father-Son-Holy Spirit. And thus we can truly speak of the Church as "the universal sacrament of salvation" which is itself sacramentalized in the seven sacraments and sacramentals, all of which are the means and signs of God's sacramental ontological communion with "all mankind."[168]

All our ritual worship, all our sacraments are but the continuing history of John's exultation at the beginning of his First Epistle (1:1–4).

> Something which has existed since the beginning, that we have heard, and we have seen with our own eyes, that we have watched and touched with our hands: the Word, who is life—this is our subject. That life was made visible; we saw it and we are giving our testimony, telling you of the eternal life which was with the Father and has been made visible to us. What we have seen and heard we are telling you so that you too may be in union with us, as we are in union with the Father and with his Son Jesus Christ. We are writing this to you to make our own joy complete.

NOTES

1. On all this, which can be discussed only very briefly here, see Robert Kress, *A Rahner Handbook* (Atlanta: John Knox, 1982) 98–103; John Baptist Metz, *Christliche Anthropozentrik* (Munich: Kosel, 1962); "Being," SM 1, 153–159; "Existence," SM 2, 297–307; "Freedom," SM 2, 349–362; "Man," SM 3, 358–370; "Person," SM 4, 404–409.

2. In 1 Sent. 15, 5,3, ad 2: "Anima verius habet suum esse ubi amat quam ubi est."

3. On this, with original texts, see Adolf Kolping, *Sacramentum Tertullianeum* 1 (Munster: Regensberg, 1948) 30.

4. On this, see L. Hodl, "Kirchliches Sakrament—christliches Engagement," *Zeitschrift fur Kirche und Theologie* 95 (1973) 3–5.

5. Odo Casel, *Das christliche Kultmysterium,* ed. Bernhard Neunheuser (Regensburg: Pustet, 1960) 79.

6. This transformation had already taken place in Plato: for example, *Phaedrus* 249a–250c.

7. On ancient Gnosticism and its surprising perdurance in contemporary phi-

losophy and politics, see Hans Jonas, *The Gnostic Religion* (Boston: Beacon, 1963); *Philosophical Essays* (Englewood Cliffs: Prentice-Hall, 1974) 21–44, 263–348. Eric Voegelin, *Science, Politics and Gnosticism* (Chicago: Regnery, 1968). Ancient texts are translated in James Robinson, ed., *The Nag Hammadi Library* (New York: Harper and Row, 1977). Modern versions and apologias are Jacques Lacarriere, *The Gnostics* (New York: Dutton, 1977): Marquerite Yourcenar, *Fires* (New York: Farrar, Straus and Geroux, 1977); *The Abyss,* 1976; Emile Cioran, *The Fall into Time* (Chicago: Quadrangle, 1970); *A Short History of Decay* (New York: Viking, 1975). Gnosticism may well be Christianity's oldest, severest and most persistent temptation. Its ''cosmic pessimism'' (Jonas, *Philosophical* 266) and utter disdain of the cosmos and matter, which it regards as essentially and inherently failed, flawed, and evil (Lacarriere 24,99) vitiate any possibility of a sacramental understanding. Of course, for Gnosticism Christian doctrines like incarnation and creation are nonsense.

8. Josef Finkenzeller, *Die Lehre von den Sakramenten im allgemeinen. Von der Schrift bis zur Scholastik* (Freiburg: Herder, 1980) 12.

9. Raphael Schulte, ''Die Einzelsakramente als Ausgliederung des Wurzelsakraments,'' MS 4/2, 78–79.

10. Heinrich Schlier, *Die Zeit der Kirche* (Freiburg: Herder, 1955) 314.

11. William van Roo, *De Sacramentis in Genere* (Rome: P.U.G., 1957) 7–9 This volume also contains a handy collection of patristic texts on mystery and sacrament in Latin and Greek.

12. Beda Rigaux, ''Revelation des mysteres et perfection a Qumran dans le Nouveau Testament,'' *New Testament Studies* 4 (1957–58) 237–262.

13. A helpful summary of the current state of the discussion is offered by H. Klos, *Die Sakramente im Johannesevangelium* (Stuttgart: KBW, 1970) 11–44.

14. Rudolf Bultmann, *Theology of the New Testament* 2 (London: SCM, 1955) 58–59.

15. Oscar Cullmann, *Early Christian Worship* (London: SCM, 1969) 37.

16. Franz Mussner, ''Kultische Aspekte im johanneischen Christusbild,'' *Liturgisches Jahrbuch* 14 (1964) 144.

17. Rudolf Schnackenburg, ''Die Sakramente im Johannesevangelium,'' *Sacra Pagina,* ed. J. Coppens et al. 2 (Gembloux: Duculot, 1959) 235–254.

18. Raymond Brown, *The Gospel According to John I-XII* (New York: Doubleday, 1966) CXIIGCXIV, with reference to his ''The Johannine Sacramentary Reconsidered,'' *Theological Studies* 23 (1962) 183–206.

19. Barnabas Lindars, ''Word and Sacrament in the Fourth Gospel,'' *Scottish Journal of Theology* 29 (1976) 63. Eucharistic act is representation and application (243–253).

20. Schnackenburg (246–248) emphasizes John 19:34 and 1 John 5:6–8. See also his *Das Johannesevangelium* 3 (Freiburg: Herder, 1975) 48–53, where he discusses the absence of the Eucharist in John's account of the Last Supper.

21. Donald Senior, ''God's Creative Word in Our Midst,'' *The Sacraments: God's Love and Mercy Actualized,* ed. Francis Eigo (Villanova: Villanova University Press, 1979) 20.

22. ''For this reason he has been called 'the creator of ecclesiastical Latin.' This however, is an exaggeration and does not do justice to the profound and lasting influence of the oldest translation of the Bible, where many of the words which were

thought to have been invented or adapted by Tertullian were first used, as recently proved for sacramentum. . . ." Johannes Quasten, *Patrology* 2 (Utrecht: Spectrum, 1953) 249.

23. *De Anima* 1

24. *De Baptismo* 1

25. *De Baptismo* 4

26. Tertullian was the first to use "Mother" as a title of the Church. *Ad Martyres* 1; *De Pudicitia* 5, 14.

27. *De Anima* 43.

28. St. Cyprian, *The Unity of the Church* 7. Ancient Christian Writers 25, Fr. Maurice Bevenot (Westminster: Newman, 1957) 48–50.

29. *Epistola* 45, 1, (CSEL 3/2, 600,4).

30. *Epistola* 74, 11 (CSEL 3/2, 808).

31. *In Lucam* 2, 79 (PL 15,1633).

32. For this reason Karl Rahner (ST 4, 379–380) has seen fit to defend the term, understanding and reality of "transubstantiation" in regard to the Eucharist. Otherwise "the act of God remains solely in the divine sphere; it is not present and transforming there where the things of the world are—the bread, the grave, etc. . . . God's deed remains beyond not only the experience of unbelief (which is, certainly, correct) but beyond the very reality of the world itself. God remains in the heavens; here, where the bread is, nothing happens."

33. Even Paul Tillich, who is exercised (excessively, it seems to me) by the idolic possibilities of sacramentality, nevertheless recognizes the inevitability and desirability of what he calls "sacred objectivities" and "Gestalt of Grace." He also notes that "the one thing needful is that the whole Protestant attitude toward the sacraments be changed. . . . For this reason the solution of the problem of 'nature and sacrament' is today a task on which the very destiny of Protestanism depends." *The Protestant Era* (Chicago: University of Chicago Press, 1957; Phoenix Books abridged ed.) 227–229; 212, 111–112.

34. Christine Mohrmann, "Sacramentum dans les plus anciennes textes chretiens," *Harvard Theological Review* 47 (1954) 141–152.

35. van Roo, *De Sacramentis* 19.

36. Charles Couturier "Sacramentum et Mysterium dans l'oeuvre de saint Augustin," in Henri Rondet et al., *Etudes Augustiniennes* (Paris: Aubier, 1953) 164. In addition to this article, one can still recommend the chapter on sacraments in Eugene Portalie, *A Guide to the Thought of St. Augustine* (Chicago: Regnery, 1960) 243–269. Portalie consistently points out the differing interpretations of Augustine by Catholic and Protestant theolgians.

37. *De Natura et Gratia* 2,2 (PL 44, 249).

38. *Sermo* 10 (PL 38, 93).

39. *Sermo* 354 (PL 39, 1563).

40. *In Psalmos* 79 (PL 36, 1021). See Emile Mersch, *The Whole Christ* (Milwaukee: Bruce 1938).

41. *De Doctrina Christiana* 2, 1, 1 (PL 34, 36).

42. *Sermo* 272 (PL 38, 1247).

43. *Ep* 98, 9 (PL 33, 364).

44. *Ep* 138 (PL 33, 527).

45. *De Civitate Dei* 10 (PL 41, 283).

46. *In Joannem* tr. 80, 3 (PL 35, 1511).

47. *Contra Faustum* 19 (PL 42: 356).

48. H. M. Feret, "Sacramentum, Res dans la langue theologique de saint Augustin," *Revue des sciences philosophiques et theologiques* 29 (1940) 242–244.

49. *Ep* 98, 9 (PL 33, 363); *De Civ Dei* 18, 48 (PL 41, 611).

50. Thomas Camelot, "Sacramentum. Notes de theologie sacramentaire augustinienne," *Revue Thomiste* 57 (1957) 445–447.

51. *En in Ps 77* (PL 36, 983).

52. *Ep* 55, 1–2 (PL 33, 205).

53. *Etymologiae* 6, 17 (PL 82, 248).

54. Joseph de Ghellinck, "Un chapitre dans l'histoire de la definition des sacraments au XIIe siecle," *Melanges Mandonnet* 2 (Paris: Vrin, 1930) 88,.

55. Jaroslav Pelikan, *The Growth of Medieval Theology* 1 (Chicago: University of Chicago Press, 1978) 184–204.

56. Ludwig Ott, *Fundamentals of Catholic Dogma* (Cork: Mercier, 1955) 370.

57. C.E. Sheedy, "Berengarius of Tours," NCE 2, 321.

58. Pelikan, *The Growth* 202–204.

59. Hugh of St. Victor, *De Sacramentis Legis Naturalis et Scriptae Dialogus* (PL 176, 33–35).

60. *De Sacramentis Christianae Fidei* 9, 2 (PL 176, 317–318).

61. *Summa Sententiarum,* tractatus 4,1 (PL 176, 117).

62. Peter Lombard, *Liber Sententiarum* 4,d. 1, c. 4.

63. Karl Rahner. *Worte ins Schweigen* (Innsbruck: Rauch, 1954) 29. The key sentence has a play on words which eludes English equivalency: "Du hast mich ergriffen, nicht ich habe dich begriffen." Both *ergriffen* and *begriffen* come from *greifen,* which means to grasp, get hold of, grab, etc.

64. ST III, q. 60, a. 2.

65. van Roo, *De Sacramentis* 52.

66. Ludger Kruse, "Der Sakramentsbegriff des Konzils von Trient und die heutige Sakramentstheologie," *Theologie und Glaube* (1955) 401–412.

67. van Roo, *De Sacramentis* 61.

68. ST III, q. 60, a. 1, ad 3.

69. ST III, q. 60, a. 5, ad 3.

70. ST III, q. 60, a. 5

71. ST III, q. 60, a. 5.

72. ST II-II, q. 81, a. 1–8.

73. The Latin text has 83:3: "Cor meum et caro mea exsultaverunt in Deum vivum."

74. Yves Congar, *Jesus Christ* (New York: Herder and Herder, 1966) 30.

75. As is, sadly, asserted by Paul Tong, "A Study of Thematic Differences Between Eastern and Western Religious Thought," *Journal of Ecumenical Studies* 10 (1973) 347.

76. R. Kress, "Worship Communal," NCE 17, 722–724.

77. James F. Ross, "Analogy as a Rule of Meaning for Religious Language," *Aquinas,* ed. Anthony Kenny (Notre Dame: University of Notre Dame Press, 1976) 132–33.

78. DS 806.

79. Karl Jaspers, *Einfuhrung in die Philosophie* (Munich, Piper, 1953) 111.

80. See Cornelio Fabro, *God in Exile* (New York: Newman, 1968) 940–945.

81. On this entire section, see Robert Kress *Christan Roots: No Alien God* (Westminster: Christian Classics, 1978).

82. Unfortunately, this aspect of God's Fatherhood is entirely overlooked by Bernard Cooke, "Non-Patriarchal Salvation," *Horizons* 10 (1983) 22–23. Can such an omission be other than a syndrome of the Gnostic strain in some contemporary feminist theology?

83. See my "Cosmos and Conscience in the History of Religious Imagination," *The Pedagogy of God's Image,* ed. Robert Masson (Chico: Scholars Press, 1982) 191–206, and "Peter, Paul and Oedipus: Truth as Light or Darkness, Vision or Blindness," *Explorations* 2:6 (July 1984); "Veritas Rerum," *The Thomist* (1984).

84. Dante, *The Divine Comedy:* "Purgatorio," XVI, 89 (New York: Random House Modern Library, Carlyle-Wicksteed translation, 1952) 285.

85. Plato, *Cratylus* 400 c; *Gorgias* 493a.

86. See Jacques Lacarriere, *The Gnostics* (New York: Dutton, 1977) 10, 24, 47, 93. Also E. Voegelin, *Science Politics and Gnosticism.* (Chicago: Regnery Gateway, 1968) 86.

87. E. de Ray, "De l'influence du Gnosticisme sur Origene," *Revue de l'histoire des religions* 43 (9123) 201, 206.

88. See Hans Jonas, *Philosophical Essays* (Englewood Cliffs: Prentice-Hall, 1974) 266.

89. For example, on Maximus the Confessor, see Hans Urs von Balthasar, *Kosmische Liturgie* (Einsiedeln: Johannes, 1961).

90. Karl Rahner, ST 10, 409, 414.

91. This is because not only Christ and grace, but even/also human nature/being is incarnational, or as Karl Rahner puts it, *Spirit in the World* (New York: Herder and Herder, 1968). See also Andrew Tallon, "Personal Becoming," *The Thomist* 43 (1979) 1–178.

92. Karl Rahner, ST 8,225.

93. Karl Rahner, ST 12, 261, 267.

94. See Karl Rahner, "Theology of the Symbol," ST 4, 221–252. A handy introduction to symbol, from a more historical approach, is Lionel Mitchell, *The Meaning of Ritual* (New York: Paulist, 1977). Also, Mary Collins, "Critical Ritual Studies: Examining an Intersection of Theology and Culture," *The Bent World,* ed. John May (Chico: Scholars Press, 1981) 127–148; Louis Bouyer, *Rite and Man* (Notre Dame: University of Notre Dame Press, 1963); James D. Shaughnessy, ed., *The Roots of Ritual* (Grand Rapids: Eerdmans, 1973).

95. See above, Augustine on *Signa Data,* 131.

96. See Robert Kress, "Religious Indifference—Definition and Criteria," *Concilium* 165 (May 1983) 11–19, and "Everyday Life and Spiritual Discipline," *Spiritual Discipline and Ultimate Reality,* ed. James Duerlinger (New York: Paragon, 1984) 13–42.

97. M.-D. Chenu, "Anthropologie et Liturgie," *Maison Dieu* 12 (1947) 65.

98. Karl Rahner, ST 13, 255.

99. Peter Berger, *Facing Up to Modernity* (New York: Basic, Harper Colophon, 1977) xvi–xvii.

100. ST III, q. 63, a.3.

101. ST III, q. 62, a.6.

102. Henricus (Edward) Schillebeeckx, *De Sacramentele Heilseconomie* (Antwerpen 'T Groeti: H. Nelissen Bilthoven, 1952) 656.

103. St. Thomas Aquinas, *Super Epistolas S. Pauli II,* "Ad Ephesios 4:5–6," IV, Lectio 2 (Turin, Marietti 1953) 200 (n. 49–50).

104. ST III, q. 63, a.4, ad 3.

105. ST I-II, q. 103, a.4.

106. *Inn IV Sent.*, d.1, p.1, a. unic, q.5 (quaracchi, p 26).

107. Karl Rahner, *The Church and the Sacraments* (New York: Herder and Herder, 1963); Edward Schillebeeckx, *Christ the Sacrament of the Encounter with God* (New York: Sheed and Ward, 1963).

108. See also Werner Stark, *The Sociology of Religion 4: Types of Religious Man* (New York: Fordham University Press, 1970) 13–79, 98–166.

109. On the objectification of experience in general, see Karl Rahner, ST 8, 197–207; 12, 550–559, 582–598; in regard to Christ, 99–101; with Wilhelm Thusing, *Christologie–systematisch and exegetisch* (Freiburg: Herder, 1972) 21–29.

110. *Ep* 187 (PL 83, 845).

111. *Sermo* 74, 2, (PL 54, 398).

112. *Apologia Prophetae David* 12 (PL 14,875).

113. *Summa Contra Gentiles* 3,69.

114. This is the import of the theological theory about the obediential capacity of human nature for grace and supernatural elevation. Karl Rahner speaks of the "Heilsempfanglichkeit" of human being for salvation (his emphasis): ST 8, 52. We can legitimately ask whether the Calvinist "human passivity" is absolutely necessary to insure the initiative of grace, the pre-eminence of the divine in the work of salvation? See Alexander Ganoczy, *Ecclesia Ministrans* (Freiburg: Herder, 1968) 83: "Der Glaube ist fur Calvin so sehr das Werk des Geistes dass er *opus passivum* genannt werden kann" (my emphasis): "For Calvin faith is so much the work of the Holy Spirit that it can be termed a passive work." Is not receptivity much more in keeping with Judeo-Christianity's creational sacrament communion ontology than Luther's contention that "Christian righteousness (holiness in general) is a purely *passive* one, which we receive only when we effect nothing, but suffer according as another is at work in us, namely God" (WA 40 I/41, 2). Also, "Thus am I justified, like matter, and I suffer something [to be done to me] but do nothing" (WA 39 I/447, 14). On this, see Otto Hermann Pesch, *Theologie der Rechtfertigung bei Martin Luther und Thomas von Aquin* (Mainz: Grunewald, 1967) 172–186.

115. See F. Chapey, "Paul Tillich," *Bahnbrechende Theologen des 20. Jahrhunderts,* ed. R. Vander Gucht and H. Vorgrimler (Freiburg: Herder, 1970) 51.

116. On this absolutely fundamental principle see the superb book of Joseph Pieper, *In Tune With the World* (Chicago: Franciscan Herald, 1973).

117. Thomas Aquinas *In IV Sent.* d. 1, q. 2, a.6, sol.3. See also ST III, q. 61, a.3, ad 2. See Schillebeeckx, *De Sacramentele* 52–61; "kosmische liturgie" 59.

118. The title of a book by Jean Cardinal Daniélou which investigates the "sacraments" of the Old Testament (Westminster: Newman, 1960). For descriptions and explanations of the sacraments of nature see the various publications of Mircea Eliade, for example, *Rites and Symbols of Initiation* (New York: Harper, 1965).

119. Edward Schillebeeckx, *De Sacramentele* 59.

120. ST I-II, q. 103, a.1; also III q. 70, a.4, ad 2.

121. ST III, q. 70 a. 4.

158   *The Church*

122. Edward Schillebeeckx, *Christ the Sacrament* 10–13.

123. Bernard Leeming, *Principles of Sacramental Theology* (Westminster: Newman, 1960) 604–614.

124. Although some theologians like to berate the sacramental practice of the Church, at least of some members of the Church and their popular, practical piety, I must say that in twenty-five years of pastoral practice and theological teaching, I have yet to meet a Catholic who thinks of or uses the sacraments magically or superstitiously. Their theological explanations may not always be highly sophisticated, but that hardly merits the epithet of magic or superstition. I am thinking of such statements in Raymond Vaillancourt, *Toward a Renewal of Sacramental Theology* (Collegeville: Liturgical Press, 1979) and the very title of George Worgul, *From Magic to Metaphor* (New York: Paulist, 1980).

125. Thomas Aquinas, ST III, q. 52, a.8, ad 2.

126. Indeed, currently there is a serious liturgical and sacramental revival within Protestantism: James J. White, "A Protestant Worship Manifesto," *The Christian Century* 99/3 (Jan. 27, 1982) 82–86. It would be a shame twice over were Catholicism, in the current wave of social concern, to abandon its own sacramental dimension at this particular moment. See Philip Murnion, "A Sacramental Church," *America* 148 (March 26, 1983) 226–228.

127. Karl Rahner (with Eberhard Jungel), *Was ist ein Sakrament* (Freiburg: Herder, 1971) 79.

128. A suspicion expressed by Walter Kasper, *Glaube und Geschichte* (Mainz: Grunewald, 1970) 292, note 20. In any case, it is not immediately evident how Kasper could reconcile this suspicion with his own statements on the bottom of page 305.

129. Heinrich Schlier, *Die Zeit der Kirche* (Freiburg: Herder, 1956) 244–264.

130. Heinrich Schlier, *Das Ende der Zeit* (Freiburg: Herder, 1971) 21–36, quotations 21, 29.

131. Walter Kasper, "Wort und Sakrament," *Theologisches Jahrbuch,* ed. A. Danhardt (Leipzig: St. Benno Verlag, 1976) 445.

132. *Sent,* d. 4, q. 8. a.1. See also St. Thomas Aquinas, ST III, q. 64, a.7; q. 72,a.6, ad 1. See also Bernard Leeming, *Principles of Sacramental Theology,* rev. ed. (Westminster: Newman, 1960), pp. 5,117, 214, 268.

133. *In IV Sent.*d. 1, q. 2, a. 6, sol 3.

134. H. Schillebeeckx, *De Sacrementele,* 617.

135. Karl Rahner, "Die Rucksicht auf die verschiedenen Aspekte der Frommigkeit," in *Handbuch der Pastoral theologie,* II/1, ed. F.X. Arnold et al. (Freiburg: Herder, 1966) 71

136. Robert Hotz, *Sakramente im Wechselspiel zwischen Ost und West* (Einsiedeln: Benziger, 1979) 266–286.

137. Ludger Kruse, "Der Sakramentsbegriff des Konzils von Trient und die heutige Sakramentstheologie," *Theologie und Glaube* 45 (1955) 401–412.

138. Yves, Congar, "The Idea of Major or Principal Sacraments," *Concilium,* I, 4, (January 1968) 4–11.

139. Of this approach a prime example is Jacques Dournes, "Why are There Seven Sacraments?" *Concilium,* I, 4 (January 1968) 35–44.

140. *De Sacramentis* 2 (PL 176, 461–471).

141. Josef Finkenzeller, *Die Lehre von den Sakramenten im allgemeinen* (HDG, IV 1a) 120.

142. *In IV Sent.* d 2, c 1.

143. Josef Finkenzeller, *Die Lehre* 166–172; Hotz, *Sakramente* 269–277.

144. Emile Rideau, "Sakramente, Geschichte, Kulturen," *Orientierung* 43/17 (15 September 1979) 187–190.

145. Yves Congar, *Le Christ, Marie et l'Eglise* (Bruges: Desclee, 1952), 16–20, 40–49.

146. Hans B. Meyer, "Die Sakramente und ihre Symbolik als Antwort auf Grundfragen menschlicher Existenz," *Theologische Akademie* 2, ed. K. Rahner and O. Semmelroth (Frankfurt: Kencht, 1966) 57, 82.

147. See Robert Kress, "Tillich's Principle of Correlation: A Method for All Seasons," *The Bent World: Essays in Religion and Culture,* ed. John May (Chico: Scholars Press, 1981) 55–81.

148. Both are cited in Bernard Leeming, *Principles* 569.

149. ST III, q. 65, a. 1.

150. DS 1311. On the mystical body, 18–20.

151. Franz Dander, *De Sacramentis Christi I* (Innsbruck: Rauch, 1950) 8.

152. On the seven individual sacraments, from various points of view, Joseph Martos, *Doors to the Sacred* (Garden City: Doubleday, 1981); William Bausch, *A New Look at the Sacraments* (Mystic: Twenty-Third, 1983); Bernard Cooke, *Sacraments and Sacramentality* (Mystic: Twenty-Third, 1983); Regis Duffy, *Real Presence* (San Francisco: Harper, 1982); John Schanz, *Introduction to the Sacraments* (New York: Pueblo, 1983); James White, *Sacraments as God's Self-Giving* (Nashville: Abingdon, 1983).

153. Robert Jones, "Metaphor and Sacrament," *The Christian Century,"* 100 (June 1, 1983) 547–549 encourages "a Roman Catholic view of the sacraments" (548). He speaks further of the Catholic "appreciation for the thingness of it all" (549). Here though, as in Worgul's book mentioned above, I cannot avoid uneasiness in regard to the word "metaphor," although it is fast gaining popularity among theologians, especially in sacramental theology, It seems to me that theologians enthralled by metaphor tend precisely to misappreciate "thingness." One does better, it seems to me, with an approach like the "mystical-biological" one of Teilhard de Chardin, *Hymm of the Universe* (New York: Harper, 1965) 19–37.

154. Karl Rahner, ST, 13, 243–45.

155. J. Lecuyer, *Le Sacerdoce dans le Mystere du Christ* (Paris: Cerf, 1957) 181.

156. Joseph Fitzmyer explains the implications of this text.

> Christians by their Baptism are deputed to the cultic service of God in Christ. In Romans 12:1 Paul appeals to Christians to offer themselves as a "living sacrifice" that would be holy and acceptable to God—this to be their "spiritual worship." The baptized Christian is therefore empowered and expected to live his whole life as if it were a cultic act, continuing in a sense the sacrifice of Christ, but also manifesting to the world that he is marked for the service of Christ.

This quotation reminds us that there are two "kinds" of sacrifice in the lives of Catholics. There is, first of all, the sacrifice of everyday living. This is the dedication of one's life—wholly and entirely—to the Kingdom of God. This is the "spiritual worship'' of which Fitzmyer speaks. Spiritual is a problematic word. Too often it is taken to mean invisible and then unreal, removed from the world, merely interior. But that is not its real meaning. Spiritual is properly contrasted to sacramental or ritual in the precisely narrow sense—contrasted, not opposed or contradictory. Joseph A. Fitzmyer, ''The First Epistle of Peter,'' in *The Jerome Biblical Commentary* (58–12), ed. R. Brown, J. Fitzmyer, R. Murphy (Englewood Cliffs: Prentice-Hall, 1968) 365.

157. Vatican II, *Constitution on the Sacred Liturgy* 61.

158. *The Liturgy,* 60.

159. W.J. O'Shea, *The Worship of the Church* (Westminster: Newman, 1957), 533.

160. *Epistola* 64 (Pl 77, 1186–1187, 1200).

161. *The Liturgy,* 21, 37, 38, 40.

162. DS 1728: ''Salva illorum substantia.'' Again, the Council did not clarify the meaning of this phrase nor did it identify the substance of each sacrament.

163. On the receptive, institutional role of the Church in the origin of the sacraments, see H. Schuster,''Ansatz einer existentialen Ekklesiologie,'' *Wagnis Theologie,* ed. Herbert Vorgrimler (Freiburg: Herder, 1979) 379–386.

164. See Franz Schupp, *Glaube-Kultur-Symbol* (Dusseldorf: Patmos, 1974) 31–77.

165. This seems to have entirely escaped Tad Guzie, *The Book of Sacramental Basics* (New York: Paulist, 1982).

166. Athanasius, *De Incarnatione,* 8 (PG 26, 996C).

167. P. Evdokimov, *L'Orthodoxie* (Paris: Neuchatel: 1959), 75, 94.

168. Vatican II, *The Church* 48, 1.

4

THE CHURCH AS COMMUNICATION

One could wonder about the title of this chapter, since it is obvious that we have been talking about the Church as communication all along. The Church as communion presupposes and describes the fact that God has communicated with the creation, in deed and sign. As sacrament, the Church is explicitly the communication of the divine life to human life in deed and sign (ritual). Hence, the topic of this chapter is by no means entirely new. In this chapter, though, we wish to emphasize the Church as a network or system of communications. System is a word to which people are sometimes allergic. But there is no need for that, since system does not necessarily entail oppression or uniformity or the ignoring of individual differences. The opposite of systematic is not free or charismatic, but unsystematic—disorderly and chaotic and anarchic. Exactly what we mean by system will become clear as we move through this chapter. Although communication is a very popular term these days—one could even call it a code or buzz word—it has not played a great role in ecclesiology.

Vatican II did issue a *Decree on the Means of Social Communication,* but it is generally regarded as by far the least successful of all the conciliar documents. More than all the other documents it least successfully fulfilled the Council's stated desire to speak the Gospel of Christ to the modern world. It remains caught up in a moralism and clericalism elsewhere diminished by the Council. Perhaps its chief value is as a sort of negative cipher, highlighting the past history of the Church as a system of communications that has not kept pace with the times.[1] Throughout this chapter we shall suggest that a communications system germane to earlier cultural conditions may no longer be effective today, and we shall try to suggest some means whereby the Church can communicate more effectively today, both within itself and with the whole world of whose salvation it is the sacrament.

The crucial question is not *whether* the Church is communication, the crucial question is ''only'' *how.* Not the fact, but the mode of the Church as communication is apt matter for discussion. As Avery Dulles has noted, ''communications is at the heart of what the Church is all about. The Church exists to bring men into communion with God and thereby to open them up to communication with each other. . . . If communications is seen as the procedure by which communion is achieved and maintained, we may also say that the Church is communications . . . a vast communications network." He goes on to note "the rich variety of modes by which Christ himself communicated" and to "suggest that the Church, too, as an incarnational reality, may utilize all the possibilities of communication at hand in a given culture."[2] As Augustine noted long ago, communication has been largely verbal. He explained the small number of other signs on the basis of the superiority of words in human activity and communication. "But, compared to words, all these signs are very few indeed. . . . But the innumerable multitude of signs, by which men express their thoughts, are constituted in and by words."[3]

However, we also know that there is non-verbal communication and that this non-verbal communication can at least sometimes be more effective than verbal. Within the Christian tradition, the Catholic Churches (Roman, Anglican, Orthodox) have especially preserved and cultivated "non-verbal" communication in the sacraments, sacramentals and other ritual actions. I have put non-verbal in quotation marks, since, as we have seen, sacraments are not really non-verbal, since human words belong to the very nature of the sacrament. We might do better to describe them as trans-verbal, since they take the word over into a more complex human phenomenon. Indeed, the Catholic tradition has maintained and emphasized nature itself as a means and place of communication between divine and human being.

Medieval theologians like Hugh of St. Victor emphasized that "the whole sensibly perceptible world is like a book written by the finger of God."[4] According to Alain of Lille, "For us the world's every creature is like a book, a picture, a mirror."[5] Unlike the "vertical" theology and ecclesiology espoused by Karl Barth and his disciples, the Catholic tradition enjoys a "horizontal" dimension.[6] In this horizontal dimension, the symbolism of nature plays a decisive communicational role. As M.-D. Chenu has noted, "knowledge of God and his designs was derived from both nature and from history. These, men said, were the two 'books' in which God taught us."[7]

Our tradition, then, allows and encourages us to think of Church and Churchly communication as other than merely verbal. As important as preaching is, it is not the only and not necessarily always the best or most effective means of proclaiming and communicating the faith. In addition to preaching, natural symbolism and sacramental ritual, the Gospel can also be communicated by charitable or social service and action. For us, even the Eucharist as the most precise and ritually emphatic communication and proclamation of Christ's sacrifice, that is, his self-reference to God in recognition and honor of God's excellence, is not absolute. We know that the good news of Christ and of "the Church's union with Christ's sacrifice could and can be manifested and achieved in other ways as well as in the sign of the eucharistic celebration. Indeed in certain circumstances it can only be convincingly demonstrated in other signs—in acts of charity to relieve urgent need, in devout prayer, etc."[8] Admittedly, this caritative communication has usually been exercised in the alleviation of misery already being endured. This remedial approach has clearly outweighed the preventive approach, if we might so call it, of establishing healthy institutions and structures in society. Not all wish to include this preventive or positive approach in the direct mission or communicational activity of the Church.[9] Their reluctance can be readily rejected as a still lingering culturally conditioned caution, which is required neither ecclesially nor theologically. Of course, one must hasten to emphasize immediately and equally that not every religiously or "evangelically" motivated and inspired interest and concern, especially reformist, in political matters is to the point. The religious motive clearly confers neither knowledge nor competence in the disciplines requisite to the structuring of the good society.[10] The journey from the good news communicated by Jesus and the New Testament to the establishment of the fair, just and good society is long and arduous. Nevertheless, the social action of Christians individually and of the whole Church officially is as much a part of the Church's communication of the good news of salvation as its remedial charity, its preaching, its sacramental celebration and its natural philosophizing. To say "as much" is not to say, of course, that all these means of communication are of equal value or that they are indifferently interchangeable. Rather, each has its own peculiar and irreplaceable value. Each belongs to the communications system which is the Church, as does still another which we shall now mention.

In this chapter we shall emphasize still another non-verbal mode of communication, one which also relies heavily on verbal communication. This mode of communication in question is that of societal organization and leadership. As we shall see, leadership is a very wide-ranging term. It includes a great number of activities within its scope. Too often, leadership is restricted to a particular kind or a few kinds of leadership in both popular and scholarly presentations. We shall suggest an expanded understanding which will enable many—in fact all—to be leaders, without, at the same time, evacuating the term "leadership" of any and all identifiable content. The arrangement of the Church's membership, their multiple interaction, especially the interrelationship of ordained, official, hierarchical leaders with all the other "leaderly" members—all this is crucial for the Church as communication. It is also crucial for the Church as communion, for if communications break down within the articulated membership of the Church, the Church's communion will also suffer. Consequently, the Church as the sacrament of the world's salvation— communication and communion of God with man and among humans—would at least be clouded and obscured. Whenever, then, we think of the Church as communication we must keep in mind all the elements we have discussed so far. And we must continue to emphasize that, precisely as a system of communication among all its members, the Church must continue to be and act in the image and likeness of the triune-communion God. As communication the Church continues its theandric nature and mission—between divinity and humanity and within humanity.

We can begin our detailed examination of the Church as communication by recalling two of the "definitions" of the Church suggested above—tradition and memory of Christ. The entire Church is entrusted with the handing on of the memory of Christ—within itself, for others and to future generations. I say "to itself" because the Church must preserve and promote the memory of Christ within its own membership as well as with others who are not in full communion with it. I say "not yet" and "full " because it is legitimate to regard all creation as radically caught up in God's self-communication to the world in Christ, explicitly in the Church, anonymously elsewhere. Although "anonymous Christianity" is most closely associated with Karl Rahner, Edward Schillebeeckx also speaks of "an at least anonymous supernatural revelation and faith . . . unconscious Christianity . . . grace remained . . . strictly anonymous . . . anonymous dialogue (of creation) with God."[11] Elsewhere, he also speaks of "implicit Christianity . . . God-centered life, albeit anonymous . . . anonymous Christianity . . . that portion of mankind that is anonymously Christian and in which the Church is anonymously present . . . mankind carries within itself and anonymously this ecclesial orientation as a grace that is accepted or rejected." Finally, "The Church is actively present even when her adequate ecclesial form has not yet appeared."[12] As communication, the Church's charge is to bring the universally, divinely communicated Christic grace into ever greater, explicit "ecclesial form," among both explicit and implicit Christians. The Church itself is not salvation purely and simply. It is, rather, the sacrament (sign and cause) of this salvation in the world.

In a word, then, the Church communicates the original theandric communication throughout time and place in word and action and sign. This communication takes place primarily in and through the very members of the Church. They are the Church communicating and communicated. They are the memory and tradition of Christ.

Memory and tradition are especially apt for a consideration of the Church as communication. Although one can well say that the Church is the tradition of the memory (of Christ), one can also simply say that the Church is the tradition of Christ. Three elements are involved in the Church as tradition: that which is handed on (the object(-s); the *traditum* or *tradita*); that which hands on (the subject or agent; the *traditor*); that by which the handing on takes place (the action or process; the *traditio*). From the viewpoint of tradition, the Church is clearly communication.

This idea is driven home in a book which describes the Church as "a *koinonia* of memory and the Spirit [within which] Christian meaning and insight took on appropriate and formal structures."[13] The title notwithstanding, *kerygma* (the authoritative proclamation, both act and message, of divine revelation) and *didache* (the authoritative doctrinal clarification, elaboration and appropriation of this *kerygma*) are not the only, perhaps not the most important categories or forms of Christian discourse and communication.

They are joined by four others which also, of course, have "Greek" names. *Propheteia* as prophecy enlists the emotions and imagination in the service and appreciation of the Gospel. *Paraclesis* or exhortational preaching is a kind of popular exegesis which uses creative imagination and rhetoric to make Christ and Christian way more appealing. *Paraenesis* or practical teaching emphasizes the application of the Gospel to the practical necessities of everyday life. In the context of baptism, it is known as catechesis. Finally, and undergirding these other three, comes *paradosis,* the tradition developing about the life, person and teaching of Jesus, understood on the basis of the Easter event of the resurrection. Like the other three, *paradosis* is rooted in the life and worship of the Church, its religious experience in general. *Paradosis* is not the Gospel, but its carrier or bearer, that which transports the Gospel: ''It presents data which must be conveyed to and grasped by the hearer if he is to understand the basis on which the Gospel can be proclaimed.''[14] It is worth making explicit that these activities were not restricted to any group selected or stipulated *a priori.* All members, in various ways and according to their various gifts, could and did participate in these forms of Christian communication. The same still holds true today. It is especially important to note that all members of the Church bear the responsibility and the capacity to participate in the Church as communication. All are communicators of the good news, all are *traditores*—handers/passers on of the memory of Christ, of Christ himself, all, of course, in their own ways. And it is these ways which we now wish to investigate.

Some years ago, Richard Dillon suggested ''a dialectic of the New Testament quest for a durable Church order. We have traced it specifically in the provisions for stewardship of the tradition which were essential to all the ministries we investigated. . . . *Traditio* is faithful mediation of the constitutive testimony of Christ in ages and circumstances which the inspired *testes* [the original inspired witnesses] could not have foreseen.''[15] Stewardship of the tradition is a formal description within which the tradition preserving and promoting contributions of the various members of the body of Christ and the various gifts of the one Holy Spirit can be coordinated. As we shall see, during the course of history, for various reasons, the stewardship of the tradition was concentrated into one kind of stewardship or ministry, the official ordained ministry of holy orders. This concentration, although not simply unjustified, did contribute strongly to an impoverishment of the Church precisely as (a system of) communications. A similar approach can be taken in regard to the Church as apostolic succession, which has wider and more restricted applications.[16] It can legitimately refer to the entire Church, to the entire tradition. On the other hand, it can also refer to a certain dimension of this Church, of this tradition, namely a particular ministry in the stewardship of the whole tradition, the hierarchical official ministry conferred by holy orders. ''Thus,'' acording to Joseph Ratzinger, ''it emerges that apostolic tradition and apostolic succession define each other. The succession is the external form of the tradition, and tradition is the content of the succession. . . Apostolic succes-

sion is essentially the living presence of the Word in the person of the witness.''[17] Here Ratzinger is speaking, directly, and rightly so, of ''episcopal
succession.'' Even in this context we can see how the concept of person-wit-
ness as apostolic successor (and steward of the tradition) can also have a wider
range than the bishops. It is necessary to accept the specialized usage which
developed in history, but at the same time we must also guard against the dangers inherent in such specialization, namely the restriction and isolation of
truths originally much wider ranging. In the rest of this chapter we shall see
how the stewardship of the tradition has been articulated in the past and how it
might be more effectively articulated today. We shall be guided by Vatican
II's statement that ''all ought to cooperate in the spreading and intensifying of
the Kingdom of Christ in the world'' (*The Church* 35). In other words, all
members of the Church are called upon to cooperate in the Church, the sacrament of salvation, as a system of communications communicating this very
salvation itself.

The scope of this cooperation is twofold: holiness and apostolate or mission, both of which involve the articulated membership of the Church. This
twofold scope is consistent with the original divine communication which is
simultaneously sanctifying and signifying. Although the two modes of coop-
erating and communicating (mission and holiness) are distinct, they are not to
be separated. The intimate relationship between personal holiness and professional ministry has been a favorite theme of theology, especially so-called
spiritual theology. This theme has usually been treated in regard to the ordained, official ministry of the priesthood, but no inherent reason restricts it
thereto. All members of the Church must be holy in the context of their vocations, the roles they play in society and Church. Of course, particular elements
in the actual constitution of the holiness of each person will vary according to
the particular conditions and circumstances, the situation, of that person.[18] For
this reason saints play an important role in the Church. They illustrate not only
the gracious gifts of God. They also illustrate the myriad responses of humankind to this grace in different times and places. ''What Christian holiness is is
revealed in the life of Jesus and his saints . . . they are the initiators and creative exemplars of precisely that holiness which is required by and proper to
any given age.''[19] Explicitly canonized saints are but more eye-catching instances or manifestations of the holiness which is possible and actual among
many other people in the Church and world, whose ''anonymous'' holiness is
celebrated on their own special feast day on November 1, All Saints. It remains unfortunate that the catalog of these explicitly canonized saints is not as
representative as it might be, straitened, as it is, by cultural, national, sexual,
and vocational strictures.[20] Such strictures both illustrate and further deficiencies in the Church as a system of communications, for they imply that certain
members have occcupied privileged positions in regard to the mission and holiness of the Church. As we shall see, privilege like this is a perversion of the

original diversity in unity and unity in diversity which is a hallmark of the Church.

The whole question is also intimately bound up with another question, namely the existence and exercise of leadership in the Church. Too often leadership has been understood very narrowly and has been restricted to only a certain kind of leadership, the ordained priest–episcopal–papal office. This overemphasis on one kind of leadership has naturally de-emphasized and underemphasized other modes of leadership and participation in the Church as communication. In this context, a cleft developed within the Church, separating the ordained, official hierarchy on the one side and the "simple" faithful, the laity, on the other. This split became so intense that one theologian has seen fit to call for a sort of ecumenical movement *within* the Church, playing on the Johannine verse so popular in ecumenical discussions, "that all might be one" (Jn 17:21).[21] Are saintly holiness and apostolic mission restricted only to a few, to a privileged few? Is the Church as communications system basically a monarchy or oligarchy in which all communication is from the top down? Is ecclesiology really hierarchology,[22] where a few tell the rest what to do and what to think and how to behave? Is the stewardship of the tradition the privileged preserve of special persons? Are a few members of the Church the active communicators, the rest a mass of passive communicatees? What happened to the great variety of gifts of the Holy Spirit proclaimed and manifested in the early Church according to the New Testament? The answers to these questions will enable us to appreciate better the Church as a system of communications and to delineate, at least initially, some future possibilities.

JESUS' DISCIPLES

As we saw earlier, the preaching and healing ministry of Jesus required and resulted in the recruiting of hearers. Of those who heard and saw Jesus, some were favorably impressed and others were not. Of those favorably impressed, some "followed" Jesus. These became his disciples.

It is clear that these disciples and followers of Jesus formed a community of differentiated membership from the very beginning.[23] The New Testament positively affirms such differentiation during the ministry of Jesus (Mk 3:13–19; Lk 10:1–20; Jn 6:1–15; Mt 10:40–42; 14:13–21). Even negative indications are available: Jesus' exhortations that his disciples not lord it over one another (Lk 22:24–27) and his negative evaluations of the leadership style of the Pharisees (Mt 23; Lk 11:37–54). Not only in the Pauline listings of various gifts of the one Holy Spirit, but throughout the other New Testament writings, this differentiation is attested by elders, presbyters, apostles, deacons, super- *episcopal* visors. A striking example of expanding differentiation of membership is the establishment of the seven "deacons"—hardly deacons according to recent theological and canonical understanding (Acts 6:1–7).[24] By the time of the pastoral epistles, "offices" and "officials" are clearly present in the Church, provoking the problem of "Fruehkatholizismus" for those reluctant about definite forms and structures (such as stable offices) in the Church.[25] Even the Johannine writings, apart from their concern with the Simon Peter–Beloved Disciple rivalry, indicate that "the community of believers gathered by those whom Jesus sent out . . . is structured . . . that the evangelist was not opposed to an organized Church. The fact, however, that the references just given came from different strains in the Johannine literature does make it difficult to make an overall judgment on the evangelist's concept of order in the Church."[26]

Even the earliest Church was not a monochromatic, monolithic uniformity. The temptation of certain types of membership to lord it over others was also there very early. Matthew's Gospel and the exhortation of 1 Peter 5:3, "Never be a dictator over any group that is put in your charge," clearly give the lie to those who would assign the temptations of authoritarianism and clericalism solely or principally to the "hierocratic papalism" of the Middle Ages. Articulation and differentiation of membership does not necessarily entail lording it over. Originally the Church was an *adelphotes,* a brotherhood or fraternity (Mt 23:8–10) in which various specialized (ruling) modes of membership were understood to be service, not domination. This brotherhood of believers was rooted in the first-born brother, Jesus (Rom 8:29), who made all to be brothers.[27] Local Churches called themselves "brotherhoods."

However, already in the third century this sense of brotherhood had thinned and waned, as the letters of Cyprian clearly confirm. "He still designates his own community as 'beloved brother,' but he uses the singular 'Brother' only for bishops and clerics." On the other hand, the Roman presbyters and deacons address him as "most blessed and glorious 'Papa.' "[28] Ratzinger detects a double reduction in the sense of ecclesial brotherliness. First, brotherhood no longer described the whole Church, but only a narrow circle within it. Second, the word brother, which carries with it something of the Gospel's simplicity and the absence of overbearing officialdom, was gradually replaced by the formal title, "collega," which was adapted from Roman law, as were other concepts such as "corpus" (body) and "ordo"(order). So, when many rejoiced at Vatican II's revival of collegiality, they were indeed rejoicing at something good, but also at something which was already a decline from the original brotherhood. As Ratzinger points out, although the Church may not be a democracy, it is also not a monarchy or modern centralized state.[29] However, both the theology and the practice of Church order certainly seem to have been monarchical. Not all of this "monarchialism" can simply be attributed to ecclesiastical lust for power.[30] Indeed, the "monarchialization" of the Church is an object lesson in the need for an adequate theory of leadership and membership in this or any other society and in the interplay of theory and praxis in the formation of a given society and its societal structures and institutions.

Unfortunately but also understandably, the early Church did not have an elaborate theory of Church order and office. Seldom do reform movements begin with elaborate schemes of social organization and plans for the permanentizing of the reform. Insofar as Jesus was a wandering, itinerant, charismatic preacher with a predilection for wide open rural spaces rather than organized urban settlements, this movement would have been especially unlikely to be preoccupied with organizational matters.[31] On the other hand, Jesus and his disciples would also have been familiar with the religious organization of Judaism and of contemporary Jewish sects, so they need not be accounted anarchists or pure charismatic enthusiasts. As members of the working class, they may indeed be considered to have been even more than a bit suspicious of pure spontaneity, knowing from their occupational experience that lack of organization produces neither freedom nor profit, but chaos and loss. However, in the case of the early Church, still another factor may have been decisive in the paucity of organizational information. The imminent eschatological expectations of the earliest Church would not have been conducive to the extensive elaboration of either the theory or the institutions of Church organization. If the present age is truly passing away (1 Cor 7:29–31), certain human considerations otherwise crucially important are considerably relativized—relativized, not completely abandoned, for Paul's response to the feasibility of marriage and his dispositions for the orderly life of the Thessalonian Church (2 Thess 2:1–3; 3:1–15) show that even a hyper-expectant, apocalyptic age is not immune from concern for orderliness. This lesson, that the natural and human are neither nullified nor superseded by the supernatural, often seems to elude enthusiasts of charismatic, structureless Church order.[32]

For a contemporary theory of Church order there is a further problem, fundamentalist, biblicist positivism. Generally associated with certain strains of Protestant Christianity, it is also operative in both liberal and conservative Catholic circles, especially in regard to locating the papal or Petrine office in the New Testament.[33] In regard to this and other institutional offices in the Church, biblical positivists both demand and find clear and distinct and detailed evidence in the New Testament writings—demand if they are Protestant, find if they are Catholic, at least conservative. Both represent illicit expectations. As we have noted already, it is unlikely that a reform movement like Jesus' would elaborate a complex theory of Church structure and order. On the other hand, since the people involved were real people and had to live and function in the real world, they would soon—immediately—find that they could not survive without some structures and order. So, the decisive question is not whether the New Testament, facts and books, offers a full blown theory and practice of an ecclesial establishment, but whether it offers data which indicate the initiation of and receptivity to an organized and structured arrangement of the people of God who are the body of Christ. To this the answer is affirmative, even when grudgingly and unnecessarily conditionedly given.[34] Furthermore, one cannot but wonder at John Meier's wonderment at the emergence, existence and "theological justification of the monarchical (single) episcopate. . . . Likewise, by the end of the second century, the single-bishop form of government had triumphed in the major churches of the Roman Empire."[35] A given of human experience was clearly if not artistically proclaimed by President Harry Truman: "The buck stops here!" Even Marxist communism discovered that a *troika* does not work for all forms of leadership and administration. However consensual and collegial leadership and decision making might be, there is always one person who is ultimately responsible. To describe this with the term monarchical is not entirely correct, for monarchy has overtones that are generally absolutist, often oppressive and repressive. But the ultimate responsibility of one person in a society or community need not necessarily imply or embody such negativity. In the long run, as we shall see, there is office and structure in the Church because the Church is composed of human beings, and human beings need order. Even Jesus' "strictures against clericalism in Matthew 23:1–12" do not advocate the disestablishment of Judaism.

This does not seem to be understood by Ursula Schnell, who contrasts Karl Rahner's "Legitimation of Office on the Basis of the Societal-Institutional Structure or Constitution of the Church" with "The Legitimation of Office on the Basis of a Divine 'Institution.' "[36] After her explanation of Rahner's position, she comments: "Of this position of Rahner's the critical question must be asked why he bases his justification of the existence of office in the Church chiefly on the Church's societal constitution and nature and why he does not trace its origin back to a divine origin (*goettlichen Ursprung*)." To this earlier explanation she contrasts a later article by Rahner in which she claims to find "a more forcefully theological justification of office in the Church." However, the contrast is not really there, for in the explanation (according to her), Rahner locates "the roots of Church office in the apostolic office, which is based on the authority of the Church founded by/through Christ." He thinks that "that starting point for the determination of the essential nature of office is to be found in the leadership (*Leitung*) of the community, which embraces both word and sacrament."[37] Schnell's biblicist and positivist orientation is most blatant when she asserts, "In contrast to Rahner, who legitimates Church office chiefly on the basis of the societal nature and constitution of the Church. Schillebeeckx, Ratzinger, Schlier, Semmelroth [and] Schmaus look to revelation for the answer to the question of the origin of office in the Church."[38] Revelation indeed! Apparently even the foundation of the Church is not sufficiently revelational for Schnell, whose approach both presumes and establishes an abyss between humanity and grace, the natural and supernatural. For her, nature is not transformed, elevated, and perfected by grace. It is, rather, bypassed and replaced. The natural need of the sociopolitical human being for orderliness and the consequent establishment of an orderly society cannot mature graciously into the ordered, orderly Church. Jesus can presume nothing from the order of creation, which can be neither elevated nor redeemed. It must be replaced, for there is an insuperable abyss between man and God at least historically, since through original sin and the fall human nature is totally corrupt. In Lutheran and Calvinist theology there is inevitably a schizophrenia between the natural and the supernatural. Especially the Barthian emphasis has been pointedly criticized by Paul Tillich, who notes that according to the supranaturalistic method (as he calls it), "man must become something else than human in order to receive divinity."[39]

This kind of biblical positivism and theological abyssism is disastrous for all theology, especially of office in the Church. The Roman Catholic version of this biblical positivism is equally unacceptable. Conservatives claim that only a fool could miss the clear New Testament evidence that Christ instituted the sacrament of holy orders with a triple gradation, namely bishop, priest, deacon. For liberals it is equally clear that only a fool could find even traces of such a sacramental institution or articulation. And why, in any case, would one want to? Unfortunately, the positive historical data required for such an approach to office in the Church are simply not available—whether to support or refute the Catholic or the Protestant positions. In any case, the general debility of this entire approach has also been noted by Tillich, for its presuppositions require Christian realities to "have fallen into the human situation like strange bodies from a strange world."[40]

This biblicist positivism is not entirely absent from recent Roman Catholic considerations of office and minstry in the Church,[41] as Bernard Cooke indicates in the following statement:[42]

> What seems quite interesting, and in the last analysis may be of basic importance, is that one finds in neither the Old Testament texts nor in the New Testament writings any claim that this "office" or elder was of special divine institution—in opposition to the claims made for kingship, priesthood and even prophecy. Rather, the role of the elders in Old Testament Israel seems to have resulted quite naturally from the needs of the group. . . . In the early Christian churches . . . the quick emergence of established groups of presbyters seems to have resulted from the possession of natural leadership plus some form of community designation. . . . In any event, it seems quite clear that the concrete needs of the Christian community dictated the existence of these Christian elders. . . . Just as the role of the elders seems to have arisen from the practical needs of the community . . .

Why would anyone postulate such a contrast between "special divine institution" and "to have resulted quited naturally from the intrinsic needs of the group" unless he had fallen prey, unawares in all likelihood, to the "supranaturalistic method"? Cooke's espousal of such a position is all the stranger, since he so obviously wants to be expansive and not exclusionary. A major source (we shall elaborate this later on) of the problem may well lie in his entanglement in customary theological categories and language, clearly illustrated by his fascination with prophecy: "Yet, the heart of the Christian leadership we are describing lies in *being* Christian; it is an 'ontological prophetism' which is more radical than the prophetic activity that flows from it" (208).

This is compounded by his concept of the ministry of the word from which he excludes the governing function (212, 337), his minimal appreciation of the managerial and administrative ministries (180–181) and his consequent meager appreciation of bishops as administrators (211) and his *simpliste* equation of leadership in the Church with faith, hope and charity (208). There is something correct and even profound about this latter statement, but it is left simply undeveloped. And it is dreadfully compromised by his contention that such ontologically prophetic, spirit-possessed leaders "are 'consecrated,' not in some unintelligible ritual way but by the fact that their consciousness is absorbed in the Christ-mystery and thus 'set apart' and Christianized" (208). Such an attitude must find very congenial the flight from the problems of differentiated Church membership in Emil Brunner's misunderstanding of the Church as "a pure communion of persons."[43] Such approaches seem to me not very helpful, for, like Hans Küng's contention that "what is really important for the leader of a church . . . is not the position he holds . . . but whether and to what extent he is purely and simply a believer,"[44] they simply avoid the entire problem of differentiated membership in the Church. Of course, faith, hope and charity are the most important. But the problem is that no one is "purely and simply" a believer. One is always a particular believer in a particular time and place, with particular abilities, gifts and responsibilities. In the Church we are clearly "brothers and sisters," but that does not describe precisely how we are to live together and bear witness to the ends of the world. Furthermore, Cooke's emphasis on prophetism, even ontological, does not take into account that prophecy is not an unequivocal term in either New or Old Testament. In both, a, if not the, critical problem was the discernment of true from false prophets and prophecy. Indeed, for Zechariah (13:2–6) prophecy is as reprobate a designation as one can imagine. Prophecy is not, then, necessarily a privileged category to describe participation in the Church as communication. Church order includes the prophetic, but is not merely or chiefly prophetic.

Of course neither is it monarchical, especially not in the heightened monistic mode which has been so dominant in recent theology.[45]

In this view the Pope rules over the whole Church. He allows bishops to rule over small parts of his Church. The bishops allow pastors to rule over even smaller parts. The mood and the mode of this ruling is truly monarchical—it is a one man show. A better illustration of this understanding than Dominic Palmieri's book, whose title itself is alarmingly revealing, would be hard to find. In 1877 he published his *Treatise on the Roman Pontiff, with a*

Prolegomenon on the Church, in which he claimed explicitly that "the form of Church government (its *regimen)* is therefore monarchical by divine law." He also explicitly distinguished this monarchy from aristocracy, democracy, and constitutional, representative forms of monarchy and democracy. Furthermore, this form was not copied from secular governments during the course of the Church's history. It was, rather, freely, positively and deliberately instituted by Christ himself. "Therefore, through the power conferred on Peter, Christ established the form of a monarchical regime in the Church. . . ." Thus "Christ himself immediately conferred supreme power on Peter alone; others share in this power only through Peter and in dependence on him."[46] That Pope Pius IX could at least have been rumored to have exclaimed, in the manner of the Sun King Louis XIV, "La tradizione sono Io," is quite consistent with this monarchical theology.[47] It enabled theologians, canon lawyers and car-dinals, if not the Popes themselves, to say: "The Supreme Pontiff occupies the summit of the Church and can be called The Church." Another curialist simply said "Papa ipse Ecclesia"—"The Pope himself [is] the Church." Most illuminating for the history of the Church's actual government is a fourteenth cen-tury cardinal's appraisal: "The Pope and the Lord cardinals [note, no longer Brother, but Lord!] are in the Roman (Catholic) Church in such way (so intensely) that they are themselves this very Roman Church itself. . . ."[48]

Although in theory, theologians like Palmieri continued to proclaim that the Church was a monarchy, the cardinals knew that it was really an oligarchy—the rule of a few privileged and powerful insiders.

And so did the Roman curia, as it does to this very day. Involved here is not only the concentration of power in a few members of the Church, but also a change in the focus of the Church's meaning and nature. It is effectively and in practice no longer a communion, brotherly sharing and communication. As F. X. Arnold emphasizes:[49]

> With almost dialectical necessity the attacks on the hierarchical structure of the Church—from Marsilius of Padua (d. 1342) through the Reformers to the seventeenth century—caused a new kind of theology of the Church. In this new approach it was no longer the Mystery of the Church which occupied the centerpiece, as in the Fathers of the ancient Church and the Masters of Medieval Scholasticism. No, now it was the power of the Church.

This emphasis on power coincides with its concentration in a very few privileged members of the Church. Is it any wonder, then, that a historian could conclude:[50]

> The Catholic Church is the Church of the clergy. Pope, bishop and priest constitute the Church. According to its canon law, the clerics

alone appear as full-fledged members. The laity are but the people who are to be led and taught.

I include all this not to beat a dead horse or a living hierarchy. However, without some idea of this history we cannot understand the present condition of the Church as communication and its leadership theory and practice. The monarchical mood and mode was also operative in the Church at large, even in religious communities which were really supposed to be brotherhoods and sisterhoods. The same mood also obtained in marriage and family life, although, St. Paul did urge husbands to love their wives as Christ loved the Church (Eph 5:22–30).

Is, then, the brotherhood of all through the first-born brother, the risen Jesus (Rom 8:19; 1 Cor 15:20) merely a utopian longing or an unreal pipedream? Must all leadership and active communication be located in either ordained monarchical officials or free-floating prophetic spirits? The Church is neither monarchy nor absolute state nor spontaneous charismatic commune. It is a communion. But how is this communion to be understood and practiced so that the Church will be an effective system of communication of the good news of salvation. Some contemporary writers have seized upon the concept of *diakonia* (ministry, service) as the means to free the Church from its monarchical and Babylonian captivity.[51] But this concept, as desirable as it may well be, is as much bane as boon. Of course, communication, authority, and leadership in the Church should be service. But, then, so should service in the state. And who is not able to summon up the energy to claim servanthood! Even Hitler regarded himself as the servant of not only the *Volk,* but also of history and humanity. Did Jim Jones think otherwise? Prelatial Popes, who so irritate contemporary *diakonia* advocates, lived under the motto "Servus servorum Dei." Unfortunately, the term service or ministry is so general that it is basically contentless. As Frans Josef van Beeck notes, "The distinction . . . here proposed tries to be a bit milder than the one proposed by John L. McKenzie in *Authority in the Church* . . . which takes a surprisingly dim view of authority in civil society and a disappointingly unrealistic view of authority in the Church. Love and service (the latter of which notions is distorted by the biased translation of *diakonos* by 'lackey') are made to sound a bit too rosy to suit my taste."[52] The hendiadys, service-ministry, remains homiletic and exhortational, a statement of the question rather than an answer. I think it unlikely that a suitable "category" to describe the communication communion of the Church will be found if we remain with the traditional theological terms. Otto Semmelroth has pointed out the deficiencies of the triad priest–prophet–king for ecclesiological considerations.[53] A major difficulty with such categories is that they came from socio-political contexts which are not necessarily congenial to the Church as communion or to the state of educated, mature Catholics today.

They can be adapted, certainly, but they will always limp, the more so as the general society changes. It is possible that we shall be able to find adequate categories to describe the Church as communication only if we relinquish those dominant until now. New ones may well be necessary and also available.

I am encouraged in this by recent writings of Thomas O'Meara, Edward Schillebeeckx and Bernard Cooke, who all call for attention to sociology and the social sciences in regard to the theology of leadership and office. Unfortunately, they do little more. This is illustrated by the indices of Bernard Cooke's volume of 677 pages. The index of names contains no managerial theorists and authors. In the subject index, management does not appear at all, adminstration only as Church administration (and that under service), and leadership only several times. On pages 190–191 there is a jeremiad about the paternalism of recent and current official Church leadership. On page 203, we read that "leadership is not to be confused with administration," but no explanation of the difference is given. On page 207–209 leadership is explained in one paragraph, contrasted to office, and more or less equated with faith, hope and charity. On page 337 leadership is distinguished from "organization, administration and service" and described as "not specifically pointing to a certain function but rather to a much more general and subtle influence that some individuals exert upon a group." The multiple entries under office are basically in the customary ecclesiastical language and concepts and display no greater acquaintance with contemporary leadership and management literature than do the other categories mentioned earlier in this paragraph. It is interesting that under clergy are contained "leadership in immigrant groups" and "lifestyle, modern professional identity, modern sociological situation." But these entries are also basically historical, at best "retrospective sociology."[54] All this is intended merely to indicate that even among major theologians the problem of leadership-membership in the Church remains mired in old states of the question and old conceptualizations. Under these circumstances "the absorption of all ministerial functions of the Church into the pastoral office [however] inconsistent with the charismatic nature of the Church"[55] is not likely to be remedied. At times Cooke drops hints about the conceptualizations and distinctions necessary for an adequate appreciation of variegated leadership within the Church's multiple membership (203, 337), but nowhere does he develop them. Such distinctions and categorializations cannot be merely urged and asserted, as if their meanings were adequately developed, understood and accepted. They must be developed, and in this development the contemporary disciplines of social psychology and leadership-management theory can make significant contributions. But they have not yet been incorporated into the theology of Church membership and leadership, of Church order and authority.

In this context Edward Schillebeeckx notes a growing acceptance of some kind of institutional, official leadership function among Protestants.[56] This type of leadership implies some sort of "over-againstness"[57] within the membership of the Church which, nevertheless, remains a brotherly-sisterly *"we."*[58] However, this "over-againstness" is not explained and remains only either a pious wish or an edifying exhortation. Schillebeeckx's recent collection of previously published articles on ministry is also concerned with leadership, as the subtitle indicates. It also contains numerous calls for a sociological analysis and approach to leadership, ministry and priesthood.[59] However, one also reads such statements as "From both sides it has become clear that a more empirical approach to the problem of the ministry and the practice of official ministry has begun to prevail in the Church. . . . Although this sociological professionalization may be the intention here and there, i.e., that the priest should ultimately be seen as a kind of social worker, this is by no means the basic tenor of these new practical and theoretical approaches, whether among theologians or among priests" (105–106). This disappointing statement reveals Schillebeeckx's continuing unsociological stance, in that he seems to accept the equation of "sociological professionalization" with a "kind of social worker." It also demonstrates the continuing absence of sociological and management theory and knowledge from the thought and conceptualization of systematic theologians. With this criticism I do not wish to indicate that I think the task I am proposing is easy, only that it is necessary and has not yet been undertaken in any significant degree. Furthermore, as long as theology remains beholden to the customary categories of theological clarification, it may not be able to develop an adequate theory of leadership in the Church and of the Church as communication.

How heavily customary categories and conceptualizations can weigh on theological discourse and how hindersome they can be in developing new insights is illustrated very well by the debates about Catholic Action earlier this century. Some thought that the definition of Catholic Action as "the participation of the laity in the apostolate of the hierarchy" was too daring. It threatened proper hierarchical power and Church order, although Pope Pius XI himself claimed to have achieved this definition "not without divine inspiration."[60] To ward off such fears, Pope Pius XII replaced "participation" with "collaboration/cooperation," without, however, according to Y. Congar, "changing the true and basic meaning of the definition."[61] Such jealous guarding of the prerogatives of the official, ordained hierarchy still persists today according to Thomas Green. Commenting on the *Schema Canonum Libri II de Populo Dei,* he notes "the schema's overly hierarchical ecclesiology."[62] Furthermore, "the schema overemphasizes the obligations and minimizes the rights of believers, which flow from baptism and other sacraments . . . overly conditions the articulation of rights so that their limitations seem essential to the rights themselves and not to their exercise." "Frequently the laity are seen as subjects of the hierarchy rather than as having a sacramentally grounded dignity and right with the hierarchy in the realization of the Church's mission. At times the schema notably lacks a profound sense of *communio* between clergy and laity which is rooted in fundamental Christian equality and strongly emphasized in LB IV (30, 32, 37)."[63] The significance of this critique is not that the schema does not conform or further Vatican II's movement. It is, rather, that the schema perpetuates and reinforces an ecclesiology which positively hinders the development of an adequate theory and practice of membership and leadership in the Church and therefore of true ecclesial communication. This ecclesiology, really the hierarchology noted by Congar, locates all responsibility for the Church originally and principally in the hierarchy, which then doles it out to others as it sees fit. In its papalist-monarchical form this results in a pyramidal model of the Church. Even in its oligarchical form, the laity remain basically "hired hands," as a statement of Luigi Civardi, a great patron of Catholic Action, clearly intimates. According to him, Catholic Action is "the *longa manus* of the ecclesiastical hierarchy."[64] Congar traces the expression to both Cardinal Gasparri and even to Pope Pius XII's landmark address to the Congress of the Laity, October 14, 1951. The papal attempt to soften the expression only points up the problematic even more sharply: "We understand the comparison in this sense, that the ecclesiastical superiors use [this hand] in the manner in which the Creator and Lord uses rational creatures."[65]

For our consideration, the key question raised by these customary understandings of membership and leadership in the Church is twofold. How can they be reconciled with the Church as communion? How do they affect the Church, the sacrament of salvation, in the communication of this salvation? The answers are as unfortunate as they are obvious. Past explanations of the "over-againstness" of leadership in the Church have been such that they have evoked not diversity and differentiation but division and social stratification. This sad situation is splendidly illustrated by Gratian's famous description of the membership and leadership of the Church.[66]

> There are two kinds (*genera*) of Christians. One kind has been freed for and is given over to divine service. Dedicated to contemplation and prayer, it is fitting that these refrain completely from the racket of temporal affairs. Such are the clerics, devoted to God. . . . God has chosen these to be his own. . . . There is another kind of Christian, namely the laity. These are allowed to own temporal things, but only for their use in the necessities of life. . . . To these it is conceded to marry, till the soil, litigate disputes and judge between man and man, place gifts on the altar, pay tithes. Thus they should be able to be saved, if only they shall have avoided vices by benefactions.

Obviously the communion of the Church is hardly brotherly in this state of affairs. Communication of salvation is restricted, in principle, to only a se-

lect few. This communication is strictly one way, from the clerical top to the
lay bottom. But Gratian's description seems almost brotherly and benign,
compared to the Council of Trent's Catechism:[67]

> In the first place, then, the faithful should be shown how great is the
> dignity and excellence of this Sacrament considered in its highest
> degree, the priesthood.
>
> Bishops and priests being, as they are, God's interpreters and
> ambassadors, empowered in His name to teach mankind the divine
> law and the rules of conduct, and holding, as they do His place on
> earth, it is evident that no nobler function than theirs can be imag-
> ined. Justly, therefore, are they called not only Angels, but even
> gods, because of the fact that they exercise in our midst the power
> and prerogatives of the immortal God.

As recently as the end of the previous century even Matthias Scheeben
was able to write: "In virtue of its higher 'order,' the priesthood constitutes,
so to speak, the nobility of the Church, a nobility whose higher dignity and
control of the society's supernatural goods in the realm of grace sets it apart
from the other members. On account of its rank, it is called upon, as a body,
to wield the pastoral power in the Church."[68] Nobility, priesthood, control,
supernatural, power—these terms readily certify Herbert Muhlen's contention
that, in the Constantinian Church, through a kind of mystical identification,
the cleric became the sacral vicar-representative of God.[69] In the same vein,
Hans Urs Von Balthasar describes this development as a false, presumptuous
and arrogant "Reprasentationsmystik."[70] The consequence of this understanding was the effective and symbolic removal of the ordained leader from
within the Church as the society of believing human beings. Ordained ministers, especially insofar as they are called priests and conceptualized in sacerdotal and cultic terms, became almost a new kind of being, floating,
demiurge-like, between heaven and earth, between and God and man.[71]
    This understanding was at least partially caused by the Arian heresy's in-
adequate understanding of the theandric communion of the divine and human
in Christ. The refutation of this heresy was accompanied by a decline in emphasis on the priestliness of Christ, which was itself accompanied by an (excessive) emphasis on the priesthood of the ordained, official ministers of the
Church.[72] Apart from the theological deterioration inherent in these developments, they are precisely relevant to our considerations, for they illustrate the
decay and decline of the Church as a brotherhood of communion and communication. How persistent this divisive ecclesiology of ecclesial leadership
has been is illustrated by provisions of the Codex Juris Canonici: "Clerics
must lead, interiorly and exteriorly, a holier life than the laity and surpass
them in virtue and good works."[73] As late as 1947, Pope Pius XII emphasized
that priestly ordination distinguishes (*discernit*) priests from laity precisely as
(*pariter*) baptism distinguishes Christians from pagans:[74]

In the same way, actually, that baptism is the distinctive mark of all Christians, and serves to differentiate them from those who have not been cleansed in this purifying stream and consequently are not members of Christ, the sacrament of holy orders sets the priest apart from the rest of the faithful who have not received this consecration.

Before we proceed to a more positive description of the Church as brotherly communication, one more remark on theological language and conceptualization is fitting. Nowadays we are frequently reminded of the important role played by language in human being and acting. Martin Luther's contribution to both theology and the German language is widely acknowledged.[75]

In this connection Franz Mayr's remark about the theological achievement of Karl Rahner is not only interesting in itself but also apropos to our specific considerations. It can provide the transition to the second part of our considerations. Mayr has pointed out that one of Rahner's major contributions has been to theologize in a truly German thought form and language rather than in the customary baroque, Latin mode and manner. "Rahner's thinking and thought were born in and out of the world of the German language (*Sprachwelt*), his theology a modern *Theologia Deutsch*." A longer explanation is germane to our point, namely, that contemporary theologians theologizing about leadership and office in the Church accomplish little because they remain beholden to an outmoded language and conceptual world.[76]

One need recall only this. Catholic theology (and in its wake Christian philosophy) was linguistically and culturally "Latin" until the twentieth century, the outcome of post-Tridentine baroque Catholicism's counter-position to the essentially German Reformation and its consequences. It was, furthermore, also signficantly the result of the centralization of post-Vatican I orthodox (if, perhaps, not always orthopractical) theological thought in the Roman theological educational institutions under the immediate directorship of the papacy and the curial bureaucracy in Rome. Theological thought was done essentially in ecclesiastical Latin, which, under the (ideological) guise of a supra-historical and supra-national language—a sort of mystified ecclesial esperanto which was widely and uncritically adhered to by the mass of the Catholic population—continued to be the courtly private language of an in-group whose life and thought style were undeniably both feudal and aristocratic. In that the Catholic Church understood the language of neither Luther nor Kant and Hegel nor, more catastrophically, of Marx, it suffered significant loss of contact with the world.

Mayr reinforces his point with references to Modernism and "the imperial pontificate of Pius XII" during which there was a return of "an almost medieval *Dictatus Papae* mentality of the eras of Gregory VII and Innocent III.'' This mentality, he notes, exists even today and severely endangers the possible development of ''native'' theologies true to the historical and linguistic *ingenium*[77] or genius of local cultures and anthropologies. Acquaintance with and use of a new language, that of sociology and management theory, might enable theologians to develop a more adequate theology of ministry and leadership in the Church and the Church itself to avoid certain leadership conflicts, to live more peacefully in all its members, and to communicate more effectively, both within and without.

COMMUNION AND COMMUNICATION OF GIFTS

At this point we should again recall and emphasize the mutuality of the ecclesiological principles of communion and unity in diversity—diversity in unity. This is utterly necessary if we are to understand the Church as communication. The monarchical and oligarchical tendencies of the past misunderstood the Church as communion and hampered the Church as communication. They restricted all the power given the Church by Christ (Mt 28:18; Lk 24:49; Acts 1:8) to a numerical few who formed a particular caste. Thus, a real sectarian and schismatic spirit was introduced into the Church itself. But this kind of divisive elitism is simply unacceptable. According to St. Paul, ''everybody has his own particular gifts from God'' (1 Cor 7:7; Rom 12:6). Since these gifts from God are the Holy Spirit (Rom 12:4) and since the Holy Spirit is God's power (Lk 24:48; Acts 1:4–8), all Christians have that power which makes active communication and leadership possible. This is completely clear in the New Testament.

> Each of us, however, has been given his own share of grace, given as Christ allotted it. It was said that he would: ''When he ascended to the height, he captured prisoners, he gave gifts to men.'' When it says, 'he ascended,' what can it mean if not that he descended right down to the lower regions of the earth? The one who rose higher than all the heavens to fill all things is none other than the one who descended. And to some, his gift was that they should be apostles; to some, prophets; to some, evangelists; to some, pastors and teachers; so that the saints together make a unity in the work of service, building up the body of Christ (Eph 4:7–13).

> In the light of the grace I have received I want to urge each one among you not to exaggerate his real importance. Each of you must judge himself soberly by the standard of the faith God has given

him. Just as each of our bodies has several parts and each part has a separate function, so all of us, in union with Christ, form one body, and as parts of it we belong to each other. Our gifts differ according to the grace given us. If your gift is prophecy, then use it as your faith suggests; if administration, then use it for administration; if teaching, then use it for teaching (Rom 12:3–8).

There is a variety of gifts but always the same Spirit; there are all sorts of service to be done, but always to the same Lord; working in all sorts of different ways in different people, it is the same God who is working in all of them. The particular way in which the Spirit is given to each person is for a good purpose. One may have the gift of preaching with wisdom given him by the Spirit; another may have the gift of preaching instruction given him by the same Spirit; and another the gift of faith given by the same Spirit; and another the gift of healing through this one Spirit; one, the power of miracles; another, prophecy, another the gift of recognizing spirits, another the gift of tongues and another the ability to interpret them. All these are the work of one and the same Spirit, who distributes different gifts to different people just as he chooses (1 Cor 12:4–11).

Now you together are Christ's body; but each of you is a different part of it. In the Church, God has given the first place to apostles, the second to prophets, the third to teachers; after them miracles, and after them the gift of healing; helpers, good leaders, those with many languages. Are all of them apostles or all of them prophets, or all of them teachers? Do they all have the gift of miracles, or all have the gift of healing? Do all speak strange languages, and all interpret them? (1 Cor 12:27–30).

These texts of St. Paul provide us with the raw material which can be developed into a theory of the Church as communication, a Church in which there are no passive members and in which differentiation leads not to domination but to, as Origen already called for, *diakonia* or service: "Whoever is called to the office of bishop is called not to domination (lording it over) but to service in [of] the whole Church."[78] However, as we have already noted, service, *diakonia,* and ministry are not adequate terms to describe how each empowered member actually communicates the good news of salvation Christ,[79] how they exercise leadership in the Church. We shall now appeal to social psychology for help in understanding the Church as communication and then we shall appeal to management theory for help in understanding various types of leadership in the Church.

THE SIGNIFICANT OTHER

Early in this century a social psychologist, George Herbert Mead, developed the theory known as ''the significant other.'' He was concerned with the interplay of the individual and the greater society and the role of this interplay in the genesis and formation of the individual personality. According to Mead, the genesis of the self and the discovery of the greater society are one and the same event. We learn who we are by learning what society is. We learn our own roles by learning to take or play the role of the other. Peter Berger sums up Mead's theory:[80]

> All this learning occurs, and can only occur, in interaction with other human beings, be it the parents or whoever else raises the child. The child first takes on roles vis-à-vis what Mead calls his ''significant others,'' that is, those persons who deal with him intimately and whose attitudes are decisive for the formation of his conception of himself. Later, the child learns that the roles he plays are not only relevant to this intimate circle but relate to the expectations directed toward him by society at large. This higher level of abstraction in the social response Mead calls the discovery of the ''generalized other.'' That is, not only the child's mother expects him to be good, clean and truthful; society in general does so as well. Only when this general conception of society emerges is the child capable of forming a clear conception of himself. ''Self'' and ''society,'' in the child's experience, are the two sides of the same coin.

We can apply this idea of the significant other to the Church and to the members who are variously gifted by the one Holy Spirit. These gifts of the Holy Spirit empower different members of the Church to be ''significantly other'' to other members of the Church (and to those not yet members) in various ways. There is not only one significant other, there are many. They all communicate the salvation of which the Church is the sacrament. They all contribute to the building up of the Church, to the formation of the identity of the new ''cosmic man'' who is the fullness of the mystery of Christ—the *totus Christus* or whole Christ of whom St. Augustine spoke so often and so eloquently. The significant others in the Church are not only Pope, bishop, priest, deacon, not only monks and religious. The significant others are all those who, empowered by their gifts from the power-ful Holy Spirit, enlarge and enrich the communion of their Church. ''From the reception of these charisms or gifts, including those which are less dramatic, there arise for each believer the right and duty to use them in the Church and in the world for the good of mankind and for the upbuilding of the Church.''[81]

One of the ''less dramatic'' gifts and forms of leadership in the Church is parenting. Since the world is not merely "natural" but already graced, parents are likewise not merely natural parents. They are already involved in the communication of salvation. They are already leaders in and of the Church, for they are em-powered by the Spirit who has called and enabled them to be parents not only for, but *of* the Church. If St. Paul could "go through the pain of giving birth to you . . . until Christ is formed in you" (Gal 4:19) and was thus a leader, how much more parents![82] St. Paul's paternity in and of the Church could lead him to boast "You might have thousands of guardians in Christ, but not more than one father and it was I who begot you in Christ Jesus by preaching the good news" (1 Cor 4:12). Who, more than parents, begets the Church by communicating the good news to new members, by incorporating human beings into the continuing memory and tradition of Christ?

In their missionary leadership parents are supported and affirmed not only by the sacrament of matrimony, but also by confirmation, as the word itself hints: strengthening, making form and powerful. In a classical explanation, confirmation is the "supernatural" correlative of "natural" maturity. Its grace makes us responsible, active adults in the Church.[83] According to St. Thomas, by confirmation we are able to "augment" the faith not only receptively, by receiving it, but also actively, by communicating it to others. In confirmation we receive "the sacrament of the fullness of the grace of Christ."[84] We are thus initiated into the Pentecostal mission of "being witnesses" to Jesus, communicating the Good News from "Jerusalem . . . to the ends of the earth" (Acts 1:8).

Parenting is not only one of the least dramatic forms of leadership in the Church, it is also one of the least appreciated. This is because we misunderstand leadership in general, not only in the Church. We restrict the term to only certain kinds of leadership, especially the administrative, directive, managerial type. As important as this form of leadership is, it is not the only one, and it may not even be the most important form. Indeed, it is essentially auxiliary and ministerial, in the service of other forms of leadership.

LEADERSHIP

Here again we can find valuable insights in Mead's social psychology. According to him,[85]

This relationship of the individual to the community becomes striking when we get minds that by their advent make the wider society a noticeably different society. Persons of great mind and great character have strikingly changed the communities to which they have responded. We call them leaders, as such, but they are simply carrying to the nth power this change in the community by the individ-

ual who makes himself a part of it, who belongs to it. The great
characters have been those who, by being what they were in the
community, made that community a different one. They have en-
larged and enriched the community.

Mead distinguishes between "great minds," "leaders," "genius" and
all the other individual members of the community, but then emphasizes that
these "leaders" are only doing in a greater manner what every member
does—"just" by being a member. In the Church nobody is "just" a member.
That is emphasized by the New Testament texts cited above. The Epistle to the
Hebrews emphasizes that "in the whole Church everyone is a first-born son"
(12:23). This means that everyone in the Church is a full-fledged, first-class
member. It also means that all differentiation of membership must not become
division, especially not over and under. Insofar as leadership means making
the community in which we live different, we all have what is essential to leadership by virtue of gracce and the gifts of the Holy Spirit. In the Church there
are not marginal members, no merely passive objects of the clergy's monarchy. Even as cautious and traditional a theologian as Hans Urs von Balthasar
insists that the Church is not a "pyramid," in which everything filters down to
the base from the point at the top.[86] The monarchical and pyramidal models of
the Church as communication are even less acceptable in that the basis of the
Church's order is not the *one* God of (monistic) monotheism, but the *triune*
God of Christianity. For this practical reason we spent so much time on the
Trinity in chapter 1. The rejection of the monarchical and pyramidal models of
Church order is not the result of either the democratic spirit or the egalitarian
ethos. It is, rather, the logical consequence of the Church's being created in
the image and likeness of the triune (sacramental-communion-ontology) God.
Because the Church is a communion, it must also *be* a communication. Its sec-
ond-act actions must be in accord with its first-act being. In the past, emperors
tried to use the doctrine of monotheism to reinforce their imperial monarchy
and totalitarianism. The Church resisted and invoked the doctrine of the Trinity to refute the emperor's claims. The same doctrine can and must be invoked
to resist similar claims when they are made within the Church, at whatever
level and in whatever position.[87] Our being is communion; therefore our behavior, our communication must be communional.

Unfortunately, the Church has frequently behaved, internally and externally, in other than a brotherly, communion manner. The causes of this mis-
behavior are many, and clerical, ambitious lust for power cannot be ignored.
But there are other equally and perhaps more important reasons. One is certainly the defective understanding of leadership and authority which we have
mentioned before and which is not restricted to ecclesial leadership. I have frequently mentioned the tendency to act as if all leadership and authority were of
only one kind, and that one kind was the official, administrative, top-of-the-
chain-of-command type. However, there are other types, and a partial cause of

the tensions in the contemporary Church is certainly the conflict of these various types of leadership.

AUTHORITY CONFLICTS IN THE CHURCH

According to James Hitchcock, four types of leadership are currently competing for hegemony in the Church: (1) mystical-hierarchical, (2) bureaucratic-legal-hierarchical, (3) learned-professional, and (4) charismatic. There may also be a fifth kind, mandarin-intellectual, which looks very much like the third. But there is a difference. These leaders probably constitute a special class, for they are "the intellectuals who have achieved political power, in advisory capacities, supposedly because of their superior rationality and objectivity."[88] They are the experts, according to whose opinion the first two types of leader, and under certain circumstances also the fourth, formulate policy and legislation. Frequently these experts are really the power behind the throne, and it is their opinions, not those of ordained or elected officials, which establish public policy. This is the case in both Church and state and one of the reasons one must always be on guard in regard to "official" proclamations and position papers.

Mystical authority designates those sacramentally ordained and empowered in the Church where mystical and legal authority tend to coincide. The bureaucracy which administers the Church's laws and structures tends to be ordained. Learned authority becomes more and more important as society and the Church become more and more complicated.

The professional advisor can effectively displace administrative authority. On the other hand, administrators tend to select experts who agree with them. Charismatic authority is more free-lancing and "personal." It rises up wherever and whenever and is very dependent on the personality of one person. It frequently flourishes when the other types of leadership are—or at least appear to be—least effective.

As such, there is nothing wrong with this variety of leadership. Diversity is usually beneficial, and competition is generally stimulating. Even conflict is not necessarily all bad, although it can easily endanger the communion and communication which the Church is to be. What is bad is the misunderstanding and misappreciation of the nature of each type of leadership and of the functions each is to perform, the service each is to provide, the ministry each is to perform. What is worse is the attempt of any to dominate the others. What is worse is the arrogation of all power and all authority by any one type of leadership. To some extent, current authority conflicts in the Church reflect all three of these misappreciations of the different types of authority in the Church.[89] It is also, perhaps even more so, rooted in the desire of all the types of leadership to exercise executive, command power *over* the Church and *upon* its members. None of the types of leadership is immune from misusing its authority, for that is precisely what leadership is—power, authority.

LEADERSHIP AND AUTHORITY

Hitchcock remarks that "the line between leadership and authority is often a very thin one."[90] In reality, there is no line at all. All leadership is the exercise of some kind of authority by one who has it in regard to others who don't. Hitchcock probably makes this distinction because he does not attend to the fact that an inept authority or one who "does nothing" is still a leader—albeit a bad one. Likewise, someone—a leader—who does not have the power of institutionalized executive authority can still have enormous power from other resources. This person too is a leader. Leadership and authority are two faces or dimensions of one reality, the ability to induce people to behave in one way rather than another. Although this is a general definition, it is not wrong. It does take into consideration the fact that there is always some kind of presiding by one or more members in a group of people.[91] We might even use the plural, kinds of presiding. These presiders bring about a certain organization within the group. Their activity may be described as personal leadership or institutional authority, inspirational or coercive, but the result is the same. Other people "do what they say," follow their lead. Social organization can be imposed but also inspired; behavior can be forced but also evoked. One could even hope that social organization and personal behavior could be reasoned to. In any case, though, it is clear that leadership is not of one kind only.

C. J. Barnard's distinction among various aspects of "executive activity"—leadership, communication, decision-making, authority and responsibility—is legitimate.[92] Nevertheless, it is clear that his elaboration equates good, effective leadership with leadership simply taken. One may also legitimately distinguish between *leadership*[93]

> as the initiation of a new structure or procedure for accomplishing an organization's goals and objectives or for changing an organization's goals and objectives

and *administrator*

> as the individual who utilizes existing structures or procedures to achieve an organizational goal or objective. As in the case of the leader, the administrator may bring to bear the authority of his role or the influence of his personality in his relationships with other members of the organization.

In any case, both the leader and the administrator are said to have authority. It is this authority which makes them able to do whatever they do. Although the distinction made here is valid, it can also be misleading. It assumes or postulates too big a gap between the old and the new. As Peter Drucker, the expert on management, points out:[94]

> In this century the managers of our major institutions have become the leaders in every developed country, and in most developing countries as well. The old leadership groups, whether the aristocracy or the priesthood, have either disappeared entirely or have become insignificant. Even the scientists, the priesthood of the post-World War II period, have lost much of their prestige. The only new leadership groups to emerge are managers, managers of business enterprises and of universities, of government agencies and of hospitals. They command the resources of society. But they also command the competence. It is, therefore, only logical that they are expected to take the leadership role and take responsibility for major social problems and major social issues.

Unfortunately, even Drucker implicitly equates leadership authority with one type, the executive, administrational, official type. But such a concentration is problematic, not only in totalitarian dictatorship, but everywhere. For, in fact, not only executives, but many others—all in fact—also command personal competencies of various kinds and the resources of society in various ways. This is especially so in the Church, and this is why we have so emphasized the Church as the many-membered body of Christ where all the various members are complementary and as the creation of the Holy Spirit whose diverse gifts are also all complementary. At Pentecost the prophecy of Joel reminds us: "I will pour out my Spirit on all mankind . . . sons and daughters . . . young men and old men . . . even on slaves" (Acts 2:17–21; Jl 3:1–5).

Because of this Holy Spiritual empowerment, all the members of the Church "Command the resources of [the] society" of the Church, in Drucker's words; all "enlarge and enrich our [ecclesial] society " in Mead's words. And because this Church is the sacrament of the world's salvation, the world is equally enriched. On this account, we would be doubly remiss to allow all power, authority and leadership to be concentrated in only a few members. This would be unjust not only to all the members, who would be deprived of their proper Spirit-ual leadership, but also and especially to the select few, who would clearly be overburdened by such a restriction. Finally, it would be unjust to the Church as such and the world as such, for they would be deprived of the adequate communication of the salvation of which the Church is the sacrament (both sign and *cause*). In any case, there is no guarantee that the ordained, hierarchical, official leadership of the Church is always or necessarily the most effective type of leadership in the Church, as the existence of so many non-ordained saints clearly indicates. This is not to advocate anarchy or even that "pure brotherhood" so romantically pined for by some. Structures and institutions are inevitable in society. So are hierarchical and executive leadership. The question is never whether to have them, but always how to enable them to be the best possible. If all power, authority and leadership is not to be collapsed and concentrated in the ordained, hierarchical leaders, what is their proper role?

SUPERVISORY LEADERSHIP

The Acts of the Apostles and the Epistles, as we have seen above, do indicate a gift of administration and governance (*kubernesis*) in the Church. They also bear witness to an activity or function of caring for the orderliness of the Church. Even the Gospels have hints of such an ordering "office" or function (Mt 16:16–20; 15–18; Jn 6:1–12) among the disciples. Not only in the pastoral Epistles, but also in the Epistles to the Corinthians the orderliness of the Church is an overwhelming concern of Paul. The orderliness of the Church is to be a support to those already members and a witness to those not yet. Its ultimate source is the very nature of God, "who is not a God of disorder but of peace"(1 Cor 14:33). There are negataive indications of such an ordering office and function in the New Testament's frequent strictures against those in authority lording it over others like dictators (1 Pet 5:1–4; 2 Cor 1:24; Mt 23). Above all, there is the image of the shepherd throughout both Old and New Testaments. Shepherd can be as wide-ranging a term as steward, so that we must admit that all members of the Church can shepherd the flock as well as steward the tradition.

Nevertheless, it seems to me that shepherd is an image that does allow for a certain type of administrative, managerial, executive, supervisory, even hierarchical authority and leadership in the Church. Only those committed *a priori* to either a biblical fundamentalist literalism which demands absolutely clear and distinct scriptural proof texts or a revolutionary "New Equality" egalitarianist world, it seems to me, want a Church without administrative, executive, pastoral authority. The former is the temptation of the conservative right, the latter of the liberal left, and it is this latter which is newly and especially virulent today. According to Robert Nisbet, there is abroad today a "New Equality" which is really "the passionate attempt to level, never equalize . . . a dogma of equality . . . extinguishing normal diversity of strength and talent . . . the kind of equality that goes with uniformity and homogeneity—above all, with war society."[95] The redress of monarchical pretensions in Church leadership must not lead to the morass of proletarianism. For the Church is, after all, a communion, not a collectivity. The New Testament would not seem to be very patient of collective monolithic leveling. It is clearly committed to diversity, within which there is an office of pastor. It also contains further evidence of authoritative pastoral governance.

Other words in the New Testament also indicate that some members enjoy a managerial, coordinating role within the Church. The Greek word for bishop is *episcopos*. Its basic connotation is overseer, superintendent.[96] Other words are presbyter or elder, deacon, *hegoumenoi* or leaders, and *poimenes*, which the Jerusalem Bible translates as pastors (Eph 4:11). Finally, there is *proistamenos*, which could be translated foreman—the one who stands in front and is thereby able to see over and also go before (lead, guide). Germans use the word *Vorsteher* (Before-stander) to designate the leader of a community or a presider at the liturgical assembly.[97] The New Testament terms are nowhere systematically explained. Their duties were many and varied, especially those of the "episcopal" and "presbyteral" leadership or pastoring. There is an overarching and all-embracing formal principle, however. As Magnus Lohrer has noted, "In fact, they do all the things which are necessary for the good order (*recto ordine*) of the community."[98]

Of course, one does not go easily from these New Testament data to the full-blown theory and practice of the ordained ministry of the papacy, episcopate, and priesthood in contemporary Roman Catholicism. And, of course, one need not, for the Church itself did not make this journey quickly and easily.[99] Indeed, the journey is not yet over, for there is still sufficient unclarity about the theory and practice of Holy Orders in the Church.

HOLY ORDERS

Unfortunately, we tend spontaneously to speak of the sacrament of the priesthood. This is misleading, not because priesthood is fundamentally an unacceptable term. It is in no better or no worse condition than many other theological terms. It is misleading, however, because of the cultic, hieratic and liturgical overtones the term priest inevitably brings with it. These overtones tend to focus, indeed restrict, the precise nature and proper functions of the office designated by the term priest to the cultic. However, the role actually played by the "priest" in the Church, past and present, is not primarily or precisely cultic and liturgical. The proper name of the sacrament is not priesthood, but the "sacrament of order," according to the Council of Trent, although it immediately speaks of this "sacrament of order" in terms of priesthood. However, even here the context emphasizes the role of the "priest" in the orderliness of the Church. It is also interesting, although not to be pressed, that one is ordained when one receives this sacrament.[100] This is not to reduce the ordained priesthood to merely a function, whatever in the world that might mean in a graced universe and Church. It is, rather, to emphasize that the chief purpose of those who are ordained is to provide for the order of that community of which they are members. Their first and greatest dignity remains to be members of this body of Christ, not officials within it. But, then, they are still to provide a special service to the whole Church, and this special service is coordination of the gifts of the Holy Spirit as they exist in members throughout the Church. This supervisory or shepherding leadership is the particular kind of leadership which the ordained ministers, the officials of the Church are to provide.

This official ministry of the ordained has been divided into three degrees or grades—deacon, priest, bishop, with the Pope being regarded as a special way of being a bishop. The theology of the papacy as episcopacy is very intriguing in itself, and also points up clearly how undeveloped our theology of the sacrament of holy orders is. For centuries theologians and hierarchs have argued about the precise nature of this sacrament and especially about its articulation into various minor and major orders. Even today there is no generally accepted theory explaining the origin and inner relationship of the four grades of this sacrament. I say four rather than the customary three, because in any straightforward appreciation of this division, the papacy must be accounted a certainly unusual way of being a bishop. Even if one persists in asserting a threefold division or participation, one has not escaped all ambiguities. For the powers allocated to these three grades have varied over the years, and could vary even more in the future.[101] Many of us can remember when only the bishop could confirm. Now even "simple" priests can. Formerly one had to be at least a deacon to distribute Holy Communion in church—and a male! Now there are other ministers. Some authorities in the Church insist on restricting this ministry as much as possible. They avoid referring to it in terms of office or ordination like the plague. They insist on calling it an extraordinary or at least special ministry, thereby hoping to keep it as low on the scale of official ministry as possible. They conveniently forget that even the deacon, universally acknowledged to be a participant in the sacrament of holy orders, is himself (still "him") an extraordinary minister of all he does, at least according to the Code of Canon Law and the theology manuals.[102]

A major part of the confusion surrounding the role of the priest and the sacrament of holy orders is, it seems to me, rooted not only in over-emphasis on the cultic dimensions of this office, but also in a misappreciation of leadership in general. Only on such a basis could, for example, Hans Küng plead for discourse about this role in terms of "ministry, not office," of "ministry of leadership, not priesthood," for priesthood is precisely one particular type of leadership.[103] The same misunderstanding may also account for the contrast between the ordained, authoritative leadership of the hierarchy and the participation-presence of the laity in a statement issued by the United States bishops:[104]

Just as by divine institution bishops, priests, and deacons have been given through ordination authority to exercise leadership as servants of God's people, so through baptism and confirmation lay men and women have been given rights and responsibilities to participate in the mission of the Church. . . . They are an extension of the Church's redeeming presence in the world.

Would not a divine and ecclesial call also provide for leadership on the part of those so gifted—unless, of course, leadership were to be restricted to only one kind, the mystical-hierarchical?

PRIESTLY IDENTITY CRISIS

I think that the misundertanding of leadership has contributed not only to the restriction of lay people (and religious brothers and sisters) in the exercise of their rights and responsibilities, but also to the identity crisis of the ordained, the bishops and priests. In my own lifetime I have witnessed a considerable change in the understanding of the priest. The priest was, for a long time, the *confector sacramentorum,* which was always transliterated instead of translated into the confector of the sacraments. This meant that the priest confected or made the sacraments. The culmination of his priestly ministry and office was the celebration of the Eucharist when, at the consecration, he "made" Christ present upon the altar (sometimes he was even said to make Christ *come down* upon the altar!) in the form of bread and wine. Admittedly, the Eucharist enjoys a particular, unequaled role and centrality within the Church and its life. But this definition has dangers for the priest as a description of his vocation, for it locates his whole life in an activity which takes up very little of his time and energy. Even the administration (note the term!) of the other sacraments still occupies only a minor part of the priest's time and energy. This was true even when individual confessions were much more frequent than now. Even if one expands this approach, so that all activity, sacramental and non-sacramental alike, is said to enjoy an inherent dynamism leading to the Eucharist, one is still without an adequate clarification of the "priest's" role in this other activity and how this activity is to be explained as sacramental and priestly. Although the priest as sacramental confector (keep in mind, though, the terminology of *administrator* of the sacraments!) is not all wrong, it is also not all right.[105]

Closely allied with the preceding was the understanding of the priest as mediator. A favorite text on First Mass cards was from the Epistle to the Hebrews 5:1: "For every high priest taken from among men is appointed for men in the things pertaining to God, that he may offer gifts and sacrifices for sins." The difficulty with this approach is that it misses the whole point Hebrews is trying to make, namely, that all previous and other possible priesthoods have been surpassed and rendered otiose by the one priesthood of Jesus Christ, the *one* mediator between God and man (1 Tim 2:4–6). As we shall see, there is a mediational dimension to ordained office in the Church. But it is not of the type sponsored by the priest-as-mediator theology, for the mediation between God and man has been perfectly accomplished once and for all by Jesus Christ. Therefore Christians do not need a mediator to bring them into union with God, for God has already established this communion. Indeed, as we have seen, the whole cosmos is a liturgy because the whole cosmos and its history have been irrevocably graced in the risen Christ, the perfect communion of the human and the divine. As Karl Rahner has emphasized, "Thus the sacred liturgy would not appear as an infrequent, isolated, separated part in a life that is really profane—as a divine liturgy *in* the world. Rather it would appear as the divine liturgy *of* the world, as the manifestation of the divine liturgy which is identical with that salvation history"[106] which is identical with the history of the world. This would also help to demystify the ordained, hierarchical official leadership which has from early on been given cultic status, responsibility and identity in the Church. Of the mediator approach to the theology of the priesthood we can say what we said of the sacramental confector approach—it is not all wrong, but it is also far from being all right.

At the time of Vatican II and the concomitant ecumenical fervor as well as the retrieval of certain lost truths, it had become popular to speak of the priest as the "minister of the word."[107] This was valuable because it helped emphasize the role of preaching in the general and ordained ministry of the Church. But it was also unhelpful, for "word" is a polyvalent term in the Christian tradition. Does it refer to the Logos–Son of the Trinity, the Divine Word, or to the Incarnate Word or to the creative word or to the word of revelation or to the word of Scripture or to the word of the Church's general proclamation/preaching or to the word of the liturgy or to the preaching that takes place at Mass or elsewhere or to the word of theology or of instruction? Indeed, as we have seen, even the sacraments can be considered words. The ambiguity of the word "word" plus the Catholic emphasis on non-verbal communication in sacrament, ritual, and Church order did not allow this manner of theologizing priesthood and ordained ministry to succeed.

At this time there were also sporadic attempts to describe the priest as prophet, witness, catalyst for social change, reformer, leader, facilitator, etc. Of course, any given priest can play one or several of these roles in any given community. They can also be played by other people, perhaps better than by the priest. Consequently, these roles cannot serve as the specification of the priestly or episcopal or ordained ministry.

A fourth approach emphasizes that the priest or bishop plays a supervisory or coordinating role in the Church. Here is the fitting time to clarify and emphasize that there is but one ordained ministry, one "office," in the Church, however it is to be named and however it is to be explained. Currently Pope, bishop, priest, and deacon participate in this office in varying degrees and ways. As we have hinted all along, the best way to think of this office is in terms of the shepherd or pastor. As we have also noted, this is a favorite image throughout the entire Bible, and it is also a favorite of Vatican II. The *De-*

cree on the Bishop's Pastoral Office in the Church (28) speaks of bishops as "pasturing a single portion of the Lord's flock." This pasturing is a leadership that can be well conceptualized as *kubernesis,* governing or, just as well, as coordinating, if governing smacks too much of politics with overtones that are domineering, dictatorial, exploitative. Such overtones are severely prohibited by Jesus (Mk 10:41–45), Paul (2 Cor 1:24), and Peter (1 Pet 5:1–4). Consequently, we know that it is at least possible to have shepherding or governing leadership, to have ruling power in a way that is not against and over people, but for them. This "for" is important for the theology of office in the Church because, as we have seen, Jesus is precisely God's *for* us, explicitly at the Last Supper, but really from all eternity in God's saving plan. [108] Even mystical–hierarchical, legal–bureaucratic, executive, managerial, administrative, supervisory, governing power is–should be–*for* people.

This is also the point which is made by the pastoral epistles. Patrick Rogers has distinguished three approaches to these epistles, whose relative later composition neither invalidates nor marginalizes them, since they remain part and parcel of the Church's foundation. The radical approach rejects them as basically "retrograde institutionalism," marking a serious decline and fall from the original structureless, enthusiastic community of believers, which this approach thinks it can find in some of the Pauline communities. The evident romanticism of this approach is enough to relativize it sufficiently if not refute it outrightly. The conservative approach is guilty of eisegesis, tending to find in these epistles overwhelming evidence of the current Roman Catholic Church order, especially in regard to the tripartite sacrament of holy orders. It is well dealt with by the old adage "Who proves too much proves nothing." A third approach is the moderate one, which finds coherent and cogent evidence that the burgeoning institutional order of the Church of the pastoral Epistles does not contradict but rather conforms to the needs of the differentiated and articulated disciples of Jesus, who are, after all, and remain human beings even in their discipleship. As Rogers points out, "Christ intends his community to have 'historical' as well as 'eschatological' existence. He thus provided for the ministerial custody of this Gospel, as well as its incorporation in sacramental signs." [109] From someone with less ideological likelihood to find institutionalized ecclesial office desirable also comes most welcome testimony: "Where a tradition is cherished, it is no good relying merely on enthusiasm. There must also be the natural preconditions to ensure the reliability of the transmission from one generation to the next." [110] And from a most unexpected source comes supporting testimony, however reluctantly given and archly hedged: "It is a truism that the so-called 'formal principle' of earlier Protestantism is a critical impossibility, and compared with it the Catholic principle is *formally* the better; but materially the Catholic principle of tradition damages history much more (both as rank growth [weeds]) and under the shears of the magisterium, because fortunately the New Testament actually comprises the best sources." [111]

Here we can recall the statement of Ratzinger cited earlier, that "apostolic succession is the external form of the tradition, and tradition the content of the succession" (note 17). This applies not only to the apostolic succession in its most formal episcopal sense, but to the whole ministry and mission of ordained office in the Church, which is a mission and ministry of stewardship in the modes of governance and coordination. This governing ministry is not sole, as if it alone "ruled" the Church. Neither is it monarchical or oligarchical, as if it "ruled over" the Church. It is, rather, a service within the Church and in regard to and in communion with the other elements of the Church—the members, the sacraments, the Scriptures. Otto Karrer has well noted that "the Church's apostolic doctrinal tradition and the New Testament form, as it were, 'the foci of an ellipse.' "[112] We would extrapolate this insight to include the *sensus fidelium* insofar as this can be distinguished from the hierarchical, official magisterium's role in preserving and promoting the orthodox apostolic doctrinal tradition. Here also the laity play a leadership role in the Church. They are not only passive recipients in regard to active hierarchs. They themselves play an active, agent role in the stewardship of the tradition, in the governance and shepherding of the people of God who constitute the body of Christ, truly human and truly divine. Precisely in regard to this truth does the past doctrinal history of the Church provide a striking example. Cardinal Newman has reminded us forcefully that "in the fourth century . . . the divine tradition committed to the infallible Church was proclaimed and maintained far more by the faithful than by the episcopate. . . . I mean still that in that time of immense confusion (the Arian heresy) the divine dogma of our Lord's divinity was proclaimed, enforced, maintained, and (humanly speaking) preserved far more by the *Ecclesia docta* than by the *Ecclesia docens;* that the body of the episcopate was unfaithful to its commission, while the body of the laity was faithful to its baptism."[113]

As must be evident by now and as Karl Rahner has explicitly noted, the ordained priest does what other people do, with a very few exceptions such as confirm, absolve and consecrate.[114] What then is specific to the ordained, official minister in the Church? For Rahner this question's difficulty is compounded by the existence of "pastoral assistants" in many German parishes, which are priestless and pastorless because of the shortage of celibate ordained priests. These pastoral assistants are fully educated theologially and pastorally. Their only "defect," that which keeps them from being fully ordained, is that they are either married or female. Nevertheless, they do play the role of the pastor, with the few sacramental exceptions mentioned above. They are the leaders of the local communities, the shepherds, the governors. As such, they should be ordained, not because this would establish them *over* these local communities or Churches, but because it would visibly, officially, and sacramentally establish them *in* these communities as pastors or leaders *for* them. It seems both capricious and obdurate to deprive them and their communities of this normal theological, ecclesial, and gracious reality known as ordination and ordained leadership. Admittedly, as Rahner notes in the same place, all sacraments, including the sacrament of holy orders, are for the normal, ordinary situation (*Normalfall* 383). In extraordinary circumstances, sacraments, since they are the means of grace/salvation and not grace/salvation itself, can be omitted, as we saw in the previous chapter. It is difficult, however, to see that the reluctance of people, otherwise qualified, to be celibate in order to be ordained constitutes an extraordinary situation. One can only hope that the law requiring celibacy of those ordained priests and bishops will be modified, especially insofar as celibacy is not required by the ordained office itself.[115]

However, the current situation does complicate our case, for it shows that even governing, shepherding leadership positions in the Church are occupied by those not fully ordained. This does not mean, of course, that the ordained do not exercise a governing, coordinating, pastoring ministry in the Church or that theirs is no different at all from that of the non-ordained "pastoral assistants," as the latter exist in Germany and elsewhere. But wherein lies the precise difference? This difference is not to be located in personal competence or holiness, not even in professional capacity and responsibility, although, of course, the non-ordained's sacramental administration is restricted as we just noted. The difference is really in the public presence that the ordained, official minister exercises in the Church. Karl Rahner has suggestd that, when all is said and done, the priest-pastor is the "Bezugsperson der Ortsgemeinde auf die Gesamtkirche hin."[116] "Bezug" comes from "beziehen," a verb which means to relate to, to refer to, to be in relationship, etc. In this understanding, the priest-pastor is the one who relates or refers the local Church to the universal Church, especially symbolically, but also practically. Both the priest-pastor and the bishop-pastor do this; they differ only in the extent of the relationship that they symbolize and effect. Again, there is a certain way in which all believers, all members of the Church relate the local Church (recall that according to a strong theological tradition, every soul, that is, every believer, is a/the Church) to the universal Church. What is peculiar to ordained pastors is the public, official status their pastoral relating enjoys. This public presence of the ordained in the Church is also what is fundamentally meant by sacramental character.[117] Through ordination, the pastoring, supervising, coordinating ministry of the ordained is given peculiar visibility and status in the Church. By this visibility of the ordained pastor, the relationship of any local Church, whether parish or diocese, to the universal Church is heightened; its general sacramentality is intensified and made official. The uniqueness of papal episcopacy is precisely that it is the focal point of ecclesial reference to which all other focal points refer. This does not elevate the papacy above, but places it precisely in relationship with all other reference points of ecclesial unity. Even minimal acquaintance with the history of the Church provides overwhelming evidence of the intense desire for Church unity which does not demote but promotes the vitality and variety of all the local Churches. That ordained office in the Church has too often been suppressive instead of supportive does not refute but only reinforces the need for a unity promoting ordained ministry at various levels.

I would like to resume this idea now. Mediation or coordination is, it seems to me, the key function of the ordained office-ministry in the Church, whether priestly (pastoral), episcopal or papal. Some people complain that bishops are not theological enough, others that they are not prophetic enough, etc.[118] The object of the "not" depends, of course, on which axe is to be ground. The *most* frequent complaint is that bishops are either too or not sufficiently liberal or conservative. I think that this complaint is basically irrelevant, for the office, duty and function of the bishop is to be neither conservative nor liberal. And most bishops in the United States have been neither, although they have tended toward the conservative. However, it would better to describe them as cautious rather than conservative, for their conduct has truly been more cautious than conservative insofar as the latter term designates an ideology that is seriously practiced.[119] Whether the bishop is personally more conservative or more liberal is really irrelevant, for the bishop's office, duty, function, role is to keep the liberal and the conservative elements (and whatever else there might be) of the Church in union with each other. The episcopal office is to coordinate the variously gifted members of the Church with each other as well as all the tolerable different shades of opinion and ideology within the Church. This is precisely what *ordained* ministers are to do, and in this sense they are truly mediators—not between God and man, as an earlier theology and piety maintained, but among the many members of the (mystical) body of Christ, variously and diversely gifted as they are by the Holy Spirit, variously and diversely minded as they are in regard to matters secular and sacred. The bishops mediate among the individual members and among the local Churches. That is their supervisory, governing, coordinating office, for which the special gift of *kubernesis* is intended.

I am encouraged in this opinion by an opinion ventured by John Meier and Raymond Brown and other supporting evidence:[120] "During his career Peter was castigated by Paul face to face while being pulled in the opposite direction by men from James (Gal 2:11–12). By a twist of history, his stance which involved being pummeled from both sides was used after his lifetime to justify a middle position between those who used James and Paul as figureheads for an ever-hardening extremism."

According to Oscar Cullmann, "Peter . . . probably had to mediate between the Hellenists and the Judaizers"[121] And John Dunn claims that "Peter was probably in fact and effect the bridge-man who did more than any other to hold together the diversity of first-century Christianity."[122] The Pope is indeed a Pontifex, a bridgebuilder—only not betweeen God and man as is so often supposed, but between man and man, that is, within the Church and among its many members and diverse local and particular Churches. The Pope is emphatically not the whole Church, not even the monarch of the Church.

The Pope is, rather, a focal point of unity—unique, certainly, but still within and for the Church, and its members. The Pope is a special *Bezugsperson* in the Church, in that he relates the universal Church to all the local, regional, and particular Churches—especially and primarily symbolically, but also practically. But he cannot do this alone. He is not the Pope without us; he cannot be and operate papally without us.[123] And among us are certain members who are also *Bezugspersonen,* whose primary role is to be official referent persons preserving, promoting, and publicly symbolizing the unity and communion of the Church in an official mode. As official, ordained ministers in the Church, they provide a particular type of leadership among the members of the Church, all of whom are leaders in various ways, for all are endowed with the gifts (*charismatic*) of the Holy Spirit. Rahner suggests that this ordained, official leadership's proper role is to be the regulator of the charismatic.[124] This is, of course, not easy, for "the difficulty is in determining the right relationship between office (organized on a legal basis) and free spiritual power."[125] And the temptation of the organized, legal office will always be "to extinguish the Spirit" (1 Thess 5:19).[126]

The role of official ministry in the Church, that is, of mystical-hierarchical and bureaucratic-legal leadership, is to encourage, enable, and coordinate all the non-official ministries in the Church. The gift of governing is for the sake of all the other gifts, not to dominate them, not to suppress them, not even to uniformize them, but to keep them all in unity and union. The role of the ordained ministers—pastor, bishop or pope—is to preserve and promote the communion within (not over) which they exist. They are to enable the communication of all the gifts of the Holy Spirit, of all the members of the body of Christ with one another and then with the greater world beyond the empirical limits of the Church.[127] The mode of communication proper and peculiar to the ordained, official ministry is not precisely proclamation of the word or distribution of the sacraments. It is the non-verbal communication of coordination. The ordained priest is not primarily preacher of the word or confector of the sacraments, but pastor, shepherding a particular portion of the Lord's flock, the communion of the Church. Of course, within this pastoring, this governing, and this coordinating, the priest will administrate the preaching of the word, the celebration of the sacraments as well as the gifts of the people. Ordained ministry is entirely for the sake of the *koinonia,* the Church as communion.

I have devoted this much time and space to ordained ministry because of its importance in itself, but also because, properly understood, it reinforces our understanding that the Church is truly a communion, a brotherhood. Even hierarchical office does not transform or deform the Church into a monarchy or oligarchy.[128] The Church is not a pyramid, but, as Otto Karrer suggested, an ellipse. Even better, perhaps, is the image of concentric circles, circles circling about each other, so that all the Churches are in communication and communion with one another, but none is lording it over the others. An adequate system of the means of communication within the one Church and among the many Churches is not readily in evidence. Perhaps none is yet available for the particular nature and needs of the Church. But there are two theological principles within the Church which can provide the basis for a communications system which takes seriously the leadership capacity and responsibility of all the members of the Church.

The first principle is reception, not a widely known term, and not contained in the latest *New Catholic Encyclopedia* and its two supplementary volumes. It is not in the *Theological Dictionary* nor even in the ten volumes of the *Lexikon fur Theologie und Kirche*. Should we be surprised, then, if Yves Congar suggests that it might be a "dangerous topic" as well as a "rare" one. Ready definitions, as one might expect, are not abundant, but Congar suggests: "By reception we understand here the process whereby an ecclesial body truly makes its own (appropriates) a determination which has not originated within itself. It does this by recognizing in the measure promulgated a rule which is in accordance with its life."[129] This definition tries to take seriously the traditional axiom which says, "What concerns everyone should be dealt with and approved by everyone."[130] This axiom does not intend that the decisions of an ecumenical council be submitted to a subsequent vote of ratification by all the members of the Church. But it does mean that the relationship between a council and the Church is not simply one of "above and below." The life of the Church is not merely one of obedient submissions on the part of some members to the superior authority of some others. In its "independent" deliberations and decisions, even ecclesial hierarchical officialdom is bound to criteria beyond its control and disposition. These criteria have their proper home in the entire Church as the tradition and memory of Christ. The ecclesiastical hierarchy does not have independent, greater authority over or access to the truth of the tradition than the other members. It has different access, different authority—but not independence. The hierarchy and its decisions are not independent of the faithful at large. The whole Church is the subject of the tradition, within which various forms of leadership co-exist and cooperate.[131] This does not make the Church a democracy, although the Church can learn from democracies. But the Church is much more than a democracy, it is a communion. The two principles being considered here can help this ontological communion become truly effective communional communication among all its members.

HOLINESS

For transition from the Church as communication in Church order to the Church as communication in holiness, no New Testament texts are more pertinent than 1 Corinthians 6:19; 7:4, 14 where St. Paul emphasized that the vocation of Christian marriage ("spousehood," we might say) is sanctifying.

Don't you know that your body is the temple of the Holy Spirit, who lives in you and who was given to you by God? You do not belong to yourselves but to God. A wife is not the master of her own body, but her husband is; in the same way a husband is not the master of his own body but his wife is. For the unbelieving husband is made acceptable to God by being united to his wife, and the unbelieving wife is made acceptable to God by being united to her Christian husband. If this were not so, their children would be like pagan children; but as it is, they are acceptable to God.''

That is, by being husband or wife, one participates in the sanctifying mission of the Church. By being husband or wife, one communicates the holiness of God and Christ in the Church, and thus to the whole world. I have chosen the above texts precisely because they refer to people who are now accounted lay people—neither clerics nor monks/religious. The participation of lay people in the sanctifying mission of the Church has long been deprived of its significance, because and insofar as holiness had been regarded as the proper preserve of the priestly, clerical, and monastic classes (lest one say castes) in the Church. One need only recall the texts from Gratian, Trent, and some Popes cited above. Clearly, there has been a two-tiered Church in regard to both Church order and ministry and in regard to personal holiness. Some members were really called to holiness, others more or less tagged along. The original brotherhood of the Church was ''fractured'' not only in regard to active leadership, but also in regard to holiness. This applies to both the holiness we are supposed to ''acquire'' or become as well as the holiness we are to share or communicate with others.

This was, of course, contrary to the best insights of the Church, according to which there are no privileged, higher states of life. No vocation is holier than any other.

There is really only one vocation, one call, of which the various gifts of the Holy Spirit are the concrete modes in the everyday life in the world. This one vocation is holiness. St. Thomas insists that this vocation is to the perfect love of God. It is universal, not restricted to any group, not even those following the so-called evangelical counsels:[132]

The precept (or command) of the love of God, which is the ultimate purpose and end of the Christian life, is not narrowed or restricted by any boundaries whatsoever, as if one could say that so much love of God falls under the precept, but greater love, surpassing the limits of the precept, would come under the counsels. Rather, each one is commanded to love God as much as he can. This is evident in the very form of the command, ''You shall love the Lord your God with your whole heart.''

The Church has had a long custom of distinguishing the *special* evangelical counsels of poverty, virginity (chastity) and obedience from the *general* command to love God perfectly and to be perfect, although the "scriptural evidence is of unequal value," as Karl Rahner and Herbert Vorgrimler point out. It is based on various isolated incidents and sayings in the ministry of Jesus (for example, Lk 18:22; Mt 19:12, 17, 21). Historically, the counsels were special commands only to certain people. Not all are, therefore, obliged to observe them. "As a response of man, freely given under the impulse of grace, they can be regarded as a possible means to perfection, provided that the other means to the same end are recognized in principle. . . . These individual vocations . . . cannot be directly compared with or claim any superiority over, another vocation."[133] But they did claim superiority, preference, and priority over the non-monks as they became the basis for organized monastic life. Thus, they furthered "a two-level morality: one reserved for the great mass, condemned to stagnate forever in a radical inferiority; the other reserved for an elite, who practice a superior kind of morality and so have a right to superior rewards."[134] This approach runs counter to the summons of Jesus which calls all of us to "be perfect just as your heavenly Father is perfect" (Mt 5:48). It also clearly violates the Church as a brotherly communion.

Practically, the elevation of the monastic way of life to a more (indeed, *the*) perfect state in life provoked a double misfortune. First of all, it obscured and deformed the call of all Church members to "perfection." It also misled both the monks and the laity, for, at their deepest level, the counsels must be practiced by all believers. In the course of life everyone is called to be poor, sexually abstinent, obedient (subject) to a higher authority. It is not that wealth, sex and independence are bad, it is only that, given the fragility of finitude, we cannot necessarily expect to be on top—victorious and vigorous—at all times. Hence, it is to be expected that during our lifetimes we shall all practice the "vows" of poverty, chastity and obedience. It is certainly inevitable that we shall practice them in our act and moment of dying/death. Neither monks nor ordained hierarchical officials have a corner on this experience. Nor does anyone have a privileged preparation for this final surrender of self into the gracious mystery of the God beyond. The mysticism of everyday life is lived out in faith, hope and charity by all in a graced universe where all are brothers and sisters.

One's entire lifetime is preparation for and initiating exercise into the final, ultimate, irreversible act of faith, hope and charity which is called death, when one's self is finally and irrevocably referred to God as the always greater. To this act all humans and all Christians are called and enabled. In the more traditional language of Vatican II, "Thus it is evident to everyone that all the faithful of Christ of whatever rank or status are called to the fullness of the Christian life and to the perfection of charity."[135]

Is there, then, nothing special about monks and ordained officials? There is, of course, but their specialness is possible and actually exists only in tandem with the specialness of those who are not (excuse the negative expression)[136] monks and hierarchs. That is, there is a specialness of monastic and hierarchical members of the Church only because and insofar as there is a specialness of the faithful which is other than the monastic and hierarchical specialness. This specialness or difference is not in the existence or degree of holiness required and expected of the various members. It is, rather, in their particular roles (function, service, ministry) within the one body and communion of the Church. And here we are brought back to the circumincession of missionary role and person holiness. Even cautious Church documents proclaim that non-ordained members of the Church, namely "husbands and wives are cooperators in grace and witnesses of faith." Indeed, "the family is the domestic Church . . . the parents . . . the first preachers of the faith to their children" (Vatican II, *Laity*, 11: *Church*, 11). The same theme of the parents and family as evangelizers is continued in *Evangelii Nuntiandi*, 71 and *Catechesi Tradendae*, 68. All the different members of the Church are both necessary and not interchangeable, as St. Paul reminded us long ago (1 Cor 12:12–26). In regard to holiness as in regard to leadership, then, monks and priests are not better, not higher than other members. They are only different.

Their difference is not only in the roles they play in the Church, the services they perform. It is also in the signification inherent in their vocations and roles. This is why it is possible to speak of the specialness of monastic and priestly members of the Church only if one can also, simultaneously and necessarily, speak of the specialness of all members of the Church. This specialness is hinted by the biblical texts we have so often cited in regard to the various gifts of the Holy Spirit and parts of the body of Christ. It can be elaborated on the basis of Mead's concepts of leadership and significant other as we have already seen. Sanctifying grace is not merely other-worldly. Really present in the real world, it is neither only internal nor only invisible. In the creational and incarnational world which God actually created, grace itself achieves public, socio-historical status. Grace is sacramental.

Similarly, Christians themselves are also sacraments, for they are embodiments of grace in the world. They, too, are causes and signs of the grace of God visibly present in both Church and world. They are, therefore, leaders in Mead's sense, for they make their community—the Church and the world—different, and they do this precisely as graced, baptized, specifically engifted members of the Church. Some are more, some less dramatic. But all are both effective and significative. To continue in Mead's conceptualization, it is already clear that precisely as such all are significant others in the life of the Church.

From this viewpoint, holiness can be regarded as the most important and most universal form of being both significant other and leader in the Church. Again, we are brought to the perichoresis of personal and professional holiness.

Holiness may very well be the fundamental form of leadership in the

Church, but it is insufficient by itself. Hagiography and Church history are important for the Church as order and holiness. Explicitly canonized saints are more dramatic instances of significant other leadership in the Church in a concrete time and place. Although they do not replace or displace ordained official ministers, they remind the whole Church that true leaders are not only hierarchs. Explicitly canonized saints also demonstrate that holiness and, therefore, leadership and significant otherness in the Church are in no wise restricted: young-old, male-female, rich-poor, stable-wandering, educated-uneducated, eremitic-reformist, married-single, secular-monastic—no particular configuration of human existing is excluded save the sinful. As our expanded understanding of leadership is apt, of itself, to prevent the concentration of leadership and authority in only certain types of leaders, namely ordained, official, executive administrators and supervisors, so is our understanding of holiness apt to prevent the concentration of holiness in only certain types of membership.

These different types of membership play different roles in the Church. There is, properly speaking, no superior and no inferior, for all are the brothers and sisters of the first-born of many brothers, Jesus Christ, risen from the dead. Although theology is never finished in its task of explaining in concepts the creed we profess and the mystery in which we believe, it does reach certain stages where certain statements and expressions are clearly seen to be unacceptable, for they do not convey the truth revealed in and by Jesus Christ to his disciples who became his memory and tradition in subsequent space and time. This memory is (supposed to be) neither a monarchy nor an oligarchy nor anything else except a communion, brotherhood and sisterhood. For this reason, we shall desist from speaking, for example, in such a way that the laity "are said to assist at Mass, at something being done by the priest . . . that the role of the priest is spoken of in terms of power, of confecting the sacraments"[137] as if the laity had no power and were simply passive recipients of distributions and dispensations from the active priest. We have shown in this chapter that all members of the Church are active and receptive (*not* passive!) participants in the Church as communion and communication. All share in the mission and apostolate of the *Church* (not of the hierarchy!), and in its holiness. Church leadership consists not only in ordering offices, but in holiness too, and indeed holiness, which signifies and effects changes in the Church, is the most important form of leadership. As Hans Urs von Balthasar, hardly an anti-institutional, flaming radical, has said, "Order is not the chief element of the Church's life. Love is . . . and being moved by the Spirit (Rom 8:14).[138]

We must sadly but still admit that there is no even nearly adequate theory of the Church as communication. We have suggested some ideas and principles which can contribute to such an elaboration. Above all, the theology of the Church as sacramental communion must guide both the theory and the practice of the Church as communication. In the meanwhile, as we await the elaboration of such a theology, all leaders in the Church, of whatever kind and type, must constantly recall that for all leadership in the Church, the first, last and all-pervading commandment is a combination of "Do not extinguish the Spirit" (1 Thess 5:19) and "Never be a dictator over any group that is put in your charge" (1 Pet 5:3) for we "are not dictators over your faith, but are fellow workers with you for your happiness" (2 Cor 1:24).

NOTES

1. This point is made repeatedly by Karlheinz Schmidthus in his introduction to and commentary on the decree in *LTK, Das zweite Vatkianische Konzil* 1, ed. Herbert Vorgrimler (Freiburg: Herder, 1966) 112–115, 118, 122, 129. He also explicitly notes the decree's deficiencies in regard to the role of and need for public opinion in the Church.

2. Avery Dulles, "The Church Is Communications," *IDOC International North American Edition* 27 (June 12, 1971) 69, 70.

3. Augustine, *De Doctrina Christian* 2:4 (PL 34:37). This idea is examined in detail by C. Couturier, "Sacramentum et Mysterium dans l'oeuvre de saint Augustin," *Etudes, Augustiniennes,* ed. H. Rondet, et al. (Paris: Aubier, 1953) 263–274.

4. Hugh of St. Victor, *De tribus diebus* (PL 176, 814).

5. Alain of Lille, *Rhythmus alter* (PL 210, 579).

6. Stanislas Jaki, *Les Tendances nouvelles de l'ecclesiologie* (Rome: Herder, 1957) 94.

7. M.- D. Chenu, *Nature, Man and Society in the Twelfth Century* (Chicago: University of Chicago Press, 1968). As Paul Tillich, *The Protestant Era* (Chicago: University of Chicago Press, 1957), concedes, "Protestant theology (as early as in Melanchthon) showed an inclination to intellectualize religion . . . made such an intellectualization almost unavoidable. But it cannot be justified" (211). He concludes, "The problem of Protestant form-creation confronts us with a far-reaching decision. Either we decide for a mere preaching of the word, unrelated to a Gestalt *of* grace and, therefore, necessarily degenerating into an intellectual report *about* grace and allowing a secular world to remain untouched by it" (221). In this chapter we are suggesting that an effective communications system is one means whereby the Church achieves a *Gestalt* of grace. Two books by Hugo Rahner offer very interesting examples of how the Church used natural and mythological symbols to communicate its Good News. *Symbole der Kirche* (Salzburg: Muller, 1964) and *Griechische Mythen in christlicher Deutung* (Zurich: Eranos, 1957).

8. Karl Rahner and Angelus Haussling, *The Celebration of the Eucharist* (New York: Herder and Herder, 1968) 33.

9. See Frances Fiorenza, "The Church's Religious Identity and Its Social and Political Mission," *Theological Studies* 43 (1982) 197–225. See also most recently Charles Murphy, "Action for Justice as Constitutive of the Preaching of the Gospel: What Did the 1971 Synod Mean?" *Theological Studies* 44 (1983) 298–311.

10. Robert Kress, "Theological Method: Praxis and Liberation," *Communio* 6 (1979) 113–134.

11. Edward Schillebeeckx, *Christ the Sacrament of the Encounter with God* (New York: Sheed and Ward, 1963) 8–11.

12. Edward Schillebeeckx, "The Church and Mankind," *Concilium 1, 1* (January 1965) 41, 42, 43, 45, 50.

13. James Hamilton, *Kerygma and Didache: The Articulation and Structure of the Earliest Christian Message* (Cambridge: Cambridge University Press, 1980) 28, 7.

14. Hamilton, *Kerygma and Didache* 115.

15. Richard Dillon, "Ministry as Stewardship of the Tradition in the New Testament," CTSA *Proceedings* 24 (1969) 61.

16. See Wilhelm, Breuning, "Apostolic Succesion," SM 1, 88–90.

17. Joseph Ratzinger (with Karl Rahner), "Primacy, Episcopate and Apostolic Succession," *The Episcopate and the Primacy* (New York: Herder and Herder, 1962) 51, 54, 50. Also in their *Revelation and Tradition* (New York: Herder and Herder, 1966) 28–31.

18. This is not an invocation of so-called situation ethics, which is an over-simplification, overlooking the fact that every ethics is situational, in that ethics always takes the situation of the ethical agent into account. At best, "situationists" could plead that some ethical systems pay too little attention to certain situations. The point I am making is better described as "existential" ethics. In this approach, one seeks to know the will of God for precisely me—beyond, over, above and in addition to the general ethical requirements which are valid for all human beings. See Karl Rahner, *The Dynamic Element in the Church* (New York: Herder and Herder, 1964).

19. Karl Rahner, ST 3, 120.

20. Lawrence Cunningham, *The Saints* (San Francisco: Harper, 1980) *passim.*

21. Jean Paul Audet (with Alfons Deissler and Heinrich Schlier), "Priester und Laie in der christlichen Gemeinde: Der Weg in die gegenseitige Entfremdung," *Der Priesterliche Dienst* 1 (Freiburg: Herder, 1970) 151.

22. Yves Congar, *Lay People in the Church* (Westminster: Newman, 1967) 42–47.

23. See Raymond Schwager, "Priesterliche Spiritualitaet," *Korrespondenzblatt des Canisianums* 112/113 (1979–80) 11–13; Karl Hermann Schelkle, *Discipleship and Priesthood* (London: Sheed and Ward, 1966) 9–32.

24. See Paul Gaechter, *Petrus und seine Zeit* (Innsbruck: Rauch, 1958) 105–154.

25. See the remarks of the earlier and less ideologically straitened Hans Küng in his *The Council in Action* (New York: Sheed and Ward, 1963) 159–195. "Fruehkatholizismus" (early Catholicism) describes a theological approach which acknowledges that tendencies, which later came to be associated with (Roman) Catholicism in contrast to Protestantism, already existed in the early Church and are evident even in the New Testament itself. These tendencies, especially those connected with institutional structures and stable, "hierarchical" offices, are regarded by some as decline and decay from the original enthusiastic, non-differentiated Church. Usually associated with Protestant theologians, this attitude also has its advocates among Catholics, for example, Gotthold Hasenhuttl, who claims that "keine Herrschaft ist heilig" (no rule is holy) in *Herrschaftsfreie Kirche* (Dusseldorf: Patmos, 1974) 144. This approach is astonishingly naive, for no social grouping exists without some articulation of the membership, which results in some kind of ruling power. This rule can be benign or harsh, promoting or demoting of the welfare of the whole. It can be good or bad, but be it will in any case. One can also hardly escape the suspicion that advocates like Hasenhuttl are ensnared by the allures of a certain primitivism and pristinism which presupposes a cer-

tain golden age at the beginning of the Church and a subsequent fall from grace in later developments, especially those they deem "retrograde institutionalism." But they presume falsely, for there was no golden age, as had been pointed out by Burkhard Schneider, "Bemerkungen zur Kritik an der Kirche," *Gott in Welt* 2, ed. Herbert Vorgrimler (Freiburg: Herder, 1964) 246–266, esp. 249.

26. Raymond Brown, *The Gospel according to John I–XII* (New York: Doubleday, 1966) cx–cxi. See also his *The Community of the Beloved Disciple* (New York: Paulist, 1979).

27. See Joseph Ratzinger, *The Open Circle: The Meaning of Christian Brotherhood* (New York: Sheed and Ward, 1966).

28. Joseph Ratzinger, *Das neue Volk Gottes* (Dusseldorf: Patmos, 1970) 209.

29. Ratzinger, *Das Neue* 117, 134, 142, 215, 221.

30. For a calm, dispassionate account of the process whereby ecclesial power became concentrated in Rome, see John Lynch, "The History of Centralization: Papal Reservation" *The Once and Future Church,* ed. James Coriden (Staten Island: Alba, 1971) 57–110.

31. On this and the subsequent struggle about the life and order of the Church, see Gerd Theissen, *Sociology of Early Palestinian Christianity* (Philadelphia: Fortress, 1978).

32. They would be well advised to ponder Norman Cohn, *The Pursuit of the Millennium* (New York: Oxford University Press, 1970).

33. Raymond Brown and John Meier, *Antioch and Rome* (New York: Paulist, 1983) 164, 211–216. Also, Raymond Brown, *Crises Facing the Church* (New York: Paulist, 1975) 63–83.

34. For example, Edward Schweizer, *Church Order in the New Testament* (London: SCM, 1961). Of course, evidence of institutional office and structure in the early Church does not automatically prove the legitimacy of the papal office as it has de facto developed and been practiced. In addition to Brown and Meier, see also Raymond Brown, *Priest and Bishop* (New York: Paulist, 1970) and Richard Dillon, "Biblical Approaches to the Priesthood," *Worship* 46 (1971) 454–472. By far more positive than Schweizer is Manuel Miguens, *Church Ministries in New Testament Times* (Westminster: Christian Classics, 1976).

35. John Meier, *Antioch* (86) seems to overlook this.

36. Ursula Schnell, *Das Verhaeltnis von Amt und Gemeinde im neueren Katholizismus* (Berlin and New York: W. de Gruyter, 1977) 210, 214.

37. Schnell 213.

38. Schnell 214.

39. Paul Tillich, *Systematic Theology* 1 (Chicago: University of Chicago Press, 1967) 65.

40. Tillich 65.

41. Note Herbert Vorgrimler's strictures on the "naive historicism" of some theologians and exegetes in "Der Theologische Ort des Priesters," *Handbuch der Pastoraltheologie IV,* ed. F. X. Arnold et al. (Freiburg: Herder, 1969) 437.

42. Bernard Cooke, *Ministry to Word and Sacraments* (Philadelphia: Fortress, 1977) 43–44.

43. Emil Brunner, *The Misunderstanding of the Church* (London: Lutterworth, 1952) 17.

44. Hans Küng, *Why Priests?* (New York: Doubleday, 1972) 118.

45. See Yves Congar, "Autonomie et pouvoir central dans l'Eglise," *Irenikon,* LIII, 3 (1980), 291–313.

46. Domenico Palmieri, *Tractatus de Romano Pontifice Cum Prolegomeno De Ecclesia* (Rome: S. C. De Propaganda Fide, 1877) 437, 443.

47. See Harding Meyer, *Das Wort Pius IX: "Die Tradition bin ich."* (Munich: Kaiser, 1965), esp. 35–40: "I am the Tradition."

48. These citations are all taken from Yves Congar, *Jalons pour une Theologie du Laicat* (Paris: Cerf, 1954) 71–73.

49. F. X. Arnold, *Glaubensverkundigung und Glaubensgemeinschaft* (Dusseldorf: Patmos, 1955) 107.

50. Ulrich Stutz, *Der Geist des Codex Juris Canonici* (Stuttgart: Enke, 1918) 40.

51. Protypical is Henri Nouwen, *Creative Ministry* (Garden City: Doubleday, 1971) whose subtitle on the jacket is positively chilling, "Beyond professionalism in teaching, preaching, counseling, organizing, and celebrating." In a sermon at St. James Cathedral in Brooklyn (April 24, 1983), Bishop James Hoffman, Chairperson of the Bishops' Committee on the Laity, notes the dissatisfaction of many with the term ministry which "needs . . . greater specification. . . . Present use of the word is broad and vague as to create difficulties." This is a theme to which we shall return repeatedly during the course of this chapter.

52. F. van Beeck, "Sacraments and Church Order," *Theological Studies* 30 (1969) 626.

53. Otto Semmelroth, "Die praesenz der drei Amter Christi im gemeinsamen und besonderem Priestertum der Kirche," *Theologie und Kirche 44* (1969) 187–188. On the other hand, Yves Congar still finds this triad important: "Sur la triologie: Prophete-Roi-Pretre," *Revue des Sciences philosophiques et theologiques 67* (1983) 97–115.

54. Jean Delumeau, *Catholicism between Luther and Voltaire* (Philadelphia: Westminster, 1977) 128.

55. Edward Kilmartin, "Office and Charism," *Theological Studies 38* (1977) 532.

56. Edward Schillebeeckx, "Catholic Understanding of Office," *Theological Studies* 30 (1969) 572–580.

57. Hans Urs von Balthasar, "Wer ist die Kirche?" *Sponsa Verbi* (Einsiedeln: Johannes, 1960) 174–202.

58. Herbert Muhlen, *Una Mystica Persona* (Paderborn: Schoning, 1964) 359–360.

59. Edward Schillebeeckx, *Ministry: Leadership in the Community of Jesus Christ* (New York: Crossroad, 1981) 1, 5, 75, 77, 79, 84, 105, 139; also already in "Catholic Understanding," 570–571. The situation is no better in Thomas O'Meara, "Philosophical Models in Ecclesiology," *Theological Studies* 39 (1978) 4, 6, 17–19. On Schillebeeckx's over-emphasis on relative as opposed to absolute ordination, see Joseph Komonchak, "Ministry and the Local Church," *CTSAP* 36 (1981) 76-80. In the church adequately understood as the communion of local Churches and universal Church, a purely and simply absolute ordination is an impossibility.

60. Congar, *Jalons,* 507:528. Here 507, 39. See also his *Sacerdoce et Laicat* (Paris: Cerf, 1962), 328-356.

61. Congar, *Jalons* 679.

62. Thomas Green, "Critical Reflections on the Schema of the People of God," *Studia Canonica,* 14 (1980) 267. See also James Provost, "The New Code of Canon Law and the Laity," *The Catholic Laity Today,* Frances Butler, ed. (Washington: FADICA, 1982) 3–8.

63. Green, 281–282, 287–288.

64. Luigi Civardi, *Manuel d'Action Catholique* (Brussels: Desclee, 1936) 99.

65. Congar, *Jalons* 519.

66. Gratian, *Concordia discordantium canonum,* C. 7, C XII, q. 1, ed. Friedberg (Leipzig, 1879; Graz, 1959) I, 678. Yves Congar describes this approach as a "juridical definition of the Church as a perfect society, hierarchical and unequal . . . of which the primary article was the distinction by *divine right* (law), between clergy and laity." "Regard sur le Concile Vatican II," *Unterwegs zur Einheit Festschrift H. Stirnimann* (Freiburg: Herder, 1980) 773.

67. J. McHugh and C. Callan, Jr., *Catechism of the Council of Trent for Parish Priests* (New York: J. F. Wagner, 1934, 16th printing, 1962) 318 ("Holy Orders").

68. Matthias J. Scheeben, *The Mysteries of Christianity* (St. Louis: B. Herder, 1946) 551.

69. Herbert Muhlen, "Sakralitaet und Amt zu Beginn einer neuen Epoche," *Catholica* 26 (1972) 78.

70. Hans Urs von Balthasar, "Das priesterliche Amt," *Civitas* 23 (1968) 794. See also note 72, below.

71. See Tom Thott "Sacerdotium—A Reconsideration," *Cross Currents* 30 (1980) 283–289, and Joseph Blenkinsopp, "Presbyter to Priest: Ministry in the Early Church," *Worship* 41 (1967) 430–434.

72. Joseph Jungmann, *Die Stellung Christi im liturgischen Gebt* (Munster: Aschaffendof, 1925) 29. Rudolf Graber, "Vom allgemeinen Priestertum der Glaubigen," *Lebendiges Zeugnis 13* (May 1952) 31, points out: "This, so to speak, vacated place of the priestly mediatorship of Christ was henceforth occupied by the sacramentally ordained priest. . . . The consequence was, if one may so speak, a mystical exaggeration and elevation of the priest, which was complicated even more by the especially privileged social status of the priest in the Middle Ages." See also, Herbert Vorgrimler, "Das allegemeine Priestertum," *Lebendiges Zeugnis* (November 1964) 92–113.

73. C.I.C., cn. 124. This canon has not been able to find its way into the latest version of the Code of Canon Law. Instead, the new Code (can. 276) states that clerics are required by a "peculiar reason" (*peculiari ratione*) because "by the reception of orders they [have been] consecrated to God by a new title" (*novo titulo*). This is much better, and acceptable insofar as this new title is not interpreted as an elevation of clerics over non-clerics.

74. Pius XII, "Mediator Dei," *Acta Apostolicae Sedis* 39 (1947) 539 (NCWC 43). H. M. Legrand "L'avenir des ministeres: bilan, defis, taches," *Maison Dieu,* 124 (1978) 29, emphasizes that this mentality dominated pontifical documents from 1850–1960, and gives other examples from Leo XIII and Pius X; from the latter comes this: "The Church is essentially a society of unequals comprising two categories of persons, pastors and flock. . . . As for the multitude, it has no other right than to let itself be led, and, a docile flock, to follow its pastors."

75. Otto Hermann Pesch, *Die Theologie der Rechtfertigung bei Martin Luther und Thomas von Aquin* (Mainz: Grunewald: 1967) 11–23, 935–956.

76. Franz Mayr, "Vermutungen zu Karl Rahners Sprachstil," in *Wagnis Theo-*

logie, ed. H. Vorgrimler (Freiburg: Herder, 1979) 148, 151–153. In 1973 Rahner was awarded the Sigmund Freud Preis fuer wissenschaftliche Prosa der Deutschen Akademie fuer Sprache und Dichtung, an award which might be noted by those who delight in berating Rahner's literary style.

77. Vatican II, *Constitution on the Sacred Liturgy,* 37.

78. Origen, *In Isaiam* 6, 1 (GCS 8, Baehrens 269).

79. I was utterly convinced that ministry was not only too vague, but also too overworked to be simply satisfactory as soon as I saw a pamphlet entitled *The Ministry of Usher.*

80. Peter Berger, *Invitation to Sociology* (New York: Doubleday, 1963) 99.

81. Vatican II, *Decree on the Apostolate of the Laity 3.*

82. On the mission of the Chuch as not only familial but also social-cultural pedagogy, see Fanz Schupp, *Glaube-Kultur-Symbol* (Dusseldorf: Patmos, 1974) esp. 31–77.

83. Bernard Leeming, *Principles of Sacramental Theology* (London: Longmans, 1960), 566–569. Most recently, Wolfgang Beinert, ''Neues Leben und neue Verantwortung in der Kraft des heiligen Geistes,'' *Militarseelsorge* 24 (1982) 251–253.

84. ST III, q. 72, a. 1.

85. George Herbert Mead, *Mind, Self and Society,* ed. W. Morris (Chicago: University of Chicago Press, 1962, 1970) 216.

86. Hans Urs von Balthasar, *Der antiroemische Affekt* (Freiburg: Herder 1974) 107.

87. See Erich Peterson ''Der Monotheismus als politisches Problem,'' *Theologische Traktate* (Munich: Kosel, 1951) 45–148.

88. Hitchcock, ''The State of Authority in the Church,'' *Cross Currents* 20 (1970) 369–381; 378.

89. It would be very interesting to do a study of the conflicts centered on Sr. Agnes Mary Mansour in Michigan in 1983. In the meantime, one can use the above typology of authority to ponder the presentation of Madonna Kolbenschlag, ''The Case of Sister Mansour,'' *Commonweal* 110, 12 (June 17, 1983) 359–364.

90. Hitchcock, 372.

91. It also takes into consideration the fact that the idea of leadership is neither simple nor clear. Under ''lead'' the unabridged edition of the *Random House Dictionary of the English Language* (New York, 1973) has fifty-four items plus four synonyms and one antonym. The single antonym is ''to follow.'' Immediately there springs to mind the age-old adage, ''Too many chiefs, not enough Indians.'' Under the four synonyms are included escort, precede (see guide), persuade, convince, excel, outstrip, surpass, head, vanguard. These give some idea of what a leader does or is. At the same time they clearly illustrate how diffuse the idea is. Unfortunately, this complexity seems to elude religious writers on the subject with great regularity, as the following selections from *Community Spiritual Leadership: Donum Dei* 18, ed. Jacques Cloutier (Ottawa; CRC, 1971) illustrate: Gilles Cusson, ''Community Leadership: A New Phenomenon?'' 9–20 and Claude Vermette, ''Community Leadership: Its Levels and Conditions'' 21–37. Most revealing and most disappointing because of his inability to appreciate the correlation between authority and leadership is Adrian Visscher, ''Leadership and the Religious Community'' 113–128. He prefers the term ''Animator,'' from the French ''animation'' or ''animateur'' to leader or leadership because

"in Webster, the term 'leader' has authoritative overtones. Funk and Wagnall's, however, brings us closer to our point of departure. . . . Apart from the still present authoritarian elements in this definition, 'leader' would be in this sense a good translation of the French word 'animateur.' " But who would want to equate authoritative with authoritarian? And what would either a leader or an "animateur" be without some kind of authority or power? For some all leadership is executive-command, for others all leadership is fundamentally oppressive. Both are wrong, as we shall see.

92. C. J. Barnard, *The Functions of the Executive* (Cambridge: Harvard University Press, 1938) 6, 21, 259. See also Bertram Gross, "The Scientific Approach to Administration," *Behavioral Science and Educational Administration*, ed. Daniel Griffiths (NSSE: distributed by Chicago: University of Chicago Press, 1964) 33–72.

93. James Lipham, "Leadership and Administration," *Behavioral Science* 122.

94. Peter Drucker, *Management: Tasks, Responsibilities, Practices* (New York: Harper and Row, 1974) 319.

95. Robert Nisbet, *Twilight of Authority* (New York: Oxford University Press, 1975) 199, 158.

96. In addition to his other works cited earlier, cf. Raymond Brown, "Episkope and Episkopos," *Theological Studies* 41 (1980) 3222–338.

97. Jochen Martin, *Der Priesterliche Dienst III. Die Genese des Amtspriestertums in der fruehen Kirche* (Freiburg: Herder, 1972) and James Mohler, *The Origin and Evolution of the Priesthood* (Staten Island: Alba, 1970) and Peter Stockmeier, "Congregation and Episcopal Office in the Ancient Church," *Bishops and People*, ed. Leonard and Arlene Swidler (Philadelphia: Westminster, 1970) 71–86.

98. Magnus Lohrer, *De Ecclesia* (Rome: Pnt. Inst. S. Anselmi, 1966, mimeo) 74.

99. As any history of the sacrament of holy orders clearly reveals—for example, Ludwig Ott, *Das Weiheskrament* (Freiburg: Herder, 1969).

100. On the sacrament of holy orders, especially as *ordo,* see the symposium *Etudes sur le Sacrement de l'Ordre* (Paris: Cerf 1957) which examines the subject from every angle. Yves Congar has pointed out the danger of dividing the Church into different orders (*ordines*), as happened in the past. However, such a division is not necessarily inherent in either the differentiation of Church membership or in the existence of an ordering office within the Church. Yves Congar, "The Laity," 239–242. Most recently Congar has spoken of the priest in terms of "organizing the faithful" (Eph 4:12). "Richesse et verite d'une vision de l'Eglise comme peuple de Dieu," *Les quatre fleuves,* n. 4 (1975) 50.

101. See K. Rahner, *Vorfragen zu einem oekumenischen Amtsverstaendnis* (Freiburg: Herder, 1974) 15–39, 61–64 as well as his ST 13, 29.

102. On the possibility of the extraordinary or special (their terms, not mine) minister of Holy Communion being an introduction into the sacrament of holy orders, see Robert Kress, *Whither Womankind?* (Westminster: Christian Classics, 1975) 311–320.

103. Hans Küng, *Why Priests?* (Garden City: Doubleday, 1972) 39, 41.

104. USCC, *Called and Gifted* (Washington: USCC, 1981).

105. This theory almost seems to have been revived and advocated most recently by Brian Daley, "Ordination: The Sacrament of Ministry," *America* 147 (1982) 365–369, although in the end, it seems to me, his article is so diffuse that the "specific role of the ordained" is left unspecified. This is partly due to an appreciation of leadership

which logically involves fear of supervision as the proper role of the ordained: "The specific role of the ordained is not to monopolize the church's ministry, nor to dominate nor even primarily to supervise the ministry of others" (368). Why put those three verbs in the same sentence? Finally, Daley seems terribly tempted by the inspirational and good example theory, "the paradigmatic role of the ordained," as he calls it, although he does also not settle for this.

From another source entirely comes a similar approach that "the special or ordained ministry brings the multi-faceted ministry of the whole Church to sharp or concentrated expression in such a way that all Christians may be stimulated and enabled to exercise the Church's ministry. . . . The metaphor of focus indicates that the special ministry is not an exclusive ministry. . . . Yet a focus is also distinctive, and this is confirmed by the notion of representation. The special character of the ordained ministry consists precisely in its being an efficacious sign in the furtherance of the divine purpose both in the Church and in the world to which the Church bears witness." Geoffrey Wainwright, "Some Theological Aspects of Ordination," *Studia Liturgica* 13 (1979) 128–129. Of course, the ordained ministry should be inspirational and stimulating, exemplary and paradigmatic. But shouldn't all ministries?

106. Rahner, ST 14, 237.

107. See Michael Richards, "Servants of the Word, Shepherds of the People," *Clergy Review* 64 (1979) 246.

108. On vicarious authority, see also J. M. Cameron, *Images of Authority. A Consideration of the Concepts of Regnum and Sacerdotium* (New Haven: Yale University Press, 1966) 1–16.

109. Patrick Rogers, "Pastoral Authority Then and Now," *The Irish Theological Quarterly* 38 (1981) 47–59, here 56.

110. Hans von Campenhausen, *Ecclesiastical Authority and Spiritual Power in the Church of the First Three Centuries* (London: SPCK 1969) 79.

111. Adolf Harnack, reply to Erich Peterson in *Theologische Traktate* (Munich: Kosel 1951) 295.

112. Otto Karrer, *Peter and the Church* (New York: Herder and Herder, 1963) 127.

113. John Henry Newman, *On Consulting the Faithful in Matters of Doctrine,* ed. John Coulson (New York: Sheed and Ward, 1961) 75, 114.

114. Rahner, ST 9, 383.

115. See Lucien Legrand, "S. Paul et le Celibat," *Sacerdoce et celibat,* ed. J. Coppens (Louvain: Gembloux, 1971) 315–319. John Lynch, "Marriage and Celibacy of the Clergy, the Discipline of the Western Church: An Historico-Canonical Synopsis," *The Jurist* 32 (1972) 14–38, 189–212. Unfortunately the latest official document on sacerdotal celibacy in the United States evidences no greater understanding of the utter relativity of the relationship between the official ordained ministry for the sake of ecclesial order and the charism of celibacy for the sake of the Kingdom of heaven. See Bishops' Committee on Priestly Life and Ministry, *A Reflection Guide on Human Sexuality and the Ordained Priesthood* (Washington: NCCB, 1983).

116. Rahner, ST 14, 139.

117. See Eliseo Ruffini, "Character as a Concrete Visible Element of the Sacrament in Relation to the Church," *Concilium* 31 (1968) 101–116.

118. See, for example, John Jay Hughes, "The Leadership We Need," *Commonweal* (1979) 331–334. It is interesting to wonder whether those who find the U.S.

Bishops' pastoral letter on nuclear armaments "prophetic" also find the same bishops' positions on the ordination of women, the ordination of married people, the morality of artificial contraception, the possibility of girl altar boys (*sit venia verbo*), the situation of former priests in regard to public ministry and position in the Church, the official policy on divorced and remarried Catholics, etc. equally prophetic. Or, can one perhaps be selectively prophetic?

119. See Robert Kress, "The Trouble with Bishops," *Review for Religious* 33 (1974) 1121–1125.

120. Brown and Meier, *Antioch and Rome* 215. Elsewhere Brown describes Peter's "theologial stance [as] intermediary." Raymond Brown, Karl Donfried and John Reumann, *Peter in the New Testament* (New York: Paulist, 1973) 162.

121. Oscar Cullmann *Peter: Disciple, Apostle, Martyr* (London, SCM, 1962) 53.

122. John Dunn, *Unity and Diversity in the New Testament* (Philadelphia: Westminster, 1977) 385.

123. Karl Rahner, *Vorfragen* 23–32.

124. Rahner, ST 9, 419.

125. von Campenhausen, *Ecclesiastical Authority* 294.

126. This text is the title and inspiration for one of Karl Rahner's most impassioned speeches, pleading for tolerance within the Church. It was given at the Austrian Katholikentag in 1962, when Rahner himself had been under considerable oppression from Church authorities. ST 7, 77–90. Yves Congar, *A History of Theology* (Garden City: Doubleday, 1968) 273 reports that "Benedict XV declared to Fr. Ledochowski, 'In matters which are not revelation, we must allow liberty of discussion:' " This is good, as far as it goes, but the wording is not as felicitous as one could desire. Rather than "allow," one would could say "encourage." Even "not suppress" or "restrict" would have been preferable to "allow," for "allow" seems to indicate that the source of the freedom is the permission or graciousness of the allower. Early in his papal career, Pope John XXIII quoted the old adage "in what is necessary, unity; in what is doubtful, liberty" (In necesariis unitas, in dubiis libertas). This is an altogether laudable attitude for one in mystical-hierarchical leadership. John XXIII, "Ad Petri Cathedram," AAS 51 (1959) 513.

127. On this see the special double volume medited by J. J. Von Allmen, "Ministeres et laicat" *Verbum Caro* 71–72 (1964), and David Power, *Gifts That Differ* (New York: Pueblo, 1982).

128. This is not to act as if clericalism had not severely and persistently infected the Church throughout history, as is so energetically chronicled by J. P. Audet, "Priester und Laie in der christlichen Gemeinde," *Der priesterliche Dienst*, with A. Deissler and H. Schlier (Freiburg: Herder, 1970), 149–175.

129. Yves Congar, "La reception comme realite ecclesiologique," *Revue des sciences philosophiques et theologiques*, 56 (1972) 369, 370. He resumes this idea and also speaks of a "re-recevoir" in cases where significant decisions have not been immediately received. *Le Concile de Vatican II: Son Eglise: Peuple de Dieu et Corps du Christ* (Paris: Beauchesne, 1984) 38, 83–84, 100–105.

130. Yves Congar, "Quod omnes tangit ab omnibus tractari et approbari debet," *Revue de l'histoire du droit francais et etranger,* 36 (1958) 210–259.

131. See Yves Congar, *Tradition and Traditions* (New York: Macmillan, 1966) 308–348. Later he has emphasized that both Church and individual members of the Church are "subjects responsible for their lives," not merely passive objects of hier-

archical care. "Les theologiens, Vatican II et la theologie," *Vingt ans de notre histoire,* ed. G. Defois (Paris: 1982) 75–77.

132. St. Thomas Aquinas, *Contra Pestilferam Doctrinam Retrahentium Homines A Religionis Ingressu (ch. 2, 759) Opuscula Theologica II* ed. R. Spiazzi (Turino: Marietti 1954) 165.

133. Karl Rahner and Herbert Vorgrimler, *Theological Dictionary* (New York: Herder and Herder, 1965) 155–156.

134. Louis Bouyer, *Introduction to Spirituality* (Collegeville: Liturgical Press, 1961) 190.

135. Vatican II, *Dogmatic Constitution on the Church,* 40.

136. Yves Congar, "The Laity." Miller, 240–242, 267–269, notes the difficulty of giving a positive explanation of the lay state in contrast to the monastic and clerical states of life in the Church. A customary distinction, being re-emphasized strongly by some today, between the laity-temporal task and the clergy-ecclesial task is by no means enlightening and by no means acceptable. It reinstates a dualism, not only between clergy and laity, but also within the one creation and its history which has been graced and which henceforth is the history of grace. For us there is really no absolute distinction, absolutely no absolute separation between the sacred and secular, the holy and the profane. What these terms signify, because of the creation, the incarnation, and the enspiritment is a relative distinction, within the one world-history of Grace, between emphases more incarnational and this-world affirming, others more eschatological and other-world signaling. Similarly, the basic difference between the monastic (dead to or "out of" the world) and the lay or "secular" (active "in" the world) ways of being Christian lies in their differing symbolic emphases, not in their possible or actual call to or degree of holiness. As "anticipated death," monastic life symbolizes the martyr's death to the world and emphasizes that the world is always finite and hence not God, and sometimes sinful and hence able to be alienated from God. Lay Christian life in and building the world emphasizes the goodness of the world as God's created image and likeness, not only as finite but even as fallen. Practically, Christians both "in" and "out of" the world may both enjoy the goodness and good things of the world and also be called upon to die for the faith.

137. Polycarp Sherwood, "Bishop, Presbyter, Clergyman," *American Ecclesiastical Review* 159 (1968) 118–119.

138. Hans Urs von Balthasar, *Sponsa Verbi* (Einsiedeln: Johannes, 1961) 420.

APPENDIX TO CHAPTER 4

In this chapter I have said little specifically about the ordination of women to the priesthood. I have done this deliberately. An adequate understanding of leadership in the Church clearly shows that women are restricted in no way whatsoever. I think that the flow of my argument in this chapter makes that point, even without explicit and repeated reference to it. If so, the argument in favor of the ordination of women is even stronger, for then the entire burden of proof rests quite clearly with the opponents. It is they who must prove that women are, for some reason or other, incapable of priestly ordination. In any case, I have already shown elsewhere that such arguments are not compelling.[1] The entire argument is based on the point that would have to be proved, namely that women, by virtue of being women, are not fit (capable) for ordination. All the other individual arguments rely on this "argument" for their basis. Since this basis does not exist, the other arguments are baseless. There is no theological reason or ground for the exclusion of women from ordination to the priesthood in the Roman Catholic Church.

1. Robert Kress, *Whither Womankind? The Humanity of Women* (Westminster: Christian Classics, 1975) especially 223–264. In Apendix II (pp. 331–320) I argue that women have already been initiated into the sacrament of holy orders by virtue of their having been "ordained" (although the *word* is assiduously avoided in the official documents) as special or extraordinary ministers of Holy Communion. Neglected rather than refuted is how I would describe this argument. In any case, one certainly would not want to insist absolutely on a tactile laying on of hands for office in the Church.

I have expanded the above chapter on the ordination of women in "The Changing Church of the Future: The Androgynous Church," *Theology Confronts a Changing World*, ed. Thomas McFadden (West Mystic: Twenty-Third Publications, 1977) 133–158.

INDEX